FLANNERY O'CONNOR'S
RADICAL REALITY

FLANNERY O'CONNOR'S RADICAL REALITY

EDITED BY
JAN NORDBY GRETLUND
AND KARL-HEINZ WESTARP

The University of South Carolina Press

© 2006 University of South Carolina

Cloth edition published by the University of South Carolina Press, 2006
Paperback edition published in Columbia, South Carolina, by the
University of South Carolina Press, 2007

www.sc.edu/uscpress

Manufactured in the United States of America

16 15 14 13 12 11 10 09 08 07   10 9 8 7 6 5 4 3 2 1

The Library of Congress has cataloged the cloth edition as follows:

Flannery O'Connor's radical reality / edited by Jan Nordby Gretlund and
    Karl-Heinz Westarp.
        p. cm.
    Includes bibliographical references and index.
    ISBN 1-57003-601-2 (cloth : alk. paper)
    1. O'Connor, Flannery—Criticism and interpretation. 2. Women and literature—
United States—History—20th century. 3. Christianity and literature—United States
—History—20th century. 4. Christian fiction, American—History and criticism.
5. Southern States—In literature. I. Gretlund, Jan Nordby. II. Westarp, Karl-Heinz.
    PS3565.C57Z669 2006
    813'.54—dc22

2005020426

ISBN-13: 978-1-57003-717-7 (pbk)
ISBN-10: 1-57003-717-5 (pbk)

Contents

Acknowledgments vii

Introduction
From the Grotesque to Terror, Flannery O'Connor's Radical Reality ix

List of Abbreviations xix

A Good Monk Is Hard to Find
Thomas Merton, Flannery O'Connor, the American Catholic Writer, and the Cold War
Michael Kreyling 1

Flannery O'Connor's Art
A Gesture of Grace
Lila N. Meeks 18

The World of the Cartoons and Their Importance to O'Connor's Fiction
Kelly Gerald 26

He Would Have Been a Good Man
Compassion and Meanness in Truman Capote and Flannery O'Connor
Marshall Bruce Gentry 42

"Then I discovered the Germans"
O'Connor's Encounter with Guardini and German Thinkers of the Interwar Period
W. A. Sessions 56

Seeking Beauty in Darkness
Flannery O'Connor and the French Catholic Renaissance
Sarah Gordon 68

The Church-Historical Origin of O'Connor's Blood Symbolism
Inger Thörnqvist 85

"The very heart of mystery"
Theophany in O'Connor's Stories
Jack Dillard Ashley 102

Metaphoric Processes in Flannery O'Connor's Short Fiction
Karl-Heinz Westarp 111

Fiction's Echo of Revelation
  Flannery O'Connor's Challenge as Thomistic Maker
  Marion Montgomery   122

O'Connor's *Everything That Rises Must Converge* and Theories of the Short Story Sequence
  Hans H. Skei   138

Flannery O'Connor as Communicant
  A Constant Devotion
  Jean W. Cash   149

Toward Discerning How Flannery O'Connor's Fiction Can Be Considered "Roman Catholic"
  Patrick Samway, S.J.   162

Life at Andalusia
  Ashley Brown   176

Contributors   185

Index   189

Acknowledgments

The editors want to thank the contributors for their cooperation and patience. We also want to thank the staff of the University of South Carolina Press for its expertise and constructive critical support.

We are grateful to the University of Aarhus Research Fund, the University of Southern Denmark, and the U.S. Embassy in Copenhagen for their support of our Flannery O'Connor research project.

For research time and other help the editors are grateful to the Center for American Studies, the Center for English, and the University Library of the University of Southern Denmark; the University of South Carolina Beaufort Library; and the Department of English at the University of Aarhus.

The editors thank John F. Desmond, Richard Gray, Bert Hitchcock, Stuart Kidd, Valeria Gennaro Lerda, and Kurt Opitz for their friendship.

We are hopelessly indebted to our spouses, Annie Sten and Jette Westarp, for their patient understanding and unwavering support.

Introduction

From the Grotesque to Terror, Flannery O'Connor's Radical Reality

After reading just a few pages of a story by Flannery O'Connor, the reader knows that this is a writer with strong religious, moral, and social convictions. Yet her grim and apparently godforsaken world is so full of fatalities, deformities, and depravity that her most common fate among readers, and even in literary histories, is to be labeled with the epithet "grotesque." So the editors of these essays were not surprised when we received this letter from Anita Moss of the University of North Carolina at Charlotte:

> Recently I have been thinking about Flannery O'Connor because of a bizarre event in the mountains of her home state. People had been delivering the bodies of their loved ones to a crematorium there to be cremated for many years; ashes in urns were duly returned. But recently a woman took her dog for a walk near the grounds of this establishment and the dog began to play with parts of embalmed corpses. Naturally, an investigation ensued in short order. People were shocked and dismayed. The excuse was "Well, the equipment don't run no more!" The investigators found embalmed corpses stacked high in sheds, crammed into vaults, thrown out into the woods . . . I hope it is not too irreverent to imagine this grotesque discovery through O'Connor's eyes. I believe she might have found it amusing. I doubt if this news was covered internationally, but Southern gothic is alive and well, despite O'Connor's derision of the concept. Oh, the ashes in urns turned out to be cement! (March 12, 2002)

As it turned out, the news was covered internationally, even in local papers, as most news is when it confirms our preconceptions. The editors have to admit that, just like Anita Moss, we also thought of Flannery O'Connor when we read about it, and we imagined how she could have used the bizarre news from northern Georgia. And this is, of course, the point, as Anita Moss is well aware, and this is also the point of this collection. O'Connor would have exaggerated the crematorium story to endow it with metaphysical presence, suffuse it with portentousness, and with mordant humor she would have shown us how mystery and grace intrude upon us when we least expect it. As religious and social thinking are integral to her art, O'Connor would probably also have noted the widely broadcast story of prearranged cannibalism, where a man in Germany recently agreed to be killed and eaten by another man, and was. She would perhaps have created a story about the Eucharist out of that material. After all, Jesus's followers asked disgustedly, "How can this man give us his flesh to eat?" (John 6:52). O'Connor sought similar extreme instances of human behavior and was inspired by them to radicalize her depiction of the human situation; she relentlessly revealed the fake security of man-made forms of escapism. Grotesque? Yes, much of her fiction is deliberately grotesque, but as the essays in this collection demonstrate, her work is so much more than that.

R. Neil Scott's 2002 survey, *Flannery O'Connor: An Annotated Reference Guide to Criticism*, proves beyond doubt that O'Connor keeps every new generation of readers and critics busy analyzing her work. Now, forty years after her death, it is still possible to gather new insights about her from people who knew her, visited with her, and corresponded with her. There are also scholars who detect new sources of influence on Flannery O'Connor, though they have been intrigued by her art for decades. As more dimensions of her work emerge, fresh eyes see new connections between her work and that of other artists of her period. What our decade's readings of O'Connor make clear is that her work also adds depth dimensions to our terror-ridden existence.

Psalm 55:4–5—"My heart aches in my breast, death's terrors assail me, / fear and trembling descend on me, horror overwhelms me"—contains central concepts connected with our postlapsarian reality, the reality of death. Death's terror causes heart-aching agony, and the body trembles with fear and horror. The Latin *tremor mortis* was in late-fifteenth-century English rendered as the "terror of death," which man had to endure in extremis. Try as much as we may, we will not escape from this ultimate reality. To bring home the universal terror and the radical reality of existence, O'Connor decided to shock her readers into awareness. She depicted everyday lives and used local language, although the point was always to show man in extreme situations. But for O'Connor death is *not* our final reality because Christ overcame death once and for all; as Paul says in 1 Corinthians 15:54, "Death is swallowed up in victory." We are offered new life, and for O'Connor this is the mysterious reality of man's life after Christ.

O'Connor did not share the Enlightenment's optimistic view of man as endlessly perfectible. For her, man is "fallen." This is a reality that we try to repress but that can only be tackled by facing it and accepting our radical helplessness and our need of God's redeeming grace. O'Connor sees man as "incomplete in himself, as prone to evil, but as redeemable when his own efforts are assisted by grace" (*MM* 197). That was the reason for O'Connor's notorious skepticism of human efforts to build an ideal society. "Since the eighteenth century, the popular spirit of each succeeding age has tended more and more to the view that the ills and mysteries of life will eventually fall before the scientific advances of man, a belief that is still going strong even though this is the first generation to face total extinction because of these advances" (*MM* 41). On July 20, 1955, O'Connor used William Butler Yeats's famous image from "The Second Coming" in her first letter to Betty Hester: "I believe that there are many rough beasts now slouching toward Bethlehem to be born and that I have reported the progress of a few of them, and when I see these stories described as horror stories I am always amused because the reviewer always has hold of the wrong horror" (*HB* 90). In the same letter, she described her contemporaries as "a generation of wingless chickens," and added, "which I suppose is what Nietzsche meant when he said God was dead. . . . I think that the Church is the only thing that is going to make the terrible world we are coming to endurable."

Therefore she felt it was her most important concern to make us "feel the contemporary situation at the ultimate level" (*HB* 90). This was her motivation for her art. Writing a novel "is a plunge into reality and it's very shocking to the system. . . . People without hope . . . don't read. They don't take long looks at anything, because they lack the courage. The way to despair is to refuse to have any kind of experience" (*MM* 78). For O'Connor, the artist, it was of paramount importance that she with all her senses was in touch with the reality that surrounded her. But her local situations become "globalized" in her fiction, as Patricia Yaeger recently suggested in her essay about O'Connor's cosmopolis.[1] O'Connor was convinced that "the artist penetrates the concrete world in order to find at its depths the image of its source, the image of ultimate reality. This in no way hinders his perception of evil but rather sharpens it, for only when the natural world is seen as good does evil become intelligible as a destructive force and a necessary result of our freedom" (*MM* 157).

She was convinced that our greatest gift, the freedom of decision, to accept the offer of grace or to refuse it, was at the center of our ethical behavior. The voice of conscience plays an important part in our moral actions. In *Wise Blood* Hazel Motes says of conscience, which is the source of terror in ourselves, in his attempt to repress it, "it don't exist though you may think it does, you had best get it out in the open and hunt it down and kill it" (*CW* 93). A little later, after Hazel's execution of his fake "twin," Solace Layfield, he repeats the phrase: "If you don't hunt it down and kill it, it'll hunt you down and kill you" (*CW* 95). The writer who has faith, O'Connor wrote, "will be interested in characters who are forced out to meet evil and grace and who act on a trust beyond themselves—whether they know very clearly what it is they act upon or not" (*MM* 42). As Susan Srigley argues in her study *Flannery O'Connor's Sacramental Art*, ethical choices are an engagement with and a response to reality, and the choices of O'Connor's characters reveal visions of reality that are either narrow and destructive or meaningful and sustainable.[2]

O'Connor was convinced that she had to shout to the almost deaf and to draw startling figures for the almost blind. "It is the extreme situation that best reveals what we are essentially, and I believe these are times when writers are more interested in what we are essentially than in the tenor of our daily lives. Violence is a force which can be used for good or evil, and among other things taken by it is the kingdom of heaven" (*MM* 113). With the last phrase, she referred to Matthew 11:12, upon which the title of her second novel, *The Violent Bear It Away*, is based. From the very beginning of her career, O'Connor was attacked for her focus on extreme situations, on violence, and even on murder. But she defended herself, arguing that her "stories are hard because there is nothing harder or less sentimental than Christian realism" (*HB* 90). "Our age not only does not have a very sharp eye for the almost imperceptible intrusions of grace, it no longer has much feeling for the nature of the violences which precede and follow them" (*MM* 112). By relentlessly exposing her characters to the grace of God, O'Connor demonstrates that life without God is not only undesirable, it is downright terrifying.

Like Thomas Aquinas, O'Connor was convinced that "the good is the ultimate reality ... [and that] the ultimate reality has been weakened in human beings as a result of the Fall, and it is this weakened life we see" (*MM* 179). But she was profoundly skeptical of "do-gooders," like her characters Sheppard and Rayber, since "sentimentality is an excess, a distortion of sentiment usually in the direction of an overemphasis on innocence, and that innocence, whenever it is overemphasized in the ordinary human condition, tends by some natural law to become the opposite" (*MM* 147–48), by which she meant violence and other forms of evildoing. She exposes her characters, not least those who in a pharisaical way extol their own value, but they too are offered a chance of *anagnorisis*, which will open them to the offer of grace. O'Connor's fictional world is so full of mental and physical deformities that her fate among readers is often to be placed among the writers of southern gothic whose horrifying characters and plots are seen as decidedly "grotesque." This should be no surprise, if we keep in mind that her artistic imagination matured during the 1940s and 1950s with newsreels about the horrors of World War II, the devastations of the atomic bomb, the bloodshed of the Korean War, the waves of hatred in the wake of the cold war and McCarthyism, and no end of acts of "ordinary" crime. All those events contributed to an increasing existential uncertainty and fear, which we tried to assuage by amassing wealth and by propagating different forms of escapism. O'Connor faced the facts and mercilessly unmasked attempts to escape as superficial, smug, and ineffectual against both the political terror of the day and the riot of inner anxiety that without warning can possess anybody at any time.

O'Connor's fiction reflects her profound worries about the degenerate state of man and where the world is headed. She saw reality in its concrete details and went to the roots in her analysis of human reality as both postlapsarian and postredemption. Now, forty years after her death and in the aftermath of September 11, existential fear is worse and has grown into worldwide paranoia of terror, from which escape seems unlikely. But O'Connor saw terror as a means to destroy, violently if necessary, our false pride in the man-made and to purify our channels of perception for a revelation of the roots of all reality.

Because they more clearly reveal the deep roots of sin and human weakness, she found extreme situations, such as grotesque news stories, more startling in their appeal, but she never stopped there, and this is what makes her fiction a lasting fascination. According to O'Connor, ultimate reality is *not* the Fall and its terrifying final consequence of death; what is real is the offer of hope in the resurrection of Christ. The close connection between human freedom and responsibility becomes of decisive importance, and *hope* is an offer that her characters may or may not recognize or accept.

The essays in the present volume address the impact on O'Connor of contemporary issues, her reaction to them, and the ways in which she aesthetically transformed the issues in her fiction. Scholars throw new light upon the complexities of the controversial phenomenon called Flannery O'Connor. Depending on their personal or scholarly relation to O'Connor, the contributors focus attention upon historical data of her life, upon her fiction, or upon the connections between her life as a believer and her work. But the essays also try to locate the sources of her strength to confront the terror of her time and in her private life. Michael Kreyling's title for his O'Connor essay, "A Good Monk Is Hard to Find," refers to Thomas Merton's interest in Communism and his view of contemporary American cold-war politics. Kreyling is convinced that the political atmosphere also influenced O'Connor—though she was apparently never as conscious of this as Thomas Merton was. Kreyling's analysis shows how the political ambience of the cold-war period lies hidden behind the forms and contents of cultural expressions. Like Stephen Whitfield in *The Culture of the Cold War,* Kreyling argues that cultural expressions of the period were "contaminated" by political interest in both their roots and consequences. Lila N. Meeks sees O'Connor's art as substantially influenced by the cruel truth, in Dr. Johnson's words, that "nothing so concentrates the mind as the verdict of death." Meeks adduces a great number of examples of sick and evil characters in O'Connor's fiction, most of them based on "true-life" prototypes, whom O'Connor shows to be sick with sin, and waiting, in Meeks's words, for a "gesture of grace."

Substantially influenced by the truth of the verdict of death, O'Connor's art *is* bitingly serious, but the nature of her either/or topics, her strong religious convictions and purpose, and her absolute earnestness do not prevent her from being one of the funniest of American writers. Through her stylistic brilliance, she can deal with spiritual values and social conventions in an entertainingly grotesque, witty, and comic language. As a result her fiction is today better known and more popular than ever. Kelly Gerald has located a number of O'Connor cartoons, approached them systematically, and analyzed their importance for O'Connor as a writer. Gerald traces the sources for O'Connor's cartoons back to her early years at Peabody High School and later at Georgia State College for Women. In this way her cartoons are a kind of history in pictures with the artist's satiric eyes turned upon people and issues of her time—and not least also upon herself. O'Connor's cartoons and her paintings proved essential for the development of the visual density of her prose, which eventually instigated a wide variety of interdisciplinary approaches to her work. Gerald's close analyses of the cartoons, with special focus on the creation of satiric distance between the subject of the cartoon and the cartoonist, add important dimensions to our way of reading O'Connor's cartoons and stories.

Gerald's analyses indicate that O'Connor's cartoons were essential for the development of the realism of her prose. It is a radical vision of reality that O'Connor passed on to other artists. Marshall Bruce Gentry, known for his study of O'Connor and the grotesque, presents O'Connor's Misfit as one of her shockingly realistic criminals—based on an actual local case—and compares her treatment of him to Truman Capote's factual murder-novel *In Cold Blood*. Gentry develops a convincing argument for O'Connor's strong impact upon Capote. *In Cold Blood*'s many borrowings from and parallels to O'Connor's "A Good Man Is Hard to Find" are striking. Both authors struggle to find the true self of their leading criminals, The Misfit and Perry Smith, but Capote clearly speaks in O'Connor's voice when he has *his* misfit killer say, "There is no answer to it but meanness. That is all anybody understands, meanness."

Some of the essays focus on the intellectual and spiritual influences upon O'Connor. To date many influences on O'Connor have not been studied at all or only insufficiently. The essays reveal how well read she was, which has not been common knowledge. Her friend and correspondent W. A. Sessions spent a formative period of his life in interwar Germany, where he met leading thinkers such as Eric Vögelin, Martin Buber, Martin Heidegger, and Carl G. Jung. He presents Romano Guardini as the great theologian in the political hothouse of Berlin, whose thinking was a response to the concrete, grotesque political situation. Sessions starts his arguments for O'Connor's awareness of these writers' works by quoting her own "then I discovered the Germans," offers references to German thinkers in her published work as well as in O'Connor material so far not available in print, and shows the influence of her acquaintance with the German thinkers on her late stories and *The Violent Bear It Away*. Based on close analysis of conversations with O'Connor and of her letters, Sessions argues convincingly for the strong influence of these German thinkers. Similarly, Sarah Gordon, whose close connection with the O'Connor collection at Georgia College has led to her many O'Connor studies, guides us in her essay to an often-ignored twentieth-century source of inspiration for O'Connor. Gordon focuses on French Catholic thinkers such as Henri Bergson and Léon Bloy, who influenced Jacques Maritain, whose importance for O'Connor is well known. Works by contributors to the so-called French Catholic renaissance—contributors such as Paul Claudel, Charles Péguy, and Georges Rouault—were known to O'Connor, but it was in Maritain's words about Bloy that she found inspiration to "seek beauty in darkness" and to try to find "hidden mystery in the things of this world." In Bloy—

according to Gordon—O'Connor found the spiritual comedy of the "horrifying extremes of human behavior."

As sources for O'Connor's prominent blood symbolism, Inger Thörnqvist looks to the early church fathers Cyril of Jerusalem and Pseudo-Dionysius, with whose lives and theology O'Connor was familiar. Thörnqvist's new critical angle upon O'Connor, which is based on church history, presents convincing material as regards the origin and importance of blood symbolism for O'Connor's fiction. Through a wealth of documentation, this learned essay establishes links between O'Connor's fiction, early Christian blood symbolism, and southern self-understanding today. Jack Dillard Ashley's essay could well be considered the quintessence of his fifty years of scholarship. He goes one step further back in looking to the Bible for the different kinds of "revelation of divine presence," such as macrocosmic theophanies or microcosmic epiphanies. Having established distinctions and definitions for his terminologies, Ashley proves O'Connor's familiarity with all shades of theophany and her use of them in her awe-inspiring fiction.

"Go warn the children of God of the terrible speed of God's mercy" is O'Connor's wording of Tarwater's prophetic calling. It is the starting point for her friend, and fellow-Georgian, Marion Montgomery's essay on "the terror of mercy." He sees the thought of Thomas Aquinas behind O'Connor's presentation of the relation between art, reason, and grace. Art, the "made thing," is "reason in making." Montgomery discusses the importance of Aquinas's aesthetic philosophy for O'Connor's way of understanding and presenting mystery and sees her fiction as revelations of "the terror of mercy." For Karl-Heinz Westarp, the incarnation of the Word is *the* central revelation in O'Connor's work. He argues that a combined linguistic, aesthetic, and theological understanding of incarnational processes as metaphorical is a key to the dimension of depth in the reality that O'Connor worked to recreate so precisely in her art. It is the interplay, Westarp claims, between surface and depth that accounts for the immediate appeal of O'Connor's fiction and its lasting effect upon many readers. Hans Skei focuses on O'Connor's presentation of reality in her posthumously published collection of short stories, *Everything That Rises Must Converge*. Do the stories comment upon each other, and can they be characterized as a short-story cycle, where the sum of the whole is more than its parts? Although he sees sequencing and the subject of death as potentially unifying elements, Skei suggests that the collection is not a cycle or composite, primarily because O'Connor in this collection also employs an aesthetic of brevity and condensation to present reality.

The final question of where O'Connor found the strength to deal with the shocking realities of life is discussed by Jean W. Cash, one of O'Connor's biographers. Cash shows how important daily religious practice was for O'Connor throughout her life. Cash traces the development of O'Connor's Eucharistic devotion from early childhood and offers new evidence about her practice as a child in Savannah, as a student in Iowa, as a young writer in New York, and as a grown-up in Milledgeville. In her discussion of the Milledgeville years Cash focuses on O'Connor's personal struggle with faith under the guidance of Fr. James McCown and on the spiritual help O'Connor offered to such close friends as Cecil Dawkins and Betty Hester. As a devout and traditional Catholic, O'Connor found peace in receiving the bread of life as often as possible. Fully aware of the philosophical and religious thinking that had influenced O'Connor, Patrick Samway, S.J., questions the legitimacy of calling her fiction "Roman Catholic." Was she an "orthodox" believer and, if so, what connotations does this categorization have considering her pre– and early–Vatican II thinking? Samway argues that O'Connor's views are wider than narrowly "Roman Catholic." Common Christian issues such as grace, revelation, inspiration, redemption, and judgment are widely present in her fiction and make its appeal more ecumenically relevant. Describing factual aspects of O'Connor's life at Andalusia, her relation to contemporaries and contemporary issues is the topic of the last essay in this volume. Ashley Brown, O'Connor's friend and correspondent since 1952 and a frequent visitor to the O'Connor farm, reveals in his reminiscences details of O'Connor's friendship with Brainard and Frances Cheney. Brown's warm relationships with the O'Connors and their mutual friends shine through and make the reading of the essay particularly rewarding. Brown throws light upon everyday life on the family farm. It was here, among a wide range of friends, that O'Connor found an inspiring reality that enabled her to cope with the ever-present threat of sudden death and to keep at bay the terror of everyday life.

O'Connor's piercing eyes—never without a satiric twinkle—fully recognized the often horrifying situations into which we maneuver ourselves. She also saw how difficult it was to resolve these, and she was not satisfied with easy solutions. Her compassionate vision saw our quintessential worries, and she understood why we find ourselves in a state of terror. She pushed her characters—and her readers—to face the terror, hinted at the possibility of new beginnings, and proclaimed that we can be redeemed only by love. Though she did not live to experience today's horrors, her stories also appeal—mutatis mutandis—to the readers of the twenty-first century in that they distance us from the threats that surround us and help us concentrate on what is essential in coping with reality. The present volume is about Flannery O'Connor and her fiction and not about being terrified by today's murdering bands, but what she wrote about the "terror within" applies to that situation as well.

The editors have previously, individually and together, worked on a wide range of southern literature focusing on Eudora Welty, Walker Percy, Flannery O'Connor, and contemporary southern authors. We are convinced that this volume on O'Connor with contributions by four of O'Connor's friends and other outstanding critics in the field will appeal to those who are grateful for new insight into O'Connor's personal and fictional universe. But we are convinced that the presentation of essential topics on her fiction and her life will also function as appetizers for newcomers to O'Connor's universe. As we move into the fifth decade of O'Connor studies, excitement about this provocative figure in southern letters is still vibrantly alive. The present volume is meant as a help to assess the directions in which O'Connor scholarship is moving and to indicate some of the new avenues into the exciting world of the wry Georgian. Her fiction, essays, and letters continue to challenge the way we live our spiritual and worldly lives. We hope the essays in *Flannery O'Connor's Radical Reality* will present horizons of relevance for the ways you spend your time.

Notes

1. Patricia Yaeger, "Southern Orientalism: Flannery O'Connor's Cosmopolis," *Mississippi Quarterly* 56, no. 4 (2003): 491–510.

2. Susan Srigley, *Flannery O'Connor's Sacramental Art* (Notre Dame, Ind.: University of Notre Dame Press, 2004).

Abbreviations

CF   *Conversations with Flannery O'Connor*, ed. Rosemary M. Magee (Jackson: University Press of Mississippi, 1987)
CS   *The Complete Stories* (New York: Farrar, Straus and Giroux, 1971)
CW   *Collected Works*, ed. Sally Fitzgerald (New York: Library of America, 1988)
HB   *The Habit of Being: Letters*, ed. Sally Fitzgerald (New York: Farrar, Straus, Giroux, 1979)
MM   *Mystery and Manners: Occasional Prose*, ed. Robert and Sally Fitzgerald (New York: Farrar, Straus and Giroux, 1969)
PG   *The Presence of Grace, and Other Book Reviews*, comp. Leo J. Zuber, ed. Carter W. Martin (Athens: University of Georgia Press, 1983)
VBIA   *The Violent Bear It Away* (New York: Farrar, Straus and Cudahy, 1960)
WB   *Wise Blood* (New York: Harcourt, Brace, 1952)

A Good Monk Is Hard to Find

Thomas Merton, Flannery O'Connor, the American Catholic Writer, and the Cold War

Michael Kreyling

Flannery O'Connor's admirers, of whom there are now generations, tend to read her and her work *sub specie aeternitatis*. Even if, like her lifelong friend and publisher Robert Giroux, one might admit that O'Connor's "work can only be understood in an American setting" (*CS* xiv), that American setting miraculously evaporates, and as John F. Desmond asserts, all historical considerations lead back to metaphysics (Desmond 2).

The main channel in O'Connor criticism, with very few exceptions, has not paused for Jon Lance Bacon's departure in *Flannery O'Connor and Cold War Culture* (1993) and made the effort to understand "the centrality of her writings in the literary history of postwar America" (Bacon 5). Indeed, as Bacon shows, O'Connor's writerly imagination was saturated with the anxieties of the cold war. Feminist critics such as Patricia Yaeger and Sara Gordon, representing successive waves of the movement, have discerned cultural narratives in O'Connor's work that link it historically and psychoanalytically to circumstances of history and gender. But as strong as their feminist approaches are, the publishing record of O'Connor criticism leans heavily toward the metaphysical conclusions that John Desmond and others advance.

I do not wish to argue that O'Connor's imagination was not equally saturated with the narrative of her Catholicism. (As a "cultural Catholic" myself, educated by nuns, priests, and brothers from kindergarten through college, I need very few footnotes to illuminate an O'Connor story theologically.) As critics such as John Desmond, Richard Giannone recently, and many others for decades have insisted, an "incarnational" aesthetic informs O'Connor's fiction. Rather than being embedded in a context, according to these critics, O'Connor possesses a "vision," an "imagination," that lifts her above or thrusts her beyond the mundane. Reading her fiction, this critical order insists, can and should do the same for the rest of us.

The beatification of O'Connor clearly sidesteps her Americanness and, just as clearly, privileges the text as doctrinal product—which is nothing new to a New Critical commune of writers and critics or to Catholics—over the text as cultural process—a paradigm more compatible to a contemporary audience. Schooled during the heyday of the New Criticism and further disciplined by Caroline Gordon, one of its strictest practitioners, O'Connor worked at her stories to burnish the contemporary signs being made. But, for better or worse, she was a cold-war writer as well as a Catholic and southern one, and her saturation in these layered cultures inflected the two masks she publicly claimed: her Catholicism and her southernness. I argue that O'Connor's "vision" was tethered to her historical circumstances, that her faith did not exempt her from the world but was tempered and compromised by the world in two ways crucial to her times. Flannery O'Connor, writer and believer, lived in an America shaped by the pressures of conformity in thought and behavior and by the upheavals of race.

Historical events have once again confirmed that "what goes around comes around": the United States, after the terrorist attacks of September 11, 2001, is in its second "cold-war culture" of official dread, anxiety, and suspicion in a half century. I use the word "official" as a qualifier, for dread and anxiety are the rhetoric of "homeland security," not necessarily the threat as felt. Some commentators, such as Bob Herbert in the *New York Times,* detect more dread on the coasts than in the hinterlands, where life seems to be going on as usual and where natural disasters like drought and wildfire seem more threatening than al-Qaeda. Nonetheless, the "official" official climate of the United States is neo–cold war. It is the announced policy of the U.S. government to remove Saddam Hussein and all other evildoers from office. President Bush has said more than once that you are either for us or against us in the war on terror.[1]

The demise of the first cold war supposedly ended the presidency of the elder George Bush, and the protracted war on terror has rescued the presidency of his son from a disputed and ambiguous first election. Americans are once again called upon to identify and cherish "our way of life" and to defend it against "evildoers" and those who hate us. Our government is revamping law enforcement, the military, and the legal system to face the threat, and this revamping takes the shape of acquiescence to increased surveillance, reduction of civil liberties, and the linking of nonconforming behavior and belief with doubts about patriotism. If the American Catholic bishops were not otherwise engaged, the church would no doubt weigh in on the issue.[2]

In the first cold war, religion played a very prominent role in identifying the American way of life as fundamentally Christian. Protestant leaders, headed by Billy Graham and Norman Vincent Peale, and visible Catholic icons, such as Archbishop (later Cardinal) Spellman and Bishop Sheen, exhorted Americans to think of Communism as Satan's latest and most insidious attack upon the faithful and to think of the Christian outlook as a spiritual fortress in a wasteland of unreligion. Allegorized as good versus evil, the narrative of cultural consciousness in the first cold war forfeited its ambiguous, contingent middle ground. Indeed, that middle ground was the fertile field for corruption of the weak- and simple-minded. Graham, whose career began with the first cold war, made the erasure of the middle ground his relentless goal. As Stephen J. Whitfield, in *The Culture of the Cold War,* notes of

Graham's sermons: "As early as 1947 Graham was denouncing Communism, for he doubted that his country was sufficiently vigilant in combating the Antichrist. Twice he delivered over the air, and distributed as a pamphlet, 'The Sin of Tolerance,' a sermon that noted 'the word *tolerant* means *liberal, broad-minded*'" (Whitfield 80). Conformity in the right translated as conformity on the right; the political and cultural center was cast into outer darkness along with the left. Catholic cultural politics were similarly drawn to reaction. The arrest and persecution of Joseph Cardinal Mindszenty in Budapest in 1948 energized Archbishop Spellman, already a social conservative in domestic matters, to perceive an international threat behind all disturbances to the status quo, and it eventually resulted in Spellman's public endorsement of Senator Joseph McCarthy in 1953 (Whitfield 95–96).

The first cold-war period generated an entire library of discourse, ranging from the sociology of David Reisman exploring the social psychology of conformity to such films as Elia Kazan's *On the Waterfront* (1954) and Stanley Kubrick's *Paths of Glory* (1957) that examine organizations of power and individual resistance. It is early in the "9/11 moment" of our cultural history, although certain political cartoons and strips like *Doonesbury*, op-ed columns, and certain satire and comedy performers have begun to cast suspicion on the culture of suspicion and patriotism.

The present is not a bad moment to interrogate the alliance of cold war and the American writer with allegiance, on the one side, to her nation and, on the other, to her religion. But let me begin with some remarks about Thomas Merton (1915–68), an American Catholic writer contemporary with O'Connor, and use Merton as a foil for O'Connor. Merton, who entered the Cistercian order at the Abbey of Gethsemani in Kentucky in 1942, had converted to Catholicism after several years studying at Columbia University in the 1930s and the early years of World War II. He had been a member of the Communist Party and active in Catholic social action in Harlem before his entry into the novitiate. Had he not taken final vows in 1948 and had he published the several novels he ritualistically burned before his entry into the monastery, he might have been called before the House Un-American Affairs Committee on the basis of his political associations. He certainly would have been a stone in the shoe of Archbishop Spellman and Senator Joseph McCarthy, two prominent cold-war Catholics.

O'Connor was half a generation younger, entering college as Merton was graduating, southern rather than internationalist in cultural outlook, born into a Catholic family rather than a convert, and by her own accounts deeply skeptical of social action in any cause. The onset of lupus, in any case, effectively ruled out any kind of social action. In the grip of the disease, O'Connor had no disposable time after writing and staying alive. O'Connor and Merton apparently never met, although in his introduction to *The Complete Stories*, Robert Giroux, who was at Columbia with Merton and later became O'Connor's publisher, describes a mutual curiosity and admiration between the monk and the writer (*CS* xiii–xv).

Yet both writers saw their faith shaping, if not overwhelming, the foreground of historical, social, and cultural events in their times. Both cite many of the same influences on their careers as Catholic intellectuals and writers, primarily Jacques Maritain and Étienne Gilson. One, Merton, withdrew from direct traffic with his time and place by entering a monastery—although his literary work kept him on the razor's edge of the kind of public fame that would have undermined his vows. The other did not so much withdraw of her own choice from the public world as she was forced out when lupus made it impossible for her to live and work on her own. The two cases are similar if not parallel.

Thomas Merton was born in southern France near the border with Spain, in Prades in the Pyrenees, in the winter of 1915. Not too far from his birthplace, he notes in his autobiography, *The Seven Storey Mountain* (1948), "they were picking up the men who rotted in the rainy ditches among the dead horses and the ruined seventy-fives, in a forest of trees without branches along the river Marne" (Merton 3). Both his parents were artists; his New Zealander father was a devotee of Cézanne, his American mother artistic by temperament. "They were in the world and not of it," Merton said of his parents, "not because they were saints, but in a different way: because they were artists. The integrity of an artist lifts a man above the level of the world without delivering him from it" (Merton 3). Merton's father died in 1931, in London, after suffering an inoperable brain tumor for more than a year. During that year Thomas pursued a peripatetic education and felt the first stirrings of a quest for faith that is the theme of his autobiography.

After schooling in England, Thomas moved with his younger brother back to the home of his maternal grandparents on Long Island and enrolled in courses at Columbia, whose dormitories were then hotbeds of Communism and whose classrooms rang with lectures on literature by Mark Van Doren. Merton nibbled at the former, for American culture and society seemed to him too bankrupt and impotent to relieve suffering, inequity, and the immense ennui permeating the modern West. He had seen much more of the world than his classmates. For the literary study modeled by Van Doren, however, Merton found a much deeper reverence and respect: "I thought to myself, who is this excellent man Van Doren who being employed to teach literature, teaches just that: talks about writing and about books and poems and plays: does not get off on a tangent about the biographies of the poets or novelists: does not read into their poems a lot of subjective messages which were never there? Who is this man who does not have to fake and cover up a big gulf of ignorance by teaching a lot of opinions and conjectures and useless facts that belong to some other subject?" (Merton 139). This tribute to "Mark," as the student Merton came to refer to his professor, continues for another paragraph. I quote this much in order to suggest Merton's esteem for literature as an autonomous entity over any other illegitimate, lesser construction of knowledge-of-the-world. This is a point on which both Merton and O'Connor agree, and both will come to see their religious faith, Catholicism, as a guarantor of their faith in literature.

During the Depression of the 1930s, the years of his undergraduate and graduate work at Columbia, Merton sought a form of this guarantee of certainty in Communism as a social system with one foot in metaphysics. In his memoir (written from a perspective that more clearly shows the faults in the Old Left), he credits himself with seeing through the sham and contradiction almost from the outset. As a teenager at a public school in England, he had displayed *The Communist Manifesto* merely as part of the "decor" of his intellectual self-fashionings (Merton 93). A few years later, at Columbia, he tried to take his faith in Communism further, but in vain. After a few marches and pledges and meetings, he concluded:

> It's a nice, complex universe, the Communist universe: it gravitates towards stability and harmony and peace and order on the poles of an opportunism that is completely irresponsible and erratic. Its only law is, it will do whatever seems to be profitable to itself at the moment.... I had thought that Communists were calm, strong, definite people, with very clear ideas as to what was wrong with everything.... But the trouble with their convictions was that they were mostly strange, stubborn prejudices, hammered into their minds by the incantation of statistics, and without any solid intellectual foundation. And having decided that God is an invention of the ruling classes, and having excluded Him, and all moral order with Him, they were trying to establish some kind of moral system by abolishing all morality in its very source. (Merton 145–46)

Merton's early conclusion about the inadequacies of Communism as a moral system approaches but is not quite the strident charge of "godless communism" that was to take hold during the cold war of the late 1940s and 1950s and widen the gap between the New Left and campus conservatives in O'Connor's late years, the early 1960s. Because of his own experience of Communism, Merton's verdict is more nuanced than Billy Graham's, but it is compatible with Graham's because both men (and O'Connor) were believers and held political and social positions up to religious scrutiny. In general the problem is that of establishing a moral order in the world on a metaphysical base not *of* that world. Merton thought through this jungle; O'Connor seems to have always stood on the firm ground Merton struggled to achieve.

To fill the void that readings in Communism and that secular life in general could not redress, Merton turned to Catholic philosophy, not surprisingly to many of the same works O'Connor would find crucial as she educated herself in faith and solidified her literary agenda. The central authors each looked to as Catholic intellectuals and writers were Étienne Gilson, whose *The Spirit of Medieval Philosophy* (1936,

1950) informed both writers' imaginations on a bedrock level (although, as I venture to guess later in this essay, O'Connor is likely to have read about Gilson rather than to have actually read his work), and Jacques Maritain, whose *Art and Scholasticism* (1935) adapted philosophical arguments for the existence of God into the relatively more worldly, and risky, realm of artistic expression and construction, finding in "Art" an absolute very similar, but subordinate, to God.

Merton's "conversion experience" is worth quoting at some length for several reasons, not least of which is its foreshadowing of O'Connor's literary philosophy. Having read Gilson's *The Spirit of Medieval Philosophy* during his Columbia years, Merton was still looking for a way to connect the centuries-old Western religious foundation of certainty to his own life on the streets of Upper West Side. He found it "one day" in November 1937, when a friend recommended Aldous Huxley's *Ends and Means* (1937). Merton not only read the book almost immediately but was so impressed that he wrote an essay on it for the Columbia University *Review*. Huxley's book opened Merton's eyes:

> Huxley had been one of my favorite novelists in the days when I had been sixteen and seventeen and had built up a strange, ignorant philosophy of pleasure based on all the stories I was reading. And now everybody was talking about the way Huxley had changed. . . . Huxley was too sharp and intelligent and had too much sense of humor to take any of the missteps that usually make such conversions [from scoffer to sincere believer] look ridiculous and oafish. . . . On the contrary, he had read widely and deeply and intelligently in all kinds of Christian and Oriental mystical literature, and had come out with the astonishing truth that all this, far from being a mixture of dreams and magic and charlatanism, was very real and very serious.
>
> Not only was there such a thing as a supernatural order, but as a matter of concrete experience, it was accessible, very close at hand, an extremely near, an immediate and most necessary source of moral vitality, and one which could be reached most simply, most readily by prayer, faith, detachment, love. (Merton 184–85)

Merton clearly indicates—at least to those with hindsight—the path that he would take out of the meretricious secular world and into a Christian *via contemplativa* inflected with medieval asceticism and Eastern philosophy. He died in Bangkok on a mission to renew his Catholic spiritual life at Buddhist wellsprings. It is the search for the religious guarantee for the literary text that links Merton and O'Connor.

At the point of conversion in Merton's memoir, when his future in the Catholic Church is not yet certain (he was not baptized until a few years later), we can also see where and how his mixing of Catholic philosophy and art diverges from O'Connor's. Whatever her sincere belief in Catholic dogma, O'Connor was never as "detached" from the circumstances of her time and place, especially the pervasive circumstances of cold-war America, as she herself claimed to be. Unlike Merton, who clearly strove to reconcile heaven and earth, O'Connor never seems to have taken "earth" as seriously as "heaven" in the equation.

O'Connor's essays on the intersection of faith and writing, in *Mystery and Manners*, might be reconsidered as a frame for assessing her stance as a religious writer vis-à-vis Merton. In "The Church and the Fiction Writer" (1957), O'Connor proposes a line of demarcation using the same concept, *detachment*, that Merton uses in the excerpt above: "Part of the complexity of the problem for the Catholic fiction writer will be the presence of grace as it appears in nature, and what matters for him is that his faith not become detached from his dramatic sense and from his vision of what-is. No one in these days, however, would seem more anxious to have it become detached than those Catholics who demand that the writer limit, on the natural level, what he allows himself to see" (*MM* 147). Using pornography as her example of the source of "anxiety" among Catholics in "these times"—the late 1950s were the salad days of Citizens for Decent Literature, the Legion of Decency, and pulpit denunciations of films and books at Sunday Mass—O'Connor's fine line between obedience to the hierarchy and support of First Amendment freedom amounts to a kind and degree of secular involvement that Merton, by contrast, had foregone: "A dimension taken away [from a writer or work in the name of dogma] is one thing, a dimension added is another; and what the Catholic writer and reader will have to remember is that the reality of the added dimension will be judged in a work of fiction by the truthfulness and wholeness of the natural events presented. If the Catholic writer hopes to reveal mysteries, he will have to do it by describing truthfully what he sees from where he is" (*MM* 150). O'Connor finishes this essay with a peroration to the fiction writer who "presents mystery through manners"; the successful religious writer will ultimately, if genuine faith be present, triumph in accessing "that sense of Mystery which cannot be accounted for by any human formula"—that is, she will see the mystery *in* the manners, the grace *in* the quotidian, a current that runs in only one direction. Merton's desire, clearly registered in *The Seven Storey Mountain*, was to rise via spirituality above "what he sees from where he is" in the world by changing the "where he is" from the secular to the not-quite-cloistered. O'Connor, by comparison, seems more trapped between the antipodes of her own formulation: manners in the world and the mystery beyond it. More than Merton, who had tried social action and opted for the cloister, O'Connor pledged to be a Catholic writer *in the world* but not to be trapped in materialist contingency. It is this "bind" that makes rereading O'Connor's fiction in the context of the cold war profitable.

The bind appears in most of her essays about being both a writer and a Catholic. In "Novelist and Believer" (1963), O'Connor recreates the fractured binary of mystery and manners, the world of the senses and the supraworld of belief: "The novelist begins his work where human knowledge begins—with the senses; he works through the limitations of matter, and unless he is writing fantasy, he has to stay within the concrete possibilities of his culture. He is bound by his particular past and by those institutions and traditions that this past has left to his society. The Judaeo-Christian tradition has formed us in the west; we are bound to it by ties which may often be invisible, but which are there nevertheless" (*MM* 155). Merton's experience told him that the "concrete possibilities of culture" were vacant of any sustaining meaning. O'Connor's bind put her into a kind of temporary hostage situation: as a writer, she must keep residence in the world of concrete possibilities shaped by historical habits of behavior and knowledge, keep the faith that the writer's theology would redeem the mundane. More specifically, that the theological, deeply embedded yet never banal and obvious, will transform the "sociological tendency"—"the notion [in reader and critic] that the writer is after the typical" (*MM* 164). Too much originality, and the writer/believer loses her audience and flirts with a sinful pride by putting her imagination over the world God has created; too little, and the writer merely recycles "the typical" and therefore forfeits any reason to be read.

In "Catholic Novelists and Their Readers" (1964), an essay that the Fitzgeralds characterize as "relatively late material" from lectures O'Connor gave a few years before her death (*MM* 237), the writer's faith is more clearly situated:

> There is no reason why fixed dogma should fix anything that the writer sees in the world. On the contrary, dogma is an instrument for penetrating reality. Christian dogma is about the only thing left in the world that surely guards and respects mystery. The fiction writer is an observer, first, last, and always, but he cannot be an adequate observer unless he is free from uncertainty about what he sees. Those who have no absolute values cannot let the relative remain merely relative; they are always raising it to the level of the absolute. The Catholic fiction writer is entirely free to observe. He feels no call to take on the duties of God or to create a new universe. He feels perfectly free to look at the one we already have and to show exactly what he sees. He feels no need to apologize for the ways of God to man or to avoid looking at the ways of man to God. For him, to "tidy up reality" is certainly to succumb to the sin of pride. Open and free observation is founded on our ultimate faith that the universe is meaningful, as the Church teaches. (*MM* 178)

The Catholic writer sure in her faith is, then, free of ideological contamination by the "merely relative." A one-armed man, a female college graduate with a prosthetic leg, a peacock in full tail-spread, an azalea festival—not to mention African American farm laborers or a jockey lawn ornament—pass frictionlessly from the world of concrete possibilities, and cliché, to the realm of the absolute by virtue of an a priori faith.

Like many Catholic writers, Merton included, O'Connor anchored her identity and work as a writer to Jacques Maritain's prescription for the Catholic writer in *Art and Scholasticism*. "It's the book I cut my aesthetic teeth on," O'Connor wrote to Betty Hester in 1957 (*HB* 216). With the "aesthetic" came a cultural infusion as well, for Maritain's elevation of form and reason above messy and disorderly content and process induced O'Connor, and most of her critics, to believe that her work had no vital connection to the American and southern world in which it was made. She invokes this book and Maritain repeatedly in her letters. However theologically compact Maritain's explanation of art and religion might be, it is also smoothly compatible with the conditions for the American artist in which O'Connor maneuvered. As a Thomistic explanation of the nature and function of art in a Christian world, *Art and Scholasticism* is also a modernist rejection of "the immense intellectual disorder inherited from the nineteenth century" (Maritain 4), a call for the reinstatement of hierarchy and authoritarian order in the world through art (a generally compatible attitude, if not a conscious act, in the direction of the cold-war conformist state), and a legitimation of a denial of political engagement, for example, in racial matters, as being among the artist's responsibilities. Maritain's view raises conformity to the unvarying rules of art to the level of godliness.

Art's *"formal* element," Maritain declares in a high scholastic vein, "what constitutes it in its species and makes it what it is, is its being ruled by the intellect. If this formal element diminishes ever so little, to the same extent the reality of art vanishes. The *work to be made* is only the matter of art, its form is *undeviating reason"* (Maritain 9). The authoritarian tone of form over matter pervades *Art and Scholasticism:* those endowed with the power to enunciate the "undeviating reasons" for behavior and belief occupy a level of hierarchy superior to the faithful, who fulfill the divine order by submitting to just authority. And since, according to Maritain, the formal purity of art subtends from the same absolute metaphorically represented in the Creator, mere secular considerations are beneath notice. In general outline, this is the shape of the cold-war state. Whereas in the religious state it is the duty and power of the hierarchy to define blessedness and the way to it, in the secular state it is the power and function of worldly powers (chairmen, directors, presidents, and the like) to define patriotism and the behaviors consistent with it. Deviants produce heresy or treason; ship of state or ship of fools, mortals may not be trusted to navigate their own fates. In the same area when O'Connor was cutting her teeth on Maritain, the Beats were toking up in rebellion against the "un-deviating reason" of form and of the state, invoking radical democracies in an age of conformity. And the existentialists, another French brigade to rival the New Scholastics, were interrogating all a priori certainties.

Maritain's absolutist philosophy provided O'Connor with a way to evade one of the most disruptive, secular issues (besides Communism itself) of the American cold-war era: post-desegregation racial politics, all-deliberate-speed versus massive resistance. Her own dislike of James Baldwin, as a "Negro" and as a novelist, personalizes O'Connor's racial standing in the 1950s (*HB* 580). She characterizes a person exploring "interracial circles" as a "liberal abolitionist," which is one of the coy, down-home quips that place her on the Dixiecrat Right (*HB* 330). In her work, there are seldom African American characters who rise above latter-day minstrel stereotypes. The two farm hands in "The Displaced Person," Astor and Sulk, are barely more than types. Coleman Parrum, in "Judgment Day," enacts the racialist "theory" that the African American, faced with the Caucasian's superior will and power, will "naturally" surrender to the white person. Tanner considers this part of the natural law and is literally surprised to death when the African American actor in his New York apartment building refuses to behave to type. But "Judgment Day" is not unalloyed evidence of inspired racial politics in O'Connor. The actor is a malevolent character, presumably the one who, finding Tanner in the throes of a probable stroke, thrusts the old white man's body between the spindles of the apartment stairwell and leaves him there to die, as if in the stocks. It would be well to remember that, taking *The Habit of Being* as text, O'Connor had no liking for any of the African American cultural leaders who were her contemporaries—not King or Baldwin, surely—except Cassius Clay, soon to become Muhammad Ali. And she liked Ali because he was just as much a separatist as she was herself (*HB* 571, 580).

Art and Scholasticism might have seemed, to O'Connor, to elevate her art above the ground of historical circumstances, of contingent rather than absolute relevance. But by a kind of surreptitious reverberation, Maritain's philosophy actually pushed her and her work more deeply into the cultural mentality of her times by reinforcing the authoritarian script. If, as Maritain claimed, forms of art must be properly admired for their "species," then so do members of the human race.

In *The Culture of the Cold War*, Whitfield characterizes the temper of the times:

> With the source of the evil so elusive and so immune to risk-free retaliation, American culture was politicized. The values and perceptions, the forms of expression, the symbolic patterns, the beliefs and myths that enabled Americans to make sense of reality—these constituents of culture were contaminated by an unseemly political interest in their roots and consequences. The struggle against domestic Communism encouraged an interpenetration of the two enterprises of politics and culture, resulting in a philistine inspection of artistic works not for their content but for the *politique des auteurs*. Censors endorsed the boycott of films that they had not seen; vigilantes favored the removal from library shelves of books that they had not read. (Whitfield 10)

The basic distinction between the culture of the cold war and the suprahistorical culture of Catholic writing is merely chronological—the former dates from the Soviet detonation of a nuclear bomb and the latter dates from the collision of the Middle Ages and bourgeois individualism. Both cultures, secular and theological, were structurally the same: the destruction of an age of faith and certainty and its replacement by an age of doubt, suspicion, and multicentered views of meaning and history that induced a turning to absolutist authority: philistine or clerical. This formula has suited many readers and admirers of O'Connor in the four decades since her death. It is immensely pleasing to think that the pleasures of reading O'Connor can also be spiritual exercises. And yet so much is lost in the myth of the "frictionless" passage from the concrete local to the absolute (a myth O'Connor herself did much to promulgate in her essays). The persistence of this habit of reading is particularly disadvantageous now for the American reading public as so much of our cultural life is being ushered into the absolute of "homeland security" by leaders who demand faith in an unexamined certainty beyond and other than democracy-as-process.

Politics is not irrelevant to O'Connor's fiction; in fact, the political circumstances of her life and times are central to the themes of her stories. Whatever they may mean on the level of theology, her stories are scripts for the cold war. If not for active participation in vigilantism, then for quietism in resignation. A story like "The Partridge Festival," which O'Connor apparently did not much like and denigrated as "that farce" (*HB* 404), may not work fully on the theological level, but it does work as a case study in enforced conformity. The town of Partridge, a generic stand-in for the American, not just the southern, small town—like the small town invaded by the pods in *Invasion of the Body Snatchers* (1956)—is having what purports to be a celebration or rite of community, an Azalea Festival. The citizens at large deem it patriotic to conform to the communal liturgy by buying and wearing a badge. One citizen, Singleton, dissents, is pressured, cracks under the pressure, and shoots six of his fellow citizens in a violent breakdown of public order that has become all-too-common in the United States since 1961, when the story was first published.

Calhoun arrives for a visit in "his small pod-shaped car," which could just simply be a Volkswagen Beetle and not an extraterrestrial vehicle suggested by the pods that infiltrate the small town in *Invasion of the Body Snatchers*. He is greeted by his maiden aunts, two women "who looked like George Washington with his wooden teeth in" (*CS* 421). In short order, O'Connor set in motion the interpenetration of the aesthetic with the political. Secular patriotism lies behind the facile surfaces of "The Partridge Festival." Calhoun fancies himself the heroic dissenter to this absolutism, and yet lurking in his character is a podlike talent for salesmanship (*CS* 424–25). Calhoun's parents smile reassuringly when he tells them he despises their values; they know, like all pod-people, that resistance is futile. Whitfield archly characterizes Billy Graham as a former Fuller Brush salesman who revealed the religious secret for his success in ironically secular terms: "I believed in the product. . . . Sincerity is the biggest part of selling anything—including the Christian Plan of Salvation" (Whitfield 82). Graham serves as Calhoun's cultural referent; salesmanship is the fatal gene of modern American life.

Calhoun fancies himself a rebel and dissenter. He is pompously confident, in the consistent fashion of O'Connor's intellectually proud fools, of his grasp on the deficiencies of the rubes in his hometown. Indeed his cross-examination of the local barber comes off as a stilted dialogue between two opponents in a debate rather than between two successful literary characters. The barber stands for the kind of philistine censoriousness that Whitfield describes:

> "He [Singleton] was an individualist," Calhoun said. "A man who would not allow himself to be pressed into the mold of his inferiors. A non-conformist. He was a man of depth living among caricatures and they finally drove him mad, unleashed all his violence on themselves. Observe," he continued, "that they didn't try him. They simply had him committed at once to Quincy. Why? Because," he said, "a trial would have brought out his essential innocence and the real guilt of the community." The barber's face lightened. "You're a lawyer, ain't you?" he asked. "No," the boy said sullenly. "I'm a writer." (*CS* 431)

Writer or lawyer, Calhoun is O'Connor's version of the proud modern: he who, as Étienne Gilson described the type, "professes to be satisfied with the state of fallen nature" (Gilson 125).

The climax of the story is formulaic: Calhoun and his female cognate, the world-weary and cynical girl-next-door, Mary Elizabeth, make the journey to the state asylum to confront Singleton, to pay intellectual homage to the outcast and outlaw. Passing themselves off as his kin, which is Mary Elizabeth's idea, they make their way to Singleton's ward and wait for two custodians to bring him out. Singleton is a perfect model of the deracinated modern. Physically unbalanced (one eye is larger and rounder than the other) and simian, he fails to live up to the existential heft of the Camusian hero. In fact, he gropes Mary Elizabeth and puts a farewell to the interview by hopping on the furniture like a chimpanzee and lifting his hospital gown for all the world to see.

"The Partridge Festival" might have ended here, and if it had, it would have been about as unsatisfying a story as O'Connor feared it might be. But after fleeing the asylum in Calhoun's pod-shaped car, the couple pauses on the side of the road. Without exchanging a word, the couple stares into each other's eyes and sees "the likeness of their kinsman [Singleton]." Calhoun has a further revelation. In the lenses of Mary Elizabeth's glasses, he watches the image of Singleton metamorphose into the visage of his great-grandfather, the "master merchant" (*CS* 422), whose immortal money bankrolls the town festival: "Round, innocent, undistinguished as an iron link, it was the face whose gift had pushed straight forward to the future to raise festival after festival. Like a master salesman, it seemed to have been waiting there from all time to claim him" (*CS* 444). Calhoun is the deepest conformist of them all, never so much the "chained" rebel than when he rebels from the most philistine grounding available to him, one utterly confident in its secular wisdom. O'Connor's absolutist elevation turns "The Partridge Festival" into a plague on all our houses: the conformity rigidly imposed by the philistines of Partridge might indeed be totalitarian, but the impulse to rebel is equally ludicrous and compromised.

"The Partridge Festival" is blatant in delivering its message, and that is probably one of the reasons O'Connor had little affection for it. "Everything That Rises Must Converge" is a different case. O'Connor lifted her title from *The Phenomenon of Man* (1959) by Pierre Teilhard de Chardin (1881–1955), a Jesuit theologian she read admiringly in the half decade before her death. "The most important non-fiction writer," O'Connor wrote to a correspondent in March 1964, "is Pere Pierre Teilhard de Chardin, S.J. who died in 1955 and has so far escaped the Index, although a monition has been issued on him. If they are good, they are dangerous" (*HB* 570–71). To me, Teilhard has always seemed an unpredictable choice for O'Connor's theological admiration, especially as her reading of him follows her "teething" stage with solid and structured Maritain. Compared to Maritain, whose Thomistic rigidity he dissolves in his concept of converging human consciousness above history, Teilhard is Whitmanic, mystical, and undisciplined. So clearly is he the opposite of the rigidly taxonomic Maritain that he seems perilously close to a parody of theology, an utterer of seemingly profound but ultimately vapid New Age babble more likely to be encountered in an episode of *Star Trek*:

> All our difficulties and repulsions as regards the opposition between the All and the Person would be dissipated if only we understood that, by structure, the noosphere (and more generally the world) represent a whole that is not only closed but also *centred*. Because it contains and engenders consciousness, space-time is necessarily *of a convergent nature*. Accordingly its enormous layers, followed in the right direction, must somewhere ahead become involuted to a point which we might call *Omega*, which fuses and consumes them integrally in itself. (Teilhard 259)

Teilhard's theology is, if anything, more like Gilson's in *The Spirit of Medieval Philosophy*, one of the foundational books both O'Connor and Merton acknowledge. Gilson's theology is more "comic" than Maritain's Scholasticism in that Gilson stresses the underlying and ultimate goodness of creation, humankind included, often regardless of the lack of apparent system. There may not, in Gilson's cosmology, be a possibility of heaven on earth, but the Creation is good (the Creator himself is on record saying so) and we are not to feel guilty when we take some pleasure in the world and our bodies. *Pace* Maritain: there is pleasure in the making of the thing, not only in the contemplation of the form from which the individual thing and its making derive. Teilhard takes the "comic" vision even further, coming quite close to believing in the perfectibility of creation in the convergence of human consciousness at the "Omega," which may be "millions of years in the future" but is nevertheless in the human future (Teilhard 192).

O'Connor usually scoffs at such airy notions as perfectibility on the human plane; grace and redemption, being essential to rescue us from sin, are reasons for central plot suspense in her fiction. The passage of centuries between the mummy and Enoch in *Wise Blood*, for example, does not augur the coming of the Teilhardian noosphere. O'Connor's comedy is deeply compromised by her buying into the authoritarian temper of her religion and her times; her comedy is almost interchangeable with her contempt. It is the interchangeability of title and story in "Everything That Rises Must Converge" that gives the story its edge.

By the very early 1960s, when the story was first published, American racial behavior was an issue in both social and political "manners." Boycotts and protests, bombings and arson were common; civil rights legislation was a few years in the future. American society, and the society of the post–*Brown v. Board of Education* South in particular, seemed locked in an anticonvergence mode: the conscious "massive resistance" policy of southern dissenters simply aimed to stop all change in its tracks. The conjunction of racial turmoil and cold-war anxieties made for a rancid brew in America. The FBI spied on Martin Luther King Jr., justifying its invasion of the privacy of an American citizen with the argument that all agitation is Communist, King agitates, ergo King is a Communist. By the rule of association, any race leader who spoke or acted to change the status quo was a Communist. The southern classic of the era is Harper Lee's *To Kill a Mockingbird*, a sentimental evasion of the issues of black rights and white responsibility. "Everything That Rises Must Converge" is anything but sentimental, but neither is it comedic or progressive. By the end of the story, the writing is on the wall: Do not rock the boat; neither progress nor improvement is attainable in the human sphere; only the deluded try.

The Julian of "Everything That Rises Must Converge" is from O'Connor's repertory company of spoiled intellectuals. That he bears the same name as Sir Julian Huxley, Aldous's brother and a coincidental reminder of the link to Merton, might be one of O'Connor's sly hints of the irony in store: Teilhard's *The Phenomenon of Man*, in English translation with an introduction by Sir Julian Huxley, was a book O'Connor often recommended. Like Calhoun in "The Partridge Festival," Julian fancies himself deserving of better places and better company. He is saddled by his overweight mother, a small southern town, and too little income to afford a car—O'Connor's favorite symbol of self-actualization. Without private wheels Julian is thrown into the cauldron of public transportation; southern municipal bus systems in the 1950s and 1960s, whatever they might symbolize in automotive terms, were sites of racial and class conflict. No surprise, then, that on the one night when Julian's mother wears her new hat on the bus to the downtown Y, an African American woman boards the same bus wearing the same hat. What registers with Julian first, however, is not the hat but the stereotype of the grotesque "colored" female body. If there is an evolutionary noosphere where human consciousness continually accumulates, shedding the burdens of the bodily self-consciousness, it is not on this bus: "There was something familiar-looking about her but Julian could not place what it was. She was a giant of a woman. Her face was set not only to meet opposition but to seek it out. The downward tilt of her large lower lip was like a warning sign: don't tamper with me. Her bulging figure was encased in a green crepe dress and her feet overflowed in red shoes. She had on a hideous hat" (*CS* 415). The racialized bodily presence of this woman in the close quarters of the bus accelerates combustion, even as Julian fantasizes interracial convergence. The process toward the racial violence in the story is blatant, but the Teilhardian discourse of convergence against which the violence is played—and which the violence denies—captures O'Connor in the religious-cultural bind.

The African American woman's child, a young boy, climbs up on the seat next to Julian's mother, and the woman herself bears "down upon the empty seat beside Julian." The irony of the interchange of sons plays in one direction, which is to infantilize Julian and his fantasy life of cosmopolitanism. But interchange also scripts the theme of convergence, and racial and biological differentiations seem mere blips on the trajectory to unity. Slowly, but in a particularly rising, convergent way, Julian becomes aware of the identical hats: "He was conscious of a kind of bristling next to him, muted growling like that of an angry cat. He could not see anything but the red pocketbook upright on the bulging green thighs. He visualized the woman as she had stood waiting for her tokens—the ponderous figure, rising from the red shoes upward over the solid hips, the mammoth bosom, the haughty face, to the green and purple hat. His eyes widened" (*CS* 416). In the upward trajectory O'Connor plots deliberately for Julian's gaze, and correspondingly for his emerging awareness, convergence is the keynote. His mother and the black woman rise and converge in his consciousness toward the omega point of their identical hats. In a positive Teilhardian register, this might be read as a hoped-for and eventual convergence of human identity leaving race distinction behind and below. Teilhard would have the ultimate progress of the human race in such a hopeful mode. In fact, his diagram 4 (Teilhard 192), representing the rising and convergence of human consciousness over millennia, uses a vertical, organic shape, bulbous through its middle and capped by a relatively tiny omega: the shape of the two mothers complete with identical hats.

Julian's sick fantasies of humiliating his mother, by confronting her with her own antiquated prejudice, are just a pale foreshadowing of what does happen. Julian's mother, acting out of unconvergent racial habit, begins to treat the young black boy like a pickaninny, or a lawn jockey. Julian senses the impending crash but does nothing to intervene. When his mother rummages in her purse for a shiny coin to give to the black boy, the detonation happens: "The huge woman turned and for a moment stood, her shoulders lifted and her face frozen with frustrated rage, and stared at Julian's mother. Then all at once she seemed to explode like a piece of machinery that had been given one ounce of pressure too much. Julian saw the black fist swing out with the red pocketbook. He shut his eyes and cringed as he heard the woman shout, 'He don't take nobody's pennies!'" (*CS* 418). The black fist with the red pocketbook is a loaded symbol for a readership immersed in racial and anti-Communist propaganda. Typically, O'Connor overloads the moment. Failing to find a coin impressed with the profile of Thomas Jefferson, Julian's mother finds one with Lincoln's. The image of the Emancipator fails to bring the two mothers, two races, together, and the story ends with a negative convergence. The clear theme is that, in the sphere of American race relations at least, nothing but animosity rises and the convergence of human interests is the last item on anyone's agenda. From a variety of directions, then, O'Connor's debt to the social status quo overrode her theology.

For a Catholic writer who claimed the certainty of the absolute, O'Connor's cultural politics proved stronger. When the issue was race, she chose the local over the absolute, manners over mystery. Nowhere is this clearer than in her refusal to meet with James Baldwin in Georgia: "No I can't see James Baldwin in Georgia. It would cause the greatest trouble and disturbance and disunion. In New York it would be nice to meet him; here it would not. I observe the traditions of the society I feed on—it's only fair. Might as well expect a mule to fly as me to see James Baldwin in Georgia. I have read one of his stories and it was a good one" (*HB* 329). For O'Connor the Catholic writer in the cold war, religious faith bowed to social conformity. On the one hand, the claim to be a Catholic writer excused her from local responsibility for the "sins" of her "traditions." On the other hand, immersion in and allegiance to those traditions (when change threatened) functioned as similar absolutes. This is the bind of the Catholic writer in the cold war. For one who believes in the risen Christ, a flying mule should be no problem.

Notes

1. The original draft of this essay was written before Gulf War II in the spring of 2002. Revising it more than a year later, in the wake of disclosures of "sexed-up intelligence" in Britain and similar suspicions in the U.S., it seems likely that a policy of fear and dread was calculated.

2. This essay was delivered first in 2002, when the U.S. Catholic bishops were deep in the throes of revelations of widespread sexual abuse of boys by past and present priests.

Works Cited

Bacon, Jon Lance. *Flannery O'Connor and Cold War Culture*. Cambridge: Cambridge University Press, 1993.

Desmond, John F. *Risen Sons: Flannery O'Connor's Vision of History*. Athens: University of Georgia Press, 1987.

Giannone, Richard. *Flannery O'Connor and the Mystery of Love*. Urbana: University of Illinois Press, 1989.

———. *Flannery O'Connor, Hermit Novelist*. Urbana: University of Illinois Press, 2000.

Gilson, Étienne. *The Spirit of Medieval Philosophy.* Translated by A. H. G. Downes. 1936. Reprint, London: Sheed and Ward, 1950.

Gordon, Sarah. *Flannery O'Connor: The Obedient Imagination.* Athens: University of Georgia Press, 2000.

Herbert, Bob. "Isn't Democracy Worth It?" *New York Times,* June 17, 2002, A21.

Huxley, Aldous. *Ends and Means.* London: Chatto and Windus, 1938.

Maritain, Jacques. *"Art and Scholasticism" and "The Frontiers of Poetry."* Translated by Joseph W. Evans. New York: Charles Scribner's Sons, 1962.

Merton, Thomas. *The Seven Storey Mountain.* New York: Harcourt, Brace and Co., 1948.

Teilhard de Chardin, Pierre. *The Phenomenon of Man.* Introduction by Sir Julian Huxley. Translated by Bernard Wall. New York: Harper and Row, 1959.

Whitfield, Stephen J. *The Culture of the Cold War.* Baltimore: Johns Hopkins University Press, 1991.

Flannery O'Connor's Art

A Gesture of Grace

Lila N. Meeks

Perhaps her life and art reflect the truth of Samuel Johnson's observation that nothing so concentrates the mind as the verdict of death. Receiving her verdict at the age of twenty-five, Flannery O'Connor, a devout Catholic, for the final fifteen years of her life never faltered in exploring things eternal and absolute in her fiction. For O'Connor the greatest literature involves the salvation or loss of one's soul. She is a break from the American tradition of artist-doubters and certainly from the nihilism of the twentieth century. Like saints of old, she faced the fires of her time—the elevation of the intellectual and the rational, the infallibility of the scientific method, the use of sociology's and psychology's data collections as explanations for what it means to be human, and America's romance with the almighty dollar and all it can buy—with an accurate assessment, a biting sense of humor, and an unfailing faith. She knew her task was a daunting one: "The novelist with Christian concerns will find in modern life distortions which are repugnant to him, and his problem will be to make these appear as distortions to an audience which is used to seeing them as natural" (*MM* 33).

She rejected the prevailing distortions, including the era's faith in humanity's progress as expressed by Swinburne when he wrote, "Glory to man in the highest, for he is the master of things," and by Steinbeck when he wrote, "In the end was the word and the word was with men" (*MM* 159). She was outraged by an article in *Life* magazine complaining that America's best writers were not adequately celebrating the joyous life of every American, a joy ensured by the country's achievements of "unparalleled prosperity," an "almost classless society," and being "the most powerful country in the world" (*MM* 25–26). This zippity-do-dah view of life in the United States reflected the country's predisposition to believe that things material and nonessential are the basis for life's joy. Walker Percy may have read a similar article just before pointing out, "When the canary gets unhappy, utters plaintive cries, and collapses, it may be time for the miners to surface and think things over."[1] O'Connor agreed that the canary had indeed expired, and after mulling things over, she decided that "at its best our age is an age of searchers and discoverers, and at its worst, an age that has domesticated despair and learned to live with it happily" (*MM* 159).

In *The Divine Milieu*, Teilhard de Chardin suggests that, even in an age of despair, divine grace is a force that refuses to be denied: "God must, in some way or other, make room for Himself, hollowing us out and emptying us, if he is finally to penetrate into us. . . . He must break the molecules of our being so as to re-cast and re-model us."² Often it is a violent assault of grace upon the nonbeliever that unnerves readers and leads them to misconstrue O'Connor's stories. O'Connor was well aware that she would likely fail to communicate but refused to give up the effort: "You can't indicate moral values when morality changes with what is being done, because there is no accepted basis of judgment. And you cannot show the operation of grace when grace is cut off from nature or when the very possibility of grace is denied so that no one will have the least idea of what you are about" (*MM* 166). "When I write a novel in which the central action is a baptism, . . . I have to make the reader feel, in his bones if nowhere else, that something is going on here that counts. Distortion in this case is an instrument; exaggeration has a purpose and the whole structure of the story or novel has been made what it is because of belief. This is not the kind of distortion that destroys; it is the kind that reveals, or should reveal" (*MM* 162).

If her distortions are still unsettling to readers today, it is because in a world content with ten-second answers to most of its questions, she digs deep, beneath the manners to the mysteries of life. Her intention was to make the supernatural as real as the natural. Flannery O'Connor believed that even the most alienated of men, through free will, could accept the undeserved, immeasurable love of God and, by accepting this gift of grace, be free to live in unity with God, his fellow man, and himself. She also believed the devil would do all he could to prevent such a reunion. And so in her first book of short stories the headnote, a quote from Saint Cyril of Jerusalem, gives the casual reader a warning that he or she is jumping into the deep end of the pool: "The dragon is by the side of the road, watching those who pass. Beware lest he devour you. We go to the Father of Souls, but it is necessary to pass by the dragon."

Like Hawthorne, she knew the devil was a presence; like C. S. Lewis, she believed that the twentieth-century world was largely a territory held by him. She believed that God would rescue us from the devil and from ourselves if we want him to, but she saw her neighbors—even church-going believers in Christ—as separated from nature, wanting salvation served up as "Instant Uplift," pleased as punch with themselves, full to the brim with self-satisfaction, and empty of belief. As a Georgian and a Catholic growing up in the rural South, the Bible Belt, she was a native and an alien at the same time. She realized that the religion of her neighbors was both diminished and distorted but felt that the North, too sophisticated, secular, and progressive to believe at all, was even more lost than the twisted and distorted South.

O'Connor did not turn from the solitary path before her because, like Faulkner, she knew that the serious writer must gnaw on universal bones, even when everyone else has gone out for fast food. For her those bones were original sin, free will, grace, redemption, salvation, and judgment. While her stories are more fleshed out than the parables of the Bible, her precision in giving just the necessary information and her insistence that there is more in life and in a story than meets the eye remind one of the parables and suggest to the reader that her stories are, indeed, parables of grace and that more than casual attention to detail is required. The setting and the characters are mundane, but the emphasis and the tone may awaken the reader to something mysterious, something mystical and holy. Struggling against one's own nature, education, and experience, the successful reader may discover essential truths beneath the kudzu and red clay of O'Connor's stories. To be captured by her prose, one must focus carefully and grasp the struggles between divine will and the human wills who are either unconscious of the possibility of grace or actively avoiding entanglement with God as best they can. If her fiction does not investigate the social concerns some critics believe it should, it is because she was attempting to dig beneath the manners to the mysteries. For her, accepting the gift of grace was not a chief issue, it was *the* issue.

Harry Ashfield in "The River" and the grandmother in "A Good Man Is Hard to Find" are innocents of different generations, who are unaware that there are spiritual mysteries beneath the surface of their everyday existences. A child held hostage in the city by self-indulgent parents, Harry recognizes his need for more than he is presently experiencing when he escapes from the city and hears the Word. The Ashfields, like many Americans, have moved to the city and become lost souls. They are alienated from nature and from God. They are too self-indulgent, self-absorbed, and self-centered to realize the stultifying effect their vacuous, hollow existence has on young Harry. Mrs. Connin, a good country woman who knows that the spirit is more important than the body, comes to rescue the boy and allows Harry to envision the possibility of something more. Almost immediately he changes his name to Bevel and accepts the idea that he can be healed, the idea that there is an opportunity for redemption. He recognizes the limitations of his own existence after experiencing something he could compare it to: "You found out more when you left where you lived.... They joked a lot where he lived" (*CS* 163). There was no chance to be healed there. At the river he was given a clear choice: "Believe Jesus or the devil." And "he had the sudden feeling that this was not a joke." But "where he lived everything was a joke" (*CS* 166–67). He prefers to go under the river to the Kingdom of Christ than to return to the secondhand smoke and stale liquor fumes of his apartment. He wants to "count," but the world he lives in does not provide an opportunity for his spirit to matter in any significant way. He does not intend to waste anymore time. At his moment of grace, as the long gentle hand pulls him forward and down, for the first time in his life he knows he is getting somewhere, and all his "fury and fear" leave him.

The grandmother is less innocent than Harry is, more responsible for her state of alienation, but as she grudgingly sets off for Florida, she is unaware that there is a deeper reality than the tedium of her life. She thinks of herself as a good Christian, but she is a foolish, silly bigot, whose worship of her ancestors leads her family into terrible danger and death. According to O'Connor, she lacks comprehension but has a good heart. Perhaps nowhere in her writings does O'Connor dramatize the need to shock a person out of the everyday for her to see the gift of grace as clearly as she does with the grandmother's encounter with The Misfit. The old woman babbles on, as she is wont to do, about family and breeding until the horror of what is happening leads her to a moment of grace, to a gesture that hollows her out and makes room for God. When she reaches out to this criminal, this twisted murderer, when she calls him "one of my babies," she is reunited with her Creator (CS 132). Her death can be seen as a victory over a vacuous life, and her reaching out clearly shakes The Misfit, touches him in his practiced alienation and atheism so that he loses his joy even in meanness.

Mrs. May in "Greenleaf" and Ruby Turpin in "Revelation" are sisters to the grandmother, other solid examples of the self-satisfied, southern women who peopled the South of O'Connor's life and fiction; but even more than the grandmother, they plan to have religion on their own terms—usually for social purposes. They believe that they are contributors to the greater good, and as such, they should receive their rewards in this life, where it counts. Mrs. May is so alienated from herself and God that she has disdain for the body and the soul. She believes that sex belongs only in the bedroom just as Christ belongs only in church. She wants her life as sanitized as her milking barn. Self-sufficient and self-satisfied, she will not seek God, so she must be brought to the point where she can no longer avoid him. The scrub bull removes the scales from her eyes, but only at the moment of her death.

Ruby Turpin seems to have a head that is not quite so hardened and a heart that is not so shriveled. Her revelation requires less violence. She is a fine, southern, white, respectable, land-owning, church-going farm lady, who is sick with sin and is waiting for the doctor. Of course, she thinks it is her husband, not she, who needs the doctor. She presides over the waiting room and divides those waiting into classes, determining their worth by looking at their shoes. Her dreams just before she dozes off depict her self-satisfaction. She'd rather be her plump self than white trash or black. She is a rather simple soul, who accepts the prejudices of her time and place: a society of hierarchies of race and class based on blood, money, and property. The image Ruby has is of cramming folks into boxcars according to how they fit her norms.

Her usual complacency is interrupted, not by a raging bull, but by a sour intellectual with a message from God wrapped in a psychology text. By the end of the story, Ruby is no longer ignoring God; she is shaking her fist at him, angry that God does not protect *her* white, middle-class values. As we watch her standing with the pigs in the scientifically designed, spotless pig parlor, we come to understand that God does not help those who help themselves, that cleanliness is not next to godliness. Ruby's salvation can only come if her pride and spiritual arrogance are burned away by God's grace. As she turns toward home in the twilight, she hears the cricket chorus and sees a vision. We come to understand that it is by the gift of grace alone, undeserved and freely given, that Ruby can join the singing souls moving toward heaven. Marching in step and singing on key will not assure salvation.

O'Connor's stories are peopled with the Ashfields, the grandmothers, the Mrs. Mays, the Ruby Turpins, and others—the innocent and the hardened, the ordinary and the grotesque, the blacks and the whites, the ignorant and the educated. For O'Connor, all are made in the image of God—these humans, no matter how distorted, maimed, or lost, are expressions of the holy—and her fiction insists that none can be dismissed as unworthy of grace. What could be a more serious focus for fiction than the salvation of the soul? For the Christian, salvation of the soul involves the crucifixion, the resurrection, the ascension, the eating of the flesh, and the drinking of the blood of Christ, all of which could make for some pretty dreadful reading if O'Connor did not bring comic relief to her storytelling with her mimic's ear and her cartoonist's eye. According to O'Connor, it is the very seriousness of her themes that necessitates the humor in her stories: "all comic novels that are any good must be about matters of life and death" (*MM* 114). At another point she says, "the maximum amount of seriousness admits the maximum amount of comedy" (*MM* 167).

Whatever the reason, everyone's delight is greater when something humorous happens at a serious moment—during a sermon, a funeral, or a stuffy lecture. Clearly O'Connor understands that humor is an important element of her fiction because the subjects are deep and often the endings are not happy, at least not in the conventional sense. The humor of her stories brings us closer to the characters and makes the sharp points of her satire easier to understand and to accept. She seeks to entrap our everydayness and force us to sense the mystery of essential things, and humor is one of her most important tools of entrapment. With the theme of the redeeming power of God's grace in an age of apostasy, her fiction would have, no doubt, been condemned to the pages of Catholic magazines if it had not been for her sureness in perceiving and depicting the absurd; her powerful, straightforward prose; her ear for authentic dialogue; and, most important, her wicked, stripped-of-all-sentimentality sense of humor.

Her brilliant use of language is one of the most successful elements of her humor. Her letters and papers are filled with ample evidence of her ability to hear and repeat the singular expressions that place the speaker in and around Milledgeville, Georgia, that ground the speaker in this particular place. She readily admitted that even if she peopled her stories with Japanese characters, they would talk like Georgia chicken farmers. Certainly the authenticity of the language adds to the reality of the natural world and thus is significant in preparing to bring on the supernatural. She knew you could not reach the supernatural except through the natural. She captures the language and the inanity of daily conversations, repeats them in her letters, and then puts them into the mouths of some of her most memorable characters. In writing to Cecil Dawkins about Dawkins's fiction, she says, "you have a very good ear and that means a lot" (*HB* 286). It means a lot in O'Connor's fiction also. One of the longer examples of her excellent recall and her keen fascination with just how banal conversations can be was an exchange she overheard between two orderlies while she was in the local hospital recovering from the flu: "What have you done with them sheets? I ain't done nothing with them. Well I tole you what to do with them. You ain't never done no suchofva thing. I know what I done. You may know what you done, but you don't know what I done" (*HB* 270). The pearls of wisdom shared endlessly by Mrs. Hopewell and Mrs. Freeman as they verbally attempt to one-up each other at every breakfast and lunch and often at supper echo the humor and the emptiness of the orderlies' dialogue: "Everyone is different." "Yes, most people is." "It takes all kinds to make the world." "I always said it did myself" (*CS* 273).

While listening, she was also watching intently, and the sharp, squinting eye of the seeress of Andalusia did not miss much that was ridiculous in the world around her, and what she saw usually found its way onto the printed page to expose one character or another. Some of the most delightful moments in reading O'Connor are when she gratuitously throws in an observation by one of the characters or includes some background information that makes us smile at the slyness of its inclusion and then wonder at the smoothness with which it fits into the story's structure and meaning. Mrs. Connin has assessed the Ashfields' apartment, and on her way out of the door, she refers to a picture saying, "I wouldn't have paid for that, . . . I would have drew it myself." Then later in the hallway, she reconsiders and says, "I wouldn't have drew it" (*CS* 158). The truth is Mrs. Connin, who works the night shift and has a picture of Jesus on her wall, has nothing in common with the Ashfields; she does not share their values in art or in life. Poor and country as she is, she is one of O'Connor's fundamentalists who know a universal truth that the middle class and the well-to-do have chosen to leave behind while striving smartly to secure their socioeconomic advancement and to establish their impeccable taste in art. Early on in Ruby Turpin's visit to the doctor's office, the background music is "wona these days I know I'll we-eara crown" (*CS* 490). Of course, she knows every line of this song because what could be a more appropriate theme song for do-gooder Miss Ruby, who is definitely expecting to arrive in heaven in style. It serves also as a meaningful anthem for the final vision of heavenly folk, when wearing a crown will definitely not move her to the front of the line.

Before O'Connor turns her wit upon her fictional folk, she gives herself a good dose of the same medicine. A disarming honesty—totally without sentimentality —and a wicked sense of humor are more than a part of her art; they appear to be part of her nature. In her letters, one is struck by her unflinching honesty in viewing people, events, and herself. There is no pretentiousness and no hypocrisy. She repeatedly uses self-deprecating humor, often with self-incriminating grammar and idiom, whenever she reports good news about her fiction, so that her achievement is put in its place, so that she reminds herself and her correspondents that the one with the most toys, prizes, victories, publications, positive reviews does not win. Following the reception of a fiction award, she writes Betty Hester that "it not only extols my merits as a writer but spells my name in two interesting ways" (*HB* 179). She is not impressed that one of her stories is to be made into a TV drama, but she is delighted she can buy Regina a new refrigerator with the proceeds: "While they make hash out of my story, she and me will make ice in the new refrigerator" (*HB* 174). She is not caught taking herself or her work too seriously. Even in the last months of her life, when she was facing a serious operation, she said, "I have a large tumor and if they don't make haste and get rid of it, they will have to remove me and leave it" (*HB* 567). After being away from Andalusia, she is "very glad to be back with the chickens who don't know I have just published a book" (*HB* 84). With similar humor, she repeatedly stomps on her characters' pride and puts them in their places to the delight of the reader and the development of the story. Time and again she tells of a character's sense of accomplishment, general satisfaction with self, and dissatisfaction with the shortcomings of others only to pull the rug out from under the self-satisfaction or self-delusion and leave the character completely exposed as foolish, fraudulent, or worse. Mrs. May offers a great example of such exposure: "'I don't like to hear you boys make jokes about religion,' she had said. 'If you would go to church, you would meet some nice girls'" (*CS* 320). Nothing could miss the point of religion any more than turning church into a dating service for the likes of Scofield and Wesley. Or nothing could be more full of hubris than Mrs. May's under-the-breath comment: "I'll die when I get good and ready" (*CS* 321).

In all of her satire, no group comes in for more scathing, more drawn out exposure than intellectuals, who are always sure they know everything, certainly more than anyone else, including God, if there were one. I am afraid she did not come to this depiction without help from professors, both individuals and as faculties, with whom she had contact. There were the Georgia State College for Women faculty members whose reactions she summed up at a poetry reading in Savannah: "One reported it was over her head—she teaches sociology; the other said it was a great waste of time to take poetry that seriously . . . she was a Doctor of Education and was only slumming that night" (*HB* 265). "I met some of the English faculty and they were a very disgruntled crew" (*HB* 185). In response to an English professor's asking about why she named Mrs. May, Mrs. May, she stated, "I knew some English teacher would write and ask me why. I think you folks sometimes strain the soup too thin" (*HB* 582). She also relates instances with a Kenyon College professor who would not believe that what he had written was not a short story (*HB* 81) and with an Emory University professor who blamed his inability to teach writing on the fact that his students were not good writers (*HB* 183).

In her fiction these professors show up in many shapes and situations, but they are never a pretty sight, and they are always wallowing in misery of their own making, taking no responsibility for their failures, and assuming that they know more than the other characters. Three of her most humorous and successful professorial caricatures are Joy-Hulga, Mary Grace, and Wesley May. For Joy-Hulga "one of her major triumphs was that her mother had not been able to turn her dust into Joy, but the greater one was that she had been able to turn it herself into Hulga" (*CS* 275). According to her mother, Mary Grace—a Wellesley student—"is a girl who can never say a kind word about anyone, who never smiles, who criticizes and complains all day long" (*CS* 499). Wesley "was thin and nervous and bald and being an intellectual was a terrible strain on his disposition. . . . He didn't like anything." He hates every detail of his life but never makes a move to change it: "He talked about Paris and Rome but he never even went to Atlanta" (*CS* 319). Clearly in the fictional world of Flannery O'Connor, education and intelligence do not lead to understanding and wisdom. Basing existence on collecting more degrees and more theories upon which to expound leads to an even narrower and more curdled existence than basing it on shallower social and economic considerations. Her silly, often grasping Christian women are humorous in a lighter vain; the nonbelieving, hardened intellectuals are amusing in a dark, hopeless satiric sense. Perhaps the fact that Catholic teachings allow salvation for those who die ignorant, but hold those who hear the Word and reject it responsible, accounts for this difference in the severity of the satire.

Flannery O'Connor did not hear the Word and reject it; from early on she was marked as Christ's own forever. She did not require "somebody there to shoot her every minute of her life" to keep her mind concentrated on the sorry state of man and the redeeming mystery of God's love as she reached out with her finely crafted gesture of grace to all of us misfits.

Notes

1. Walker Percy, *The Message in the Bottle* (New York: Farrar, Straus and Giroux, 1975), 101.
2. Pierre Teilhard de Chardin, *The Divine Milieu* (New York: Harper, 1960), 61.

The World of the Cartoons and Their Importance to O'Connor's Fiction

Kelly Gerald

> For the writer of fiction, everything has its testing point in the eye, and the eye is an organ that eventually involves the whole personality, and as much of the world as can be got into it. It involves judgment. Judgment is something that begins in the act of vision, and when it does not, or when it becomes separated from vision, then a confusion exists in the mind which transfers itself to the story.
>
> O'Connor, *Mystery and Manners*

Principally represented in the reminiscences by school friends Betty Boyd Love and Elizabeth Shreve Ryan published in the *Flannery O'Connor Bulletin* and in a brief article by Juniper Ellis in *Studies in the Humanities*, the cartoons of Flannery O'Connor have been neglected by critics. While occasionally some cartoons have been reproduced, mainly in the *Flannery O'Connor Bulletin*, David Farmer's *Flannery O'Connor: A Descriptive Bibliography*, and Jill P. Baumgaertner's *Flannery O'Connor: A Proper Scaring*, the vast majority of her work as a cartoonist for the student publications of Georgia State College for Women is unavailable for public viewing and therefore generally unknown. The Flannery O'Connor Collection of Georgia College and State University in Milledgeville, formerly GSCW, retains original newsprint copies of the *Colonnade* and the *Peabody Palladium*; however, the holdings of the latter are quite spotty and incomplete, and the archive's copies of both student publications are quickly deteriorating. Some of the newspapers are torn or otherwise damaged, and there is no restoration project underway to preserve them. Needless to say, handling these artifacts adds to their deterioration, and access to the cartoons in the original publication is necessarily limited.

The Flannery O'Connor Collection contains nearly 150 of O'Connor's marginal drawings, linoleum-block cuts, prints, paintings, watercolors, and sketches. This essay will consider a small selection of O'Connor's linoleum-block-cut cartoons from the *Colonnade*, the Georgia College student newspaper, and from the *Corinthian*, the school's journal for creative writing and the arts, that will illustrate the ways O'Connor's work in the visual arts, specifically her work as a cartoonist, informs her technique as a fiction writer.

O'Connor's cartoon "Targets are where you find 'em!" in the *Colonnade*, March 27, 1943, provides an interesting beginning to any discussion of the context for these drawings (Farmer 92). This cartoon appeared more than a year after the arrival of the WAVEs (women in the navy's emergency reserves) on the Georgia

College campus in the winter of 1942, one of a series of wartime cartoons that feature the ongoing conflict between the women attending the WAVE school on campus and the regular students of Georgia College. Signed with O'Connor's bird anagram at the lower left, "Targets are where you find 'em!" depicts a girl in the foreground with her back to the viewer. She holds a bow and arrow in one hand while the other hand rests on her hip. In the background to the right of the frame stands a bull's-eye target. A column of WAVEs marches into the distance at the left. The girl's head turns toward the column of WAVEs indicating her choice of targets.

As with many of her other cartoons, this image and its caption seem in dialogue with articles that appear in the same issue of the *Colonnade*. Her use of cartoons to comment on current events and on how they are reported in the paper indicates that O'Connor's targets lie beyond the limits of the cartoon's frame. Many of her cartoons' meanings are lost when the immediate contexts are not considered. Two articles in this issue of the *Colonnade* help inform the understanding of this particular cartoon. The first of these articles bears a possible tangential connection and comes from the initial sentence of "Parking Space," a regular column by Betty Park, that appears directly below the cartoon: "The time has come when I feel that I must take up arms and defend a little item that has long been close to my heart and which of late seems to be suffering from violent attacks by members of the elder generation." The subject is chewing gum. The resonance between the article and the cartoon is not merely coincidental, since O'Connor's image, directly above the opening line of "Parking Space" in the same column, also shows a student taking up arms against representatives of an older generation, the WAVEs. O'Connor almost exclusively represents the WAVEs as women, or at least as adults, while her depictions of the regular students at Georgia State College for Women always present them as young girls or children. This contrast can be most clearly observed in cartoons like "Our Naval Escort" in the 1945 *Spectrum* (Farmer 105), the Georgia State College for Women yearbook, "Counter-Attack" in the April 18, 1944, issue of the *Colonnade* (Farmer 96), and "Oh, give me back my raincoat; you still look more like a moron than a WAVE" in the March 6, 1943, issue of the *Colonnade* (Farmer 91).

More to the point of the particular cartoon under discussion, "Targets are where you find 'em!," is an article titled "400 More Waves Expected in July; Junior Colleges May Be Dropped," which appears on the facing page and addresses the difficulty colleges face when flooded by both armed forces trainees and regular students. The reason the students resent the WAVEs on the campus of Georgia State College for Women becomes clear. Without considering the image in its historical and textual environment, the joke of the cartoon remains largely lost, revealing that O'Connor's cartoons are not strictly a world unto themselves and should not be considered in isolation.

The first known O'Connor cartoon for the *Peabody Palladium* appeared on October 28, 1940. "One Result of the New Peabody Orchestra" (Farmer 87) is clearly designed to comment on two articles in the same issue of the paper, "Students Join Concert Group" and "Orchestra and Music Club Are Organized," both of which were front-page news. O'Connor's cartoon appears on the second page of the issue. In it a girl in the foreground, wearing a tasseled hat, sweater, pleated skirt, and saddle oxfords, blows a large saxophone as the expression "BLAH" emerges from the instrument. In the background, a thin figure in a jacket and skirt frowns and holds her hands over her ears. The O'Connor Collection contains only nine cartoons by O'Connor from the *Peabody Palladium*. The greater portion of the run has been lost, though copies occasionally resurface as in the 1990 article by Elizabeth Shreve Ryan, "I Remember Mary." Two of O'Connor's cartoons from the *Peabody Palladium* accompany the article: "Music Appreciation Hath Charms" and "These two express the universal feeling of heart-brokenness over school closing." The O'Connor Collection holds neither copies of these cartoons nor the issues of the *Peabody Palladium* in which they originally appeared, and Ryan's reminiscence offers no publication dates for these images. In instances like these, exact historical references for the cartoons are completely lost. In any case, issues of the *Peabody Palladium* remain relatively scarce compared to the O'Connor Collection's complete run of the *Colonnade*, which contains fifty-seven of O'Connor's original linoleum-block-cut cartoons. In the pages of the *Colonnade*, many more instances of parallels between O'Connor's cartoons and articles surface.

The very first cartoon by O'Connor to appear in the *Colonnade*, "The Immediate Results of Physical Fitness Day" (Farmer 88), removes any doubt about whether references to articles in the paper are coincidental or not. The cartoon shows a girl in a baggy sweater, skirt, and saddle oxfords. Slightly crouched, she is unsteadily supporting herself between a cane and the edge of a table, and her tongue hangs out, indicating extreme fatigue. An article on the third page of the same issue, dated October 9, 1942, clarifies exactly what issue the cartoon addresses: "Keeping Fit: Physical Fitness Program to be Daily Feature at GSCW" reports the initiation of a new program. Each dormitory on campus is to compete with the others through a regimen of exercises and other physical activities. The paper gives scores for each dorm on page four in the article "Ennis [Hall] Ranks Top in Physical Fitness." Of course, not all the girls may feel as rewarded as those lucky inhabitants of Ennis Hall. Another article, "Oh, How We Hate to Get Up the Week after Being Fit," also on the fourth page, offers a parallel commentary, one more closely in line with the joke made by O'Connor's cartoon. Both of these articles, "Ennis Ranks Top" and "How We Hate to Get Up," appear on the same page as O'Connor's cartoon "The Immediate Results of Physical Fitness Day," which makes it a compelling start for her work in the *Colonnade*.

Almost every cartoon by O'Connor that appears in the student newspaper points to articles in the paper and is based on events on campus reported either in this publication or in others. Some of her cartoons are intended specifically to operate as illustrations for articles written by her or other students, such as those that accompany Joyce Moncrief's 1944 *Corinthian* article "You Can Have My Share." To provide a quick indication of the range: O'Connor's cartoon in the October 17, 1942, issue of the *Colonnade*, "Why Don't We Do This More Often" (Farmer 88), responds to the presence of family members on campus for Parents' Day; her October 24, 1942, cartoon, "Aw, nuts! I thought we'd have at least one day off after the faculty played softball!" (Farmer 88), comments directly upon a softball game between the faculty of Georgia State College for Women and the senior class (apparently the faculty played hard to win with a final score of 13–12). Her *Colonnade* cartoon from November 14, 1942, "Doggone this Golden Slipper contest. Now we have to wear saddle oxfords" (Farmer 88), documents both the annual drama competition, the Golden Slipper Contest, held by the school and the result for the losing class. This brief list represents only the very beginning of her work as a cartoonist for the *Colonnade*, which evolved into a sustained series of biweekly contributions over three years' time.

Clearly O'Connor did not limit her targets to the WAVEs on campus, nor did her cartoons exist in creative isolation. In addition to quite literally representing a history in pictures, her cartoons comprise an impressive collection of single-frame satires anchored by human interaction. Very often O'Connor includes herself in the cartoon, either symbolically, as the bird anagram she created with her initials, or in caricature, as her friend Betty Boyd Love indicates. Love writes that her favorite cartoon "is a drawing of four students, three of them frilly-haired, frivolous-looking types wearing the exaggeratedly long sweaters popular at the time, the fourth a harried-looking limp-haired 'studious' type, staggering under a huge stack of books—probably meant to be Flannery herself" (Love 66). The particular cartoon that Love describes is called "Wayfarers" (Farmer 105), and it appears twice in the 1944 issue of the *Spectrum*. Other cartoon figures bear a canny resemblance to the artist and may also be self-portraits: the seated figure with the dark cropped hair and glasses in the December 5, 1942, *Colonnade* cartoon "Are you glad to be back?" (Farmer 88); the girl in glasses and raincoat addressed in the January 9, 1943, *Colonnade* cartoon "Aw, don't worry about not getting on the Dean's List. It's no fun going to the picture show at night anyway" (Farmer 91)—the dean's list published on the front page of this issue does not bear O'Connor's name; again the O'Connor-like girl with glasses under attack in the January 30, 1943, *Colonnade* cartoon "But I tell you, you don't have to get a rooster to tell you what time to get up; all you have to do is set your clock back" (Farmer 91). O'Connor may have occasionally drawn herself as a character in her cartoons, but more often she allowed the bird anagram that she used as her signature to represent her presence and herself as an important witness. The signature might be that "little bird" that witnessed events on the sly and told the artist what it saw. Very often O'Connor positioned the bird anagram signature so that it appeared to observe events either from an inconspicuous position on the ground or from above while in flight.

O'Connor's cartoons comment on the predictable range of student experiences: preoccupation with school holidays, dating, teachers, and exams. They target the anti-intellectualism and the various conceits of the students as well as the shortcomings of the school that is the physical and historical setting. In her cartoons, however, O'Connor does not merely satirize the typical issues and events of student life, she documents the character of the students themselves, including settings from the college campus. These cartoons offer not only an accurate documentary of life at Georgia State College for Women but also a running commentary on the times. O'Connor's cartoons are a history in pictures, and her work largely functions as a social satire that clearly includes herself.

The most conspicuous correlation between O'Connor's cartoons and her fiction is her use of repeated jokes. A. R. Coulthard in "Flannery O'Connor's Backtracking Muse" was the first to point out some instances in which O'Connor recycles jokes and images in her fiction. Considering how her work as a cartoonist might expand what scholars have previously considered the author's canon, it becomes apparent that some jokes that O'Connor first told in cartoons were later restyled in prose. As with any favorite joke, repetition generates a unique morphology. The joke changes and grows with each retelling. The few cartoons selected for this section of the analysis show the migration of jokes from visual texts to prose form. The cartoon "Coming Back Affects Some People Worse Than Others" from the *Colonnade*, March 20, 1943 (Farmer 91), represents a type of joke-telling that O'Connor used repeatedly in her fiction. Signed with her bird anagram in the lower left of the frame, the image includes three figures. In the left background two girls walk side by side; in the right foreground one girl reads a book while standing on her head. One of the girls in the background gestures with her open hand toward the girl doing the headstand, while the other one glares at the upside-down reader. Accompanying articles in this issue help to make sense of the action. The March 20, 1943, issue of the *Colonnade* marks students' return to campus for the beginning of spring quarter.

In "Coming Back Affects Some People Worse Than Others," as in other cartoons, the disruption of the expectation established by the image by the understatement of the caption makes the situation comical. But this is more than a simple or generic disturbance. It is a disruption of a particular kind: a near complete reversal, an inversion, the creation of a negative image. O'Connor shows her viewers the starkly unusual in the ordinariness of an everyday occurrence. As Sura Prasad Rath observes in "Comic Polarities in Flannery O'Connor's *Wise Blood*," the viewer who is also a fan of O'Connor's fiction will recognize the issue of visual and physical disorientation and radical inversion as a distinct characteristic of many of her stories.

Consider Mrs. Turpin's vision in the story "Revelation," where she sees a ladder of blacks and white trash, freaks and lunatics filing into heaven ahead of her own kind. Or in the story "Everything That Rises Must Converge," consider the image and its negative created by Julian's mother meeting a black woman wearing the same atrocious purple and green hat and the rift that their confrontation ultimately creates. Some of the many comic opposites O'Connor creates are represented by the contrast between Hazel Motes and Enoch Emory and their negative images in Hoover Shoats and Solace Layfield; between O. T. and E. T. Greenleaf and the May brothers, Wesley and Scofield; the contrast in the comic polarity of Tarwater and Rayber, Sheppard and Johnson, the tattooed, foulmouthed ex-sailor O. E. Parker and his sharp-eyed, straight-Gospel love, Sarah Ruth. These kinds of wild reversals represent one of O'Connor's favorite comic ploys, crucial to the way she generates ironic and multileveled discourses.

The artificial intellectual? O'Connor more than covers this subject in her cartoons, targeting this fault among her fellow students. One in particular, "I don't enjoy looking at these old pictures either, but it doesn't hurt my reputation for people to think I'm a lover of fine arts," from the *Colonnade* of January 16, 1943 (Farmer 91), is a telling satire of this character type. An interesting historical note for this cartoon exists: it directly relates to an art exhibit at Georgia College and offers a clear example of the correspondence between a cartoon and the text of the publication in which it appeared. In the January 9, 1943, issue of the *Colonnade*, an article titled "Art Exhibition in Second Week" reminds students that paintings by van Gogh and Cézanne among others were on display in the library. The first sentence of the article reads, "The appreciation of good art especially today, means a great deal." Furthermore, it specifies that 333 students had signed the guest register during the first week of the exhibit. The register of visitors, which could verify O'Connor's visit to the exhibit, has been lost. She certainly had something to say about it; though her observation was not directed toward the paintings themselves but toward their reception by the student population. Her cartoon about attendees at the exhibition in the very next issue of the *Colonnade* shows exactly how sardonically O'Connor viewed the "appreciation of good art" on the Georgia College campus.

The cartoon "I don't enjoy looking at these old pictures either, but it doesn't hurt my reputation for people to think I'm a lover of fine arts" was signed with a small "c" inside of a large "O" in imitation of the copyright symbol and as a representation of O'Connor's initials. The image features two girls regarding a cubist-style painting. The girl in the foreground speaks and stands with her back to the viewer; however, her face is turned in profile as she addresses her companion, and her open hand extends in an entreating gesture. The girl in the background at the left of the frame stands in profile. Her face is turned away from the viewer toward the painting. "Art Exhibition in Second Week" from January 9, 1943, is not the only *Colonnade* piece engaged by O'Connor's cartoon. The article "Favorite Pictures," front-page news in the January 9 issue, identifies the students' favorite paintings, "according to the latest tabulation, in the Modern Art Exhibit, [as] 'Nor' Easter,' by Homer, 'Little Margot Bernard,' by Renaud, and 'Woman with Pearl Ring,' by Carot."

Exposing the pretensions of her fellow students represents one of O'Connor's pervasive agendas in her cartoons. Targeting intellectual pretensions corresponds to a particularly recognizable and pervasive issue in her fiction. The concern with appearances and with the posturing of pseudointellectuals emerges in the character of Asbury in "The Enduring Chill," who fails as an artist but succeeds as an invalid; in the intellectual egotism and presumptuousness of women scholars like Joy-Hulga Hopewell; and in the vanity of Sally Poker Sash in "A Late Encounter with the Enemy," whose grandfather sees the advancing academics as ushering the way to death. Women obsessed with the social significance of appearances are also part of O'Connor's creative stock-in-trade. The grandmother in "A Good Man Is Hard to Find" wants whoever finds her dead body to recognize she was a lady by the way she was dressed. In "Greenleaf," Mrs. May's greatest anxiety is that the sons of the Greenleafs will one day become "Society" (CW 508), while her own sons, Wesley, a third-rate insurance salesman, and Scofield, an ineffectual, balding, and nervous intellectual, show no promise of ensuring their mother the social position she believes is her natural right. These stories, and others, indicate that the attack on social and intellectual pretensions, which forms the substance of many of O'Connor's cartoons, is a subject the author returns to with enthusiasm in her fiction.

In cartoons like "Do you think teachers are necessary?" from the October 5, 1943, *Colonnade* (Farmer 92), O'Connor salutes the individualist and anti-intellectual. Signed with her bird anagram in the lower left, this is one of the cartoons in which the artist may have drawn herself as a character. It features two figures walking toward the viewer. The figure on the left may depict O'Connor herself wearing a black raincoat, hands hidden in her pockets. She has a sharp angular nose, simple frown, and one eyebrow arches in an expression of annoyance. Short with wide hips and bushy hair, the figure on the right speaks. Her face drawn in profile, she addresses her companion and carries a stack of seven books supported by her folded arms. The hard-boiled anti-intellectual seems a favorite comic subject, one that resurfaces most famously in the tensions between Tarwater and Rayber in *The Violent Bear It Away*. Not an isolated subject of scrutiny, it also appears in "The Enduring Chill" in the portrayal of Asbury's sister, Mary George, who is eight years his senior and the principal of the county elementary school. Her steely competence, lack of sentimentality, and aesthetic sensitivity confront Asbury at every turn and remind him of his failure. If there is anyone Asbury would be happily rid of, it is the schoolteacherish Mary George.

Outside of her fiction, O'Connor seemed to have made plenty of surly, more than half-mocking comments about teachers. To give one example, in her lecture "The Nature and Aim of Fiction" O'Connor observes, "A teacher who tries to impose a way of writing on you can be dangerous. Fortunately, most teachers I've known were too lazy to do this. In any case you should beware of those who appear overenergetic" (*MM* 85). Several comments of this kind appearing in her letters and lectures demonstrate that her cartoon characters are not the only ones to have ever wondered if teachers are really necessary. In the same essay O'Connor writes, "I don't know which is worse—to have a bad teacher or no teacher at all"; she follows this attack with another: "There's many a best-seller that could have been prevented by a good teacher" (*MM* 83). She resumes the assault in her lecture "Total Effect and the Eighth Grade" when she states, "English Teachers come in Good, Bad, and Indifferent, but too frequently in high schools anyone who can speak English is allowed to teach it" (*MM* 137). And what is the result of such proceedings? O'Connor speculates in "The Teaching of Literature": "I believe that it's perfectly possible to run a course of academic degrees in English and to emerge a seemingly respectable Ph.D. and still not know how to read fiction" (*MM* 123).

Some of O'Connor's cartoons, though admittedly few, offer a more coherent sense of the repetition that sometimes occurs in her work. Not only does she reproduce comic subjects in accordance with her sense of humor and her growing narrative dexterity, but she also duplicates physical images. As with the retelling of jokes and stories, it is impossible to argue that such reproductions are conscious and deliberate. They seem to grow more from habit or from particularly striking, memorable, or humorous situations. Similarly, repeating images may be representative of general types, representative of her particular comic sensibility, or borrowed from her recollection of certain persons or events. It is impossible to determine intentionality in these visual and comedic reproductions, but the fact of their existence indicates some degree of reprocessing took place between her early work as a cartoonist and her later work in fiction. "Business as Usual" in the *Colonnade*, January 4, 1943 (Farmer 88), demonstrates that correspondences between cartoons and fiction can be very precise. This cartoon shows a tangle of bodies outside the college bookstore. Signed with a "c" inside of an "O" at the bottom center of the frame, this cartoon features a mob scene. Seemingly disconnected arms and legs emerge from the tangled mound of bodies to create an impression of the chaos and struggle of the girls fighting to get their textbooks. Only two images in this cartoon remain unfragmented, the sign in the background to the left that reads, "BOOKSTORE" and a single figure in a shapeless raincoat and a head scarf who stands watching the mob with her back to the viewer. As with many of O'Connor's other cartoons, "Business as Usual" indicates her response to events and situations reported by several articles that appear in the same issue of the *Colonnade*. "College Aims Rejuvenated," placed directly next to the cartoon addresses the recent return of students to campus for the beginning of the new term. The tone of the article becomes ironic given the proximity of the cartoon. Consider the following lines from the article in relation to the chaos shown in the cartoon: "Our nation, as a whole, has abandoned boisterous carelessness for the duration to settle into a serious effort to earn peace. We, as are other college students, are obligated to make every effort to cooperate with our government in spirit as well as in defense work. At a new quarter and a new year's beginning, we now have an opportunity to 'pull in our belts' and determine that our men in service shall not do all of the fighting." Another article, "Rationing in Relation to College," which also appears on the same page as "Business as Usual," speaks to the difficulty of balancing supply with demand on college campuses during the war years, apparently the cause of the difficulty at the bookstore.

Appearing roughly one year after the United States had entered the war, "Business as Usual" seems reminiscent of the entangled bodies of Holocaust victims. When O'Connor recycled the image a decade later in the description of a newsreel in "The Displaced Person" (1954) the recurrence is striking: "Mrs. Shortley recalled a newsreel she had seen once of a small room piled high with bodies of dead naked people all in a heap, their arms and legs tangled together, a head thrust in here, a head there, a foot, a knee, a part that should have been covered up sticking out, a hand raised clutching nothing" (*CW* 287). O'Connor uses the image a second and a third time in the story, when Mrs. Shortley offers her "prophecy," saying "legs where arms should be, foot to face, ear in the palm of hand. Who will remain whole?" (*CW* 301), and again when she suffers *tremor mortis* in the car as she and her family flee the McIntyre farm: Mrs. Shortley "was sitting in an erect way in spite of the fact that one leg was twisted under her and one knee was almost into her neck, but there was a peculiar lack of light in her icy blue eyes. All the vision in them might have been turned around, looking inside her. She suddenly grabbed Mr. Shortley's elbow and Sarah Mae's foot at the same time and began to tug and pull on them as if she were trying to fit the two extra limbs onto herself" (*CW* 304). The description of this chaos continues until Mrs. Shortley dies.

O'Connor first visits a well-worn joke in the April 3, 1943, *Colonnade* cartoon "Oh, well. I can always be a Ph.D." (Farmer 92), a joke that later informs the development of one of her most popular characters, Joy-Hulga Hopewell. The cartoon is an interesting one, not simply because O'Connor recycles the butt of the joke (the sexual desirability of the lady intellectual) in the character Joy-Hulga, but because O'Connor's joke extends beyond the frame of the cartoon in this case. Directly above the cartoon in the same column of the paper appears an article called "Them's What Has 'Em Entertain 'Em," which addresses the opening of the gym on Saturday and Sunday so that students can entertain male visitors. A revealing line from the article asserts that "students who get dates deserve help in entertaining them." So much for the unlucky girls who do not get dates. Oh, well. They can always be Ph.D.s.

While the cartoon "Oh, well. I can always be a Ph.D." does not involve a particularly pronounced physical distortion related to the main character's sexual desirability (or lack of it); O'Connor does draw sexualized girls as grotesques. She presents the girl at the dance who says, "Oh, well. I can always be a Ph.D.," as rather childlike and physically underdeveloped in comparison to the girls and boys dancing in the background. One example of the distortion O'Connor uses to communicate sexuality appears in an untitled illustration for an article by Joyce Moncrief called "You Can Have My Share" published in the Fall 1944 issue of the *Corinthian*. The illustration contains a single figure, a girl seated with her legs curled under her. Her arms undulate erotically at her sides in an exotic, Egyptian-like pose. Her face, turned toward the viewer, has exaggerated features: full, oversized lips, and large and languid, half-closed eyes. The description of this character from Moncrief's article reads, "Who's that? Oh. Her. That's Glamourpuss. Haven't you seen her around here before? You could hardly miss her. Those eyes look like she must have run into a coupla doors in the dark, but confidentially—she puts that stuff on with a brush. No, that brick-dust complexion is no indication that she doesn't wash; she simply goes in for the heavy cake make up, that's all . . . she likes that lipstick so well that she measures it in cubic inches" (Moncrief 15). Although Moncrief seems to have written the description, the four linoleum-block cuts accompanying Moncrief's two-page article belong to O'Connor. The text is not O'Connor's, but the distortions of this image certainly are her creation. They represent a kind of sexualized distortion that the author re-envisaged in characters like the seductive and perverse Sarah Ham in "The Comforts of Home," whose face Thomas describes as "like a comedienne's in a musical comedy—a pointed chin, wide apple cheeks and feline empty eyes" (*CW* 573) and whose body he reports as giving "the immediate impression of being physically crooked" (*CW* 578).

A similar phenomenon surfaces in the fat prostitute, Mrs. Leora Watts, in *Wise Blood*, whose lecherously distorted face Haze regards in a bedroom mirror. Such images help to make the case that the sexual woman comprises a special category of the grotesque in O'Connor's work, a comic fascination that did not begin with writing fiction. Another instance of physical distortion accompanying the sexualized girl appears in a 1945 issue of the *Colonnade* in her cartoon "Isn't it fortunate that Genevieve has completely escaped that boy-crazy stage?" (Farmer 97). In this cartoon, Genevieve, the subject of the illustration, cranes her neck to look at a boy as her eyes leave her head to follow him snakelike around the corner of a building. This image represents the most extreme of O'Connor's physical distortions in any of her drawings.

Many of O'Connor's cartoons represent studies in types—the bookish type, the athletic type, and so on—but she is interested not only in examining the sexualized girl as a type but also in seeing how class, attitude, and intellectual disposition could be communicated in the minutiae of facial distortion, clothing, and physical bearing. Some of her clearest representations of physical and social types appear in the cartoons she created for the 1944 *Spectrum*. A few of her most pronounced character studies can be seen in three untitled segments featuring a girl with a book in her hand (88), one with a gavel (74), and another with a tennis racquet (74). The cartoon of the girl with the book, shows the long-haired, overly dramatic, round-figured, sensitive type, complete with props: an open book in her extended hand and pince-nez glasses trailing a long ribbon. The second, the girl with the gavel, represents the serious, fastidious overachiever. Her cropped and meticulously combed hair, tall forehead, deeply furrowed brow, and her frown indicate a sobriety and seriousness in keeping with the many academic medals attached to the lapel of her jacket. The athlete with the tennis racquet represents the complete opposite. Her appearance is rumpled, if not slovenly, and the intensity and size of her physical presence together with her close-cropped hair, jutting ears, and small eyes give her a masculine appearance.

Ellis's article "Flannery O'Connor and Her World: The Visual Art of *Wise Blood*" is the first work comparing O'Connor's cartoons to images in her fiction. Ellis discusses O'Connor's descriptions of characters as fundamentally grotesque and cites Ewa Kuryluk's *Salome and Judas in the Cave of Sex* (1987) and Wolfgang Kayser's *Das Groteske* (*The Grotesque in Art and Literature,* translated 1963) to establish a working definition of the grotesque. Ellis then applies this concept to the visual descriptions of characters: "O'Connor's drawings evince the playful and violent disruption of order, the grotesque, which, as Ewa Kuryluk and Kayser propose, is most visible in drawings and prints whose stark lines convey the fracturing and reconstruction of the human figure, reassembled with heterogenous elements, endless variety, and blurred boundaries between people, objects, animals, and plants" (Ellis 81). Ellis cites numerous descriptions from *Wise Blood* to demonstrate how O'Connor's visual language may be understood in terms of Kuryluk's and Kayser's observations on the grotesque: "On the train for instance, Mrs. Hitchcock has 'pear-shaped legs,' 'fox-colored hair,' and she appears dressed for the night with her 'hair in knots around her head' and 'the knobs fram[ing] her face like dark toadstools.' In the dining car, the steward 'moved like a crow, darting from table to table'" (Ellis 87). Ellis extends her examination, though in a more limited way, to descriptions of characters from *The Violent Bear It Away* and *A Good Man Is Hard to Find.*

In addition to forming visual grotesques, O'Connor's visual descriptions of characters represent social types in a more general way. The eye of the beholder in these observations seems crucial to understanding how visual perception and judgment occur simultaneously. Her use of description to examine and satirize social types from the perspective of the subject and the object may be observed in the following passage from "Revelation": "Next to the ugly girl was the child, ... and next to him was a thin leathery old woman in a cotton print dress. She and Claude had three sacks of chicken feed in their pump house that was in the same print. She had seen from the first that the child belonged with the old woman. She could tell by the way they sat—kind of vacant and white-trashy.... And at right ... was a lank-faced woman who was certainly the child's mother. She had on a yellow sweat shirt and wine-colored slacks, both gritty-looking, and the rims of her lips were stained with snuff. Her dirty yellow hair was tied with a little piece of red paper ribbon" (*CW* 635). While O'Connor's interest in distortion remains apparent and undeniable, her visual descriptions of characters are generally of social and physical types, not exaggerated or freakish, but recognizable. As Mrs. Turpin observes the other people in the doctor's waiting room, O'Connor uses Mrs. Turpin's visual perspective to stimulate the reader's prejudices and to show Mrs. Turpin's own prejudices regarding the visual appearance of others.

Similar uses of visual tagging can be observed in stories such as "Everything That Rises Must Converge," in which O'Connor employs description to indicate a physical type: "a thin woman with protruding teeth and long yellow hair" (*CW* 490). The woman is later identified not by name but by the shoes she wears. She becomes "the woman with the red and white canvas sandals." Longer descriptions of a character's appearance often involve a report of dress and mannerisms to complete the impression as in the portrait of Mr. Cheat in "A Temple of the Holy Ghost": "He was baldheaded except for a little fringe of rust-colored hair and his face was nearly the same color as the unpaved roads and washed like them with ruts and gulleys. He wore a pale green shirt with a thick black stripe in it and blue galluses and his trousers cut across a protruding stomach that he pressed tenderly from time to time with his big flat thumb. All his teeth were backed with gold and he would roll his eyes at Miss Kirby in an impish way and say, 'Haw haw,' sitting in their porch swing with his legs spread apart and his hightopped shoes pointing in opposite directions on the floor" (*CW* 198). Ellis's treatment of the grotesque would isolate the comparison of Mr. Cheat's face to the rutted, unpaved roads.

While O'Connor describes Mr. Cheat in terms of an object, that relatively minor aspect of the description does significantly more than point to the confusion of a person with an object as a feature of the grotesque. It alludes to the world of the character, the unpaved back roads from which he emerges, the culture and manner of rural southern folk. The physical description extends far beyond the parameters of the grotesque to place Mr. Cheat in a particular social and geographical context that provides the lens through which his appearance and behavior may be recognized as both realistic and humorous. While her descriptions of characters are sometimes grotesque, O'Connor also seems interested in showing how "folks" look and behave. In "Writing Short Stories" she reports, "I lent some stories to a country lady who lives down the road from me, and when she returned them, she said, 'Well, them stories just gone and shown you how some folks *would* do,' and I thought to myself that that was right" (*MM* 90).

As in her portrait of the girl-athlete for the *Spectrum,* O'Connor seems no stranger to creating female characters who evoke an immediate physical presence that can easily become intimidating, even appear violent. The girl with the tennis racquet calls to mind the bodily force of the athlete, but other cartoons evoke a more direct physical threat. The 1945 *Colonnade* cartoon "She says we're on the threshold of social revolution" features an angry student shoving her book in the face of an urbane, condescending matron (Farmer 97). O'Connor repeats this scenario in "Revelation" when the blue-stocking Wellesleyan girl, Mary Grace, hits Mrs. Turpin in the head with a book. Described as "the ugly girl" (*CW* 638), Mary Grace's "eyes were fixed like two drills on Mrs. Turpin . . . there was no mistaking that there was something urgent behind them." Mrs. Turpin answers Mary Grace's seething glares with this smug and dismissive accusation: "You must be in college" (*CW* 642–43). The revelation that follows upon this violent encounter does represent a kind of social revolution, when Mrs. Turpin's anticipated heavenly ascent is disclosed as reversing the social order that ranks her and her kind first. In her cartoons, as in her fiction, O'Connor takes violence to an extreme. There is nothing unexpected in the idea that she uses physical violence as comic force and decision maker, often allowing it to resonate as the final action of a story.

The particular joke in the 1944 *Colonnade* cartoon "Madam Chairman, the committee has reached a decision" seems to be the incongruity of this skirt-clad scrapper who has just licked a whole pile of girls; her decision reigns supreme due to her use of superior physical force. Such behavior surely contradicts the ladylike comportment cultivated among the girls at Georgia State College for Women. O'Connor retells this joke in the brawl between Mary Fortune Pitts and her grandfather, Mr. Fortune, in "A View of the Woods." The fight ensues when Mr. Fortune walks Mary Fortune Pitts into the woods to beat her for her disagreeable behavior after Mr. Fortune has sold the front yard of the family home, where the new owner will build a gas station. When he tries to slap Mary Fortune Pitts with his belt, she attacks him with a kind of unforgiving violence completely unexpected in a child, particularly a little girl: "Then with horror he saw her face rise up in front of his, teeth exposed, and he roared like a bull as she bit the side of his jaw. He seemed to see his own face coming to bite him from several sides at once but he could not attend to it for he was being kicked indiscriminately, in the stomach and then in the crotch. . . . 'Have you had enough?' she asked. The old man looked into his own image. It was triumphant and hostile. 'You been whipped,' it said, 'by me'" (*CW* 545). While Mary Fortune Pitts's victory arrives too late to alter her grandfather's decision to allow someone to build a gas station in the front yard, the physical brawl with the child results in the more significant loss, and provides the conclusion for the story. Here, as in the cartoon, violence settled the issue.

The recurrence of physical images and jokes between the cartoons and O'Connor's fiction provides substantial material for consideration, but these recurrences do not represent the most pervasive influence her cartoons have had upon her work as a writer. O'Connor's strategy of using a witness to construct irony in almost all of her cartoons of this period is a recognizable and repeated narrative technique in her fiction. Unless O'Connor uses an observer within the frame of the cartoon, the subject threatens to lose a necessary barometer that tells the viewer how to interpret the action or what exactly the viewer should find funny. Other persons involved as witnesses in the scene instruct the viewer how to respond. Active comedy requires the verification of participants, an audience. O'Connor provides this form of verification in several ways. This strategy appears in the 1943 *Colonnade* cartoon "They give us entirely too much work. I can't manage but six outside activities!" (Farmer 92). As seen in this cartoon, and in many others, O'Connor usually makes the speaker the butt of the joke and provides a second person whose silent observation, physical posture, and facial expression tell the viewer how to view the behavior of the first. Sometimes O'Connor will draw herself as a character in the frame as the second observer, as she does in the cartoons "Coming Back Effects Some People Worse Than Others" and "Do you think teachers are necessary?" O'Connor is present as the "little bird" that witnesses events anonymously and whispers to the artist; O'Connor as the artist becomes the secondhand witness. In a letter to Betty Hester dated June 28, 1956, O'Connor wrote, "I come from a family where the only emotion respectable to show is irritation. In some this tendency produces hives, in others literature, in me both" (*HB* 163). It seems correct to read O'Connor as the disapproving observer, no matter how far removed from a physical representation she may construe herself. Irritation appears an emotion suitable for the production of cartoons as well as of literature.

The viewer or audience outside of the frame is sometimes incorporated into the action as well. When a single figure has its back turned to the viewer as witness of a scene or when a group gathers at the edge of a frame with its back to the viewer, the group or figure sees the scene from the same perspective as the external viewer —as if the person seeing the cartoon is looking over the shoulders of those viewers portrayed in it. The line of sight between the internal and external perspectives is joined in a common object, and the external viewer comes into visual sympathy with the witnesses within the cartoon itself. This strategy appears in cartoons like "Business as Usual" and "Targets are where you find 'em." Also, the primary figure in the cartoon will directly address the external viewer, thus including the viewer as witness and addressee, as in the case of the cartoons "Oh, well. I can always be a Ph.D." and "Madam Chairman, the committee has reached a decision." This method of creating visual distance between the primary level of action in the cartoon and the viewer is O'Connor's way of generating the irony that allows the joke to succeed. Her cartoon "They give us entirely too much work . . ." might still seem funny if the speaker were isolated. But O'Connor certainly increases the complexity of the scenario by adding the annoyed witness. The speaker, if presented alone, risks making a very flat impression.

O'Connor knew how to carry a joke visually before she knew how to construct one in writing. She uses the same strategy of providing a witness, at least one, to create ironic distance in her fiction. Would Hazel Motes's behavior on the train to

Taulkinham appear amusing if O'Connor had not included the porter as an annoyed witness? Would Mrs. Hopewell seem comical if O'Connor had not created Joy-Hulga as the witness and allowed the reader to see the daughter's expression? The text of "Good Country People" re-creates the comic distance found in the great majority of her cartoons: "Nothing is perfect. This was one of Mrs. Hopewell's favorite sayings. Another was: that is life! And still another, the most important, was: well, other people have their opinions too. She would make these statements, usually at the table in a tone of gentle insistence as if no one held them but her, and the large hulking Joy, whose constant outrage had obliterated every expression from her face, would stare just a little to the side of her, her eyes icy blue, with the look of someone who has achieved blindness by an act of will and means to keep it" (*CW* 264–65). Mrs. Hopewell speaks, but what she says is not funny, merely trite. She becomes comical only when O'Connor permits the reader to see Joy-Hulga's expression as the witness to these speeches. The comic scenario of speaker and witness, which creates ironic distance, is reproduced without change between the cartoons and her fiction.

In many instances O'Connor employs this technique as a systematic and habitual part of her narrative repertoire; yet, what should appear clear from my examination is that the carefully crafted images in her stories often owe their genesis to her work in the visual arts. O'Connor practiced to master with language the skills of depiction and the power of evocation she had come to know intimately in the construction of visual representations with their narrative power. O'Connor plainly understood the nature of the relationship between her pursuit of the visual arts and her fiction writing. Her claim that anything that helps the writer to see will help his writing seems more justified now than ever before.

Works Cited

Baumgaertner, Jill P. *Flannery O'Connor: A Proper Scaring*. Wheaton, Ill.: Harold Shaw, 1988.

Coulthard, A. R. "Flannery O'Connor's Backtracking Muse." *Studies in American Fiction* 11, no. 2 (1983): 247–53.

Colonnade (Georgia State College for Women). Unsigned articles, 1942–43.

"Art Exhibition in Second Week," January 9, 1943, 3.

"College Aims Rejuvenated," January 4, 1943, 4.

"Ennis Ranks Top in Physical Fitness," October 9, 1942, 4.

"Faculty Score 13 over Seniors' 12: Close Softball Game Played at Annual Hike," October 24, 1942, 1.

"Favorite Pictures," January 16, 1943, 1.

"400 More Waves Expected in July; Junior Colleges May Be Dropped," March 27, 1943, 3.

"Frosh Bow to Mighty Sophs in Annual Slipper Contest," November 14, 1942, 1.

"Keeping Fit: Physical Fitness Program to Be Daily Feature at GSCW," October 9, 1942, 3.

"Oh, How We Hate to Get Up the Week after Being Fit," October 9, 1942, 4.

"Orchestra and Music Club Are Organized," October 28, 1940, 1.

"Parents' Day Attracts Many Here Today," October 17, 1942, 1.

"Rationing in Relation to College," January 4, 1943, 4.
"Students Join Concert Group," October 28, 1940, 1.
"Them's What Has 'Em Entertain 'Em.," April 3, 1943, 2.
"Welcome, Parents and Friends," October 17, 1942, 1.
Ellis, Juniper. "O'Connor and Her World: The Visual Art of *Wise Blood.*" *Studies in the Humanities* 21, no. 2 (1994): 79–95.
Farmer, David. *Flannery O'Connor: A Descriptive Bibliography.* New York: Garland, 1981, especially 87–102.
Love, Betty Boyd. "Recollections of Flannery O'Connor." *Flannery O'Connor Bulletin* 14 (1985): 64–71.
Moncrief, Joyce. "You Can Have My Share." *Corinthian,* Fall 1944, 14–15.
O'Connor, Flannery. Untitled cartoons. *Spectrum,* 1944, 74, 74, 88.
Park, Betty. "Parking Space." *Colonnade,* March 27, 1943, 2.
Rath, Sura Prasad. "Comic Polarities in Flannery O'Connor's *Wise Blood.*" *Studies in Short Fiction* 21, no. 3 (1984): 251–58.
Ryan, Elizabeth Shreve. "I Remember Mary Flannery." *Flannery O'Connor Bulletin* 19 (1990): 49–53.

He Would Have Been a Good Man

Compassion and Meanness in Truman Capote and Flannery O'Connor

Marshall Bruce Gentry

Flannery O'Connor's critics have occasionally noted similarities between O'Connor and Truman Capote. Usually they contrast them in terms of their writing styles and theological assumptions and then, as a rule, find Capote lacking in the comparison. I think the connections are so numerous and interesting that we may learn about O'Connor through Capote. Both writers were capable of impressive meanness and compassion toward both literary characters and real people. Moreover, there are important similarities between O'Connor's "A Good Man Is Hard to Find" and Capote's 1965 nonfiction novel, *In Cold Blood* (a study of Perry Smith and Dick Hickock's murder of the Clutter family in Kansas in 1959), and between Capote's "Handcarved Coffins" and O'Connor's "The River." Capote's novel about a mass murder is, among other things, a tribute to O'Connor; I say that despite the extent to which "Handcarved Coffins" may seem to recant part of that tribute. An examination of Capote's borrowings from O'Connor's fiction indicates his sometimes grudging respect for the power of her work, from which he probably acquired increased compassion toward the meanness in criminals, as shown in *In Cold Blood*. Capote seems unsure at times of what to do with his own meanness, for he directs some of it at O'Connor in "Handcarved Coffins." This analysis also suggests we should reconsider O'Connor's treatment of criminality and the extent to which O'Connor may have meant it when she said she admired her Misfit. O'Connor's compassion for criminals is greater than Capote's, in part because O'Connor has a better understanding of how the expression of meanness is an essential element of compassion. I believe that O'Connor's fascinating struggle with how to treat The Misfit leaves open the possibility of his goodness and that O'Connor is ultimately compassionate toward him.

The relationship between Truman Capote and Flannery O'Connor was strained, and if one judges by their published comments, one concludes that the strain existed primarily because of O'Connor. Capote, famous for his sarcastic comments, apparently had a high opinion of O'Connor. He told Pati Hill in an interview that O'Connor was one "of the younger writers who seem to know that style exists," adding, somewhat patronizingly, "she has some fine moments, that girl" (Capote 1957, 29). He has also been quoted as saying "Flannery O'Connor had a certain genius" (qtd. in Grobel 36). O'Connor's level of enthusiasm for Capote was considerably lower. In a letter to Betty Hester dated December 8, 1955, O'Connor wrote, "Mr. Truman

Capote makes me plumb sick" (*HB* 121). Why would O'Connor react with such meanness toward Capote? Ted R. Spivey argues that O'Connor's distaste for Capote has to do with "her revulsion at the frankly sexual in literature" (Spivey 31). Spivey believes that O'Connor also envied Capote's success (Spivey 82). After all, Capote was only about six months older than O'Connor, and perhaps O'Connor was troubled to see another southerner so readily accepted by a northern literary establishment. Spivey suggests that her "fanatical denunciations" actually show she was "caught up unconsciously in some of [his] views" (Spivey 53).

Capote himself discouraged investigations of his connections to other writers. Peter G. Christensen complains that "Capote pretended to be above questions of literary influence." Christensen adds, "he bristled when it was suggested that he borrowed" (Christensen 221–22). Nevertheless, Capote did borrow from O'Connor. Helen Garson suggests Capote takes from O'Connor the name Hulga for a character in his last, unfinished novel, *Answered Prayers* (Garson 70), and she sees connections between Capote's "Handcarved Coffins" and two O'Connor stories, "Greenleaf" and "The River" (Garson 26). His most significant borrowings appear in a work Capote claimed was nonfiction, *In Cold Blood: A True Account of a Multiple Murder and Its Consequences*. Why would Capote borrow from O'Connor for this book? A practical connection, though perhaps Capote did not know it at the time, is that both writers were inspired by newspaper crime reports, but more significantly, he knew O'Connor's fiction had the psychological and mythic depth his work needed. Capote was insecure about needing to be inspired by another writer, but I believe his goal was to learn from O'Connor, not to plagiarize her.

O'Connor might have been on Capote's mind because they each had a story in the second edition of an important textbook, *The House of Fiction*, edited by Caroline Gordon and Allen Tate, which was published in 1960 as Capote was starting work on *In Cold Blood*. O'Connor's "A Good Man Is Hard to Find" appears next to Capote's "The Headless Hawk" in the anthology, and the two stories undergo comparison by the editors. "Commentary on Capote and O'Connor" ends with the significant observation that Capote's stories lack "the theological framework" of O'Connor's, in part because "there is in his stories no one like 'The Misfit,' with his crisp, dogmatic explanation of why he is compelled to commit murder" (Gordon 386). I know of no reason to believe Capote was reading O'Connor's works while he worked on *In Cold Blood* (1959–65), but Capote would surely have been reminded of O'Connor's works when she died, eight months before the executions of Hickock and Smith in 1965. Many of the final pages of Capote's book were written following the executions.[1]

Several critics have noted significant borrowings from "A Good Man" for *In Cold Blood*. Jon Tuttle has noted two. First, citing the similarities between O'Connor's grandmother and Mrs. Bonnie Clutter, who both suffer moments of mental instability and who both are the last members of their families to be shot, Tuttle suggests

Capote borrowed a speech O'Connor gives the grandmother as she is about to be killed (Tuttle 193–94). The grandmother insists, "I know you're a good man. You don't look a bit like you have common blood. I know you must come from nice people!" Then she adds, "I know you're a good man at heart. I can just look at you and tell" (*CW* 147). In *In Cold Blood* words similar to Mrs. Clutter's are reported by Perry Smith: "she felt I was a decent young man, I'm *sure* you are, she says, and made me promise I wouldn't let Dick hurt anybody" (Capote 1965, 242). The second borrowing Tuttle sees is of The Misfit's words about how one ought to live if Jesus did not do what he said he did: "it's nothing for you to do but enjoy the few minutes you got left the best way you can—by killing somebody or burning down his house or doing some other meanness to him. No pleasure but meanness" (*CW* 152).[2] *In Cold Blood* attributes similar sentiments to York and Latham, two killers on death row with Hickock and Smith: "They shared at least one firm opinion: the world was hateful, and everybody in it would be better off dead. 'It's a rotten world,' Latham said. 'There's no answer to it but meanness. That's all anybody understands—meanness. Burn down the man's barn—he'll understand that. Poison his dog. Kill him'" (Capote 1965, 323). Tuttle believes that Capote ignores the religious significance of The Misfit's speeches (Tuttle 194), though there is certainly plenty of talk about religion in *In Cold Blood*.[3] Another significant borrowing, noted by David Guest, has to do with passages in which The Misfit and Dick Hickock describe their varied experiences. Here is The Misfit:

> "I was a gospel singer for a while," The Misfit said. "I been most everything. Been in the arm service, both land and sea, at home and abroad, been twict married, been an undertaker, been with the railroads, plowed Mother Earth, been in a tornado, seen a man burnt alive oncet," and he looked up at the children's mother and the little girl who were sitting close together, their faces white and their eyes glassy; "I even seen a woman flogged." (*CW* 149)

And here is the passage from *In Cold Blood* in which Capote uses The Misfit's syntax and rhythm as Dick Hickock demonstrates he is more experienced than another killer:

> I've walked a lot of mean streets. I've seen a white man flogged. I've watched babies born. I've seen a girl, and her no more than fourteen, take on three guys at the same time and give them all their money's worth. Fell off a ship once five miles out to sea. Swam five miles with my life passing before me with every stroke. Once I shook hands with President Truman in the lobby of the Hotel Muehlebach. Harry S. Truman. When I was working for the hospital, driving an ambulance, I saw every side of life there is—things that would make a dog vomit. (Capote 1965, 333)

Among the many other similarities between O'Connor's "A Good Man" and Capote's *In Cold Blood* are the extreme foreshadowing, the premise of an edenic American landscape violated by an invader, the similarities between the murdered families, the similarities between the killers, revelations of mistrust among members of an apparently normal and complacent American community, the satirizing of average Americans, skepticism about the ability of the legal and penal systems to understand the mysteries of the human heart, the suggestion of a motive for murder in a dysfunctional child-parent relationship, the significance of religion to criminals who consciously deny its relevance, killers who wander the countryside aimlessly but who know there are only two paths one can take, and heavy use of animal imagery—especially in the form of cats, parrots, and snakes. Perry Smith's fantasy of a parrot that defeats a snake (Capote 1965, 92–93) is uncannily similar to the ending of "A Good Man," where The Misfit, wearing a parrot shirt, shoots the grandmother at the moment when she appears snakelike (*CW* 152). One sometimes wonders whether Capote's killers patterned their lives after the fiction of Flannery O'Connor.[4]

The most interesting similarity between *In Cold Blood* and "A Good Man Is Hard to Find," the one that brings up fresh questions about O'Connor, is that surrounding both works we find instances of the authors' admiration for their murderous characters. Just as O'Connor tried to discover ways in which her Misfit could in a profound sense be a good man, throughout *In Cold Blood* Capote searches for the soul of a poet within Perry Smith. In real life Truman Capote was helpful to both Dick Hickock and Perry Smith, assisting them with their appeals and stays of execution and even buying their tombstones. And he befriended the murderers as he interviewed them for his book. Alvin Dewey—the primary detective in the Clutter case and a major character in *In Cold Blood*—told George Plimpton that Capote "saw himself in Perry Smith . . . in their childhood." Joe Fox went further: "He adored Perry" (qtd. in Plimpton 173–74). Harold Nye went furthest, speculating that Capote and Perry Smith "had become lovers in the penitentiary" (qtd. in Plimpton 188). And yet, when the time came to turn all his work into a book, Capote refused to let his emotional involvement get in the way of his art. Ned Rorem told Plimpton that Capote was finally eager to see Hickock and Smith die, and Rorem quotes Capote as once saying that *In Cold Blood* "can't be published until they're executed, so I can hardly wait" (qtd. in Plimton 300). It is the nature of Plimpton's work that things are sometimes reported fourthhand: Kathleen Tynan told Plimpton that Capote, upon hearing that Hickock and Smith would be executed, said to Kenneth Tynan, "I'm beside myself! Beside myself! Beside myself with joy!" (qtd. in Plimpton 215–16). Of course, Capote could be hiding his true feelings, but clearly there is a limit to Capote's friendship.

The most significant debate has to do with whether *In Cold Blood* is sufficiently fair to Perry Smith. The book does claim to be fair, even compassionate. The book's epigraph, from François Villon's "Ballade des pendus" (Ballad of the Hanged), surely works to emphasize the similarities between Capote and the two murderers. Villon's poem was written while the fifteenth-century French criminal and poet was himself in danger of being hanged (Bonner xxii–xxiii), and the speaker in Villon's poem is one of the criminals already hanged. Surely Capote could see himself in Villon, an outsider who desired a general amnesty.[5]

One could defend *In Cold Blood* as being fair to Perry even while it labels him as unlike other humans. The primary theme of all of Capote's work up to and including *In Cold Blood* has been described by William L. Nance as "acceptance of the unconventional, of the misfit in others and in oneself," an interpretation Nance says Capote personally endorsed (Nance 220–21). Or one could argue that Capote is fair because he tries to prove that Smith is actually like everyone else, including his victims. This may be Capote's goal in pointing out that, when the surrounding community learns that the Clutter family has been killed, some at first consider Mrs. Clutter responsible (Capote 1965, 61, 70). According to George R. Creeger's study of animal imagery in *In Cold Blood,* Capote shows that conventional people label criminals as animals rather than as humans in order to hide from themselves their own capacity for violence against fellow humans (Creeger 6). This argument implies that *In Cold Blood* actually shows everyone to be essentially the same in that we are all capable of violence. As Nance points out, the fictional final scene in *In Cold Blood* equates all the book's "dreamer[s] of unfulfilled dreams," all the book's "victims," so it is no stretch to say the ending compares Perry Smith and the murdered daughter, Nancy Clutter (Nance 210). It is also easy to compare Perry with Mrs. Clutter in their habits of collecting things, for they both have sentimental attachments to possessions that others see as having little value. Another version of this defense of Capote is that he proves that average Americans made Perry a killer; David Galloway claims that what happens in *In Cold Blood* is "not so much murder as suicide: in a real sense America was both killer and victim, turning the deferred-payment shotgun against herself" (Galloway 161).

The opposing argument is that *In Cold Blood* proves that Smith and Hickock really are different from the rest of us, less than human, and therefore undeserving of our sympathy. The insanity defense that Capote promotes for pages could be a concession of this major point. Even Capote's title, which could be a nod to O'Connor's *Wise Blood,* may constitute a betrayal of Hickock and Smith, since most readers will think the title refers to the killers' being cold-blooded rather than to, say, a cold-blooded American legal system. David Guest makes the amazing argument that O'Connor's Misfit is Capote's "model psychopath" and that Capote was not therefore as inclined to defend Smith and Hickock as he claimed to be (Guest 129–30). Another interesting charge against Capote is that, within the book, he never takes an explicit stand on Perry's behalf. The peculiar insistence on objectivity and near invisibility in the narration of *In Cold Blood,* a stylistic choice Capote often insisted was crucial to his book's success, can be considered a cop-out. As Guest claims, "Capote's narrator is both omniscient and impotent" (Guest 109). I can agree with Guest that Capote's choice of narrator forced him into a weaker presentation of a case on the murderers' behalf, but at the same time, I can testify, based on years of teaching *In Cold Blood*, that the book does open many students' eyes to the case against capital punishment. Here, however, it is not necessary to reach a conclusion about whether Capote did the right thing. What is clear is that O'Connor helped Capote write a great book in that he took from her lessons in seeing the potential good in a bad person, in putting aside meanness for the sake of compassion.

I hope it is already apparent that the issues raised by Capote's book are issues worth raising in O'Connor's works. But before I shift from Capote, it is worth noting that he wrote another "nonfiction" piece about murder, "Handcarved Coffins," which clearly alludes to O'Connor's "The River," a story that combines drowning and baptism. While Jack De Bellis speculates that *In Cold Blood* was Capote's revenge on the South and "a way of release from his psychological bondage to the South" (De Bellis 535), a better case can be made that it is in "Handcarved Coffins," published in 1980, that Capote most forcefully pushes O'Connor away. I should begin by clarifying that I do not consider "Handcarved Coffins" to be nonfiction; even Gerald Clarke, who generously accepts most of *In Cold Blood* as "uncompromising realism" of a basically accurate sort, sees "Handcarved Coffins" as "mostly fictional" (Clarke 359). Clarke says, "The idea for *Handcarved Coffins* came from Al Dewey" (Clarke 516), but most of the crimes in "Handcarved Coffins" are so cartoonish as to be almost beside the point.[6]

Although he clearly considered "Handcarved Coffins" similar to *In Cold Blood*, Capote's focus in the story, in contrast to his nearly invisible presence in *In Cold Blood*, is on himself as an active character and narrator imagining the criminal's motives. Capote becomes aware that Robert Hawley Quinn is killing people because his friend Jake Pepper, a detective, introduces Capote to the case. When Jake's fiancée, Adelaide Mason, drowns or is drowned, Capote becomes the superior detective, probably because he bears none of Pepper's guilt over failing to save Adelaide. Robert Siegle is correct in suggesting that in "Handcarved Coffins" Capote discovers the truth about the killer "by identifying him with a character in his own private psychodrama" and thus the process of creating fiction is demonstrated to be the way to produce nonfiction (Siegle 445–46).

The central symbol in "Handcarved Coffins" is the Blue River, which probably provides the motive for the murders. Capote's story equates the killer Quinn with the Reverend Bobby Joe Snow, who forcibly baptized the young Truman. It is no secret that Capote hates the reverend. The most important O'Connor connection here, which Helen Garson has noted but which nobody has analyzed, is the character Marylee Connor. Flannery O'Connor's first name was Mary. The sister of

Adelaide, Connor seems unable to stomach discussions of murder when she first appears, but she is the one able to figure out that her sister's life is being threatened (Capote 1980, 89), and we later realize that Connor denies that Quinn is a murderer. Detective Jake Pepper, perhaps unfairly, explains that she is "sweet but not too bright" (Capote 1980, 102). She is with Adelaide at the Blue River, reading as Adelaide drowns, and she is sure Quinn was not involved (Capote 1980, 124–25). She finally moves to Florida, mails Capote a picture of Adelaide holding a cat (Capote 1980, 136), and gets a job as a receptionist for a circus. This character in a story with a baptism scene reminiscent of "The River" is surely meant to comment on O'Connor. Jake Pepper takes a swipe at all "female literature" (Capote 1980, 94), but Capote knows better than to endorse Pepper on that point. If he is rejecting O'Connor here, it is because Capote objects to her writing about baptism in a way that simply strikes too close to home for him.[7] The major accusation that "Handcarved Coffins" makes against O'Connor is that she seems too comfortable around a murderer—too inclined to see a good man in one. It is as if Capote were complaining that O'Connor made him too compassionate toward Perry Smith.

According to Jack Hicks, the river in "Handcarved Coffins" carries significant symbolism for Capote's career: "The Blue River is a metaphor for the author's desire for historical/mythic continuity, his hope for a revivified narrative flow. It is first a source of life.... But it is soon treacherous ... and finally demonic and death-dealing, a mirror in which to see his own forced, infernal baptism forty years earlier. To be born ritually into this world, Capote implies, is to be dragged in unwillingly, to be ceremonially drowned, inundated first beneath the waters of a hell-on-earth" (Hicks 172–73). It is no stretch to apply Hicks's comment to Capote's true feelings about O'Connor. Perhaps he has to reject the inspiration he took from her in order to declare his personal and artistic independence. Hicks reads the final scene of "Handcarved Coffins" as showing that Capote refuses to join the probable murderer Quinn when invited into the middle of the Blue River, because Capote's "own sense of power grows, out of his knowledge that historical, literary, and literal rivers are all poisoned, and out of the desire not to be submerged" (Hicks 176) by the man whom Capote imagines as a substitute for the preacher who baptized him. If the story is read this way, at the end of it Capote frees himself from several oppressive ghosts. If freedom is Capote's goal in this story, he may be thinking of O'Connor as another authority figure he is ready to rebel against. In other words, one might be tempted to say that in "Handcarved Coffins" Capote, as a sort of O'Connoresque Misfit, feels he is confronting the fact that he is one of O'Connor's own children, and thus he must symbolically shoot her. And Capote as Misfit might even experience a bit of an O'Connoresque religious insight at the end of "Handcarved Coffins." Robert Siegle sees Capote becoming one with the murderer in the work's final references to acts of God (Siegle 449–50), in the claim that everything is ultimately mysterious: Quinn says, with intentionally ambiguous pronouns, "The way I look at it is: it was the hand of God" (Capote 1980, 146).

Of course, if Capote finally has some appreciation of Quinn, a man he hated, then the character Marylee Connor / O'Connor might be right after all in finding something of value in Quinn. And what Capote ends up demonstrating in "Handcarved Coffins" is that, as he pronounces his rejection of O'Connor, he seems closer to her spirit than he was in *In Cold Blood*. While *In Cold Blood* attempts an objective compassion that is ultimately fragile, "Handcarved Coffins," for all its possible artistic faults, brings Capote closer to his murderer (and to O'Connor) because Capote's meanness is not masked.

So what do all of these speculations about Capote's uses of and opinions about O'Connor teach us about her? I hope I have indicated enough of the wealth of connections between the two of them to suggest that we may learn something about O'Connor through Capote. The primary issue raised here is how well, how justly and compassionately, O'Connor treats her Misfit. I believe that O'Connor, fascinated as she had to be in order to create them, rarely went all the way in endorsing the voices of her misfit characters and misfit narrators. I have a renewed sense of her struggle to affirm her own "meanness"—her unswerving insistence on following her own path—and I have an increased appreciation for the times when her misfit voice is allowed to speak. O'Connor was finally able to endorse meanness, not as a place to stop, but as a stage in a process, a stage one might revisit repeatedly.

Of course, there are moments in real life when O'Connor identified with The Misfit. For example, writing to Betty Hester on November 10, 1955, O'Connor reported that after a woman who saw her on crutches exclaimed, "Bless you, Darling!" and obliquely tried to remind O'Connor that "the lame shall enter first," O'Connor "felt exactly like the Misfit" (*CW* 969). But the primary issue is what she did in her fiction, and O'Connor seems to have been quite conflicted about her Misfit. In "On Her Own Work," O'Connor makes some comments about the grandmother and The Misfit that suggest the complexities in how she regards both of them. Many of O'Connor's comments here seem intended to prove that the grandmother's moment of grace is the key to the story. And yet notice how indirectly and tentatively O'Connor can go about making claims for the grandmother: she says, "I think the unprejudiced reader will feel that the Grandmother has a special kind of triumph in this story which instinctively we do not allow to someone altogether bad," but O'Connor makes this claim only after admitting "that the old lady is a hypocritical old soul; her wits are no match for the Misfit's, nor is her capacity for grace equal to his" (*MM* 111).

O'Connor could be quite harsh toward The Misfit; in a letter to Andrew Lytle dated February 4, 1960, she seems to equate The Misfit and Satan, writing that the grandmother's "moment of grace excites the devil to frenzy" (*CW* 1121). On the other hand, in a letter dated October 6, 1959, O'Connor told John Hawkes that "I can fancy a character like The Misfit being redeemable" (*CW* 1108). And two pages after O'Connor calls The Misfit "altogether bad" in "On Her Own Work," she amazingly reverses herself: "I don't want to equate The Misfit with the devil." O'Connor tries to explain herself by adding, "I prefer to think that, however unlikely this may seem, the old lady's gesture, like the mustard-seed, will grow to be a great crow-filled tree in the Misfit's heart, and will be enough of a pain to him there to turn him into the prophet he was meant to become" (*MM* 112–13).[8] O'Connor immediately adds, "But that's another story." Of course one can conclude O'Connor is claiming that she did not really make The Misfit redeemable, but when one compares O'Connor with Capote, one is led to ask why O'Connor seems to have left The Misfit's potential only partially investigated. There is something about The Misfit that is crucial to the power of O'Connor's fiction. Did she abandon him in a manner at all comparable to what might be interpreted as Capote's abandonment of Perry Smith? Capote might reasonably have worked to get Smith a life in prison, where he might have developed some of his talents or might have rediscovered his affection for his religious friend Willie-Jay. What could O'Connor do (or what did she do) for her potential prophet, The Misfit, that would be the right thing? I will discuss five possible answers, some of which overlap.

First, O'Connor could prove that The Misfit is something other than human, that other rules apply to him. Josephine Hendin argues that The Misfit is finally shown to be an animal like Pitty Sing, the cat he picks up at the story's end (Hendin 151), and although Hendin probably does not want The Misfit to be good, one could probably adapt her argument and argue that it is enough for O'Connor to show that The Misfit is a good, even prophetic animal. I do not think O'Connor did, and I do not think this is good strategy. The Misfit is altogether human.

Or, O'Connor could make The Misfit good in that he puts his independence first, totally rejecting the grandmother's attempted influence. Those who see The Misfit taking over the story through the force of his fascinating personality and having the final word, in a meaningful sense, may prefer this view. This strategy would also probably be the most straightforward one, but there is reason to doubt whether O'Connor used it. I have argued elsewhere that The Misfit suffers a crucial failure of courage, hypocritically refusing to live up to his own principles (Gentry 108–12).

A third way is that O'Connor could make The Misfit good is that we could see him starting to change into a good man. When The Misfit tells henchman Bobby Lee to "Shut up" after Bobby Lee says that killing is "fun," and when The Misfit adds, "It's no real pleasure in life" (*CW* 153), he may be starting to suffer the kind of "pain" that O'Connor said could change him. Laura Mandell Zaidman proposes another version of this argument; she claims that as O'Connor revised the story, she transformed the grandmother "from a woman desperately in need of God's grace to a medium of grace for The Misfit" (Zaidman 43) and that when The Misfit acceptingly touches Pitty Sing, "the reader considers the possibility, however remote, of The Misfit's becoming a good man by the end of his life" (Zaidman 50). I do not believe that this action makes it absolutely clear that The Misfit is on his way to a new life. Picking up a cat is the sort of false kindness he has exhibited throughout the story, and his final statement of his own misery can be read as a sign that he will become worse, not better, after the story ends. Furthermore, it may be a bad sign that he recommends silence to Bobby Lee—not to mention that he seems to lapse into silence himself—immediately after he has agreed that the reason the grandmother could "have been a good woman" was that "she was a talker" (*CW* 153).[9] As much as O'Connor loved her Misfit, in the final version of the story, she identified more with the grandmother's normality than with The Misfit's profound meanness. I have argued elsewhere that the narrator of "A Good Man" becomes good by dropping a tone of meanness in the course of telling the story (Gentry 37–39), but perhaps giving up one's meanness causes the same problems that Capote encountered when he retreated into the narratorial objectivity of *In Cold Blood*.

Fourth, O'Connor could make The Misfit good by making him similar to everyone else in the story who exhibits some goodness. I am interested in the other ways the story breaks down distinctions between The Misfit and the grandmother, although I still see O'Connor as identifying with the more conventional and less interesting grandmother. Critics continue to uncover similarities between The Misfit and the grandmother. For example, J. Peter Dyson's study of "A Good Man Is Hard to Find" in relation to *The Mikado* emphasizes the sense in which The Misfit and the grandmother take on the paradoxically combined role of judge and executioner from the Gilbert and Sullivan operetta (Dyson 144). Frederick Asals also suggests a way to see the grandmother as a bit of a Misfit. Asals perceptively notes that when the grandmother lets the cat loose, what we see is "her visceral acknowledgement of her *own* failure" (Asals 20), her rejection of herself before The Misfit gets around to rejecting her.

Finally, when O'Connor wrote that The Misfit could become a prophet, she added, "But that's another story." The best argument I can make that O'Connor granted The Misfit justice is that she wrote about him in other guises. But what is striking is the struggle she went through to endorse his potential. One could say that O'Connor finds value in a murderous protagonist in both of her novels or perhaps in Thomas in "The Comforts of Home," but all of these characters lose their personalities as they become good. The exception might be Enoch Emery, but O'Connor drops his story even more abruptly than she drops The Misfit. In reexamining "The River," the story that apparently bothered Capote so much, one could interpret Harry/Bevel Ashfield as a good little Misfit, rejecting his parents, Mrs. Connin, and Mr. Paradise, as he grabs what he wants. Perhaps it is significant that "The River" immediately follows "A Good Man Is Hard to Find" in O'Connor's first story collection. But Harry/Bevel cannot survive the experience, so he may fall short of being the model Misfit.

One can find spots in O'Connor's fiction where she did justice to the mean voice of the misfit. One is in the narrative voice of "The Lame Shall Enter First," the story that provoked O'Connor to write to John Hawkes on February 6, 1962, "In this one,

I'll admit that the devil's voice is my own" (*CW* 1157). I can easily imagine a version of The Misfit as the narrator of that story. There are other O'Connor stories in which the narrator's voice never drops its tone of satirical meanness, notably "A Late Encounter with the Enemy," in which the narrator rips apart Gen. George Poker Sash and the Old South. Another spot is in a character that some critics equate with O'Connor herself: the unnamed little girl in "A Temple of the Holy Ghost," the mean child who, at the end of the story, starts to pray "Hep me not to be so mean" (*CW* 208), but who then gets an answer to her prayer from the sideshow hermaphrodite, who tells her, using ambiguous pronouns, that her meanness is good, just as the hermaphrodite's "freakishness" is good. The hermaphrodite says "I don't dispute hit. This is the way He wanted me to be" (*CW* 209). The little girl learns to affirm her own meanness, and at her best, O'Connor did too.

In Truman Capote, O'Connor had a disciple who, first, profitably misunderstood her. *In Cold Blood* was a compassionate book in which meanness had little value. In "Handcarved Coffins," as Capote expressed his anger toward his misfit and his resentment of O'Connor (in part for her being too compassionate), he revealed the value he found in his misfit, in O'Connor, and in meanness. Rereading "A Good Man Is Hard to Find" in the light of Capote, we see more of the value of meanness. In the passages cited earlier about The Misfit's varied experiences, which Capote transformed into the experiences of Dick Hickock, I think we can see Capote reversing O'Connor's effect. Dick Hickock is the ultimate loser, at a dead end no matter how much he brags. The Misfit, in contrast, shows us that he is fond of changing, so that even his final change, his sudden claim that life has "no real pleasure" (*CW* 153), can leave open the strong possibility that The Misfit will continue to change.

When I think of The Misfit's struggle toward goodness as an ongoing process with value assigned to various forms of his meanness, it is easier to conclude that O'Connor is compassionately searching to discover a way to find in him a good man. When O'Connor said "But that's another story" in discussing The Misfit's transformation into a prophet, I think she was referring to other stories she did write. In "A Good Man Is Hard to Find" she makes use of what may seem like meanness, the inclination to shoot The Misfit every minute of his life. Her compassion is evident in her refusal to excuse him as simply being crazy or an animal, in her analysis of his excuses, in her dramatizations of the opportunities for change that he lets slip by, and in her suggested denials of his pride in uniqueness. O'Connor's most compassionate act toward The Misfit is to leave him alive and wandering, disgusted with himself, still "aloose from the . . . Pen" (*CW* 137), not yet forced or willing to shut up. The fact that O'Connor leaves us with the creepy image of The Misfit holding that cat indicates that O'Connor always saw a function for meanness.

Notes

1. Not all of the O'Connor connections in *In Cold Blood* have to do with intentional borrowing or with borrowing specifically from "A Good Man." Melvin J. Friedman notes that "the Kansas

Capote writes about is not significantly different from Flannery O'Connor country" (Friedman 168). Friedman sees an "O'Connor reminder in *In Cold Blood* . . . when we are told . . . that Perry Smith's sister Fern changed her name to Joy" (Capote 1965, 185). This sounds like an inversion of the name change in "Good Country People." Friedman also suggests that "Willie-Jay, in *In Cold Blood,* whose name Capote admits he has invented, resembles in many ways O'Connor's 'Bible Belt' preachers, both in name (think of Onnie Jay Holy in *Wise Blood*) and in evangelical manner." Still, Friedman concludes "that the connections which involve *In Cold Blood* are largely fortuitous" (Friedman 167–68).

2. One might also compare this speech by The Misfit, about there being only two paths from which to choose, to Perry Smith's thoughts about his situation as *In Cold Blood* opens: either he will meet up with his religious friend, Willie-Jay, or he will join Dick Hickock's plan to commit a crime (Capote 1965, 45).

3. Capote once opined about mass murderers, "They all believe in God" (qtd. in Grobel 126).

4. One also wonders what Capote might have said if confronted with all these similarities and the specific borrowings. I suspect he would reply that what he did is far from plagiarism, and that in two places in *In Cold Blood* he criticizes those who commit plagiarism. When Perry Smith learns that a copycat killer in Florida has duplicated the Clutter murders, he says he "wouldn't be surprised" to learn the killer was "a lunatic" (Capote 1965, 200). And late in *In Cold Blood,* we learn that the poem handed to Dick Hickock by the unredeemable Lowell Lee Andrews on his way to being executed is actually a plagiarism of Gray's "Elegy" (Capote 1965, 332). It is this passage that precedes Hickock's borrowed speech about his varied experiences.

5. Here is Anthony Bonner's translation of the beginning of the first stanza of Villon's poem, also called "XIV—Villon's Epitaph":

> Brother men who after us live on,
> harden not your hearts against us,
> for if you have some pity on us poor men,
> the sooner God will show you mercy.

This is the end of the epigraph for *In Cold Blood;* here is the rest of the first stanza:

> You see us, five, six, strung up here:
> as for our flesh, which we have fed too well,
> already it has been devoured and is rotten,
> and we, the bones, now turn to dust and ashes.
> Let no one laugh at all our miseries,
> but pray to God that He absolve us all. (Villon 163)

6. John Hersey considers "Handcarved Coffins" to be "a gobbet of commercial trash" and uses a quotation from Flannery O'Connor to argue that one must not mix fiction and nonfiction (Hersey 1–3). Several other critics have been more positively disposed toward "Handcarved Coffins."

7. John C. Waldmeir says the river in "Handcarved Coffins" contributes to "the theological complexity" of *Music for Chameleons,* the collection in which it appears, so it is probably not safe to conclude that Capote rejects religion in "Handcarved Coffins." Waldmeir sees the story "dramatizing all that is at stake in the ritual of baptism, the complex and dangerous exchange between life and death that Saint Paul described a[s] 'dying to Christ'" (Waldmeir 165).

8. Capote described for Plimpton his goals in writing *In Cold Blood* in a manner reminiscent of O'Connor's statement about the grandmother's effect on The Misfit: "I've always thought of

[*In Cold Blood*] as being like something reduced to a seed. Instead of presenting the reader with a full plant, with all the foliage, a seed is planted in the soil of his mind" (qtd. in Plimpton 203).

9. When one considers the extreme extent to which "absolute silence" was insisted upon in O'Connor's first Catholic elementary school, St. Vincent's in Savannah (Cash 14), the value for O'Connor of being able to be "a talker" becomes even more apparent.

Works Cited

Asals, Frederick, ed. *A Good Man Is Hard to Find*. Women Writers: Texts and Contexts. New Brunswick, N.J.: Rutgers University Press, 1993.

Bonner, Anthony. "A Short Biography." In *The Complete Works of François Villon*, trans. by Anthony Bonner, xvii–xxiii. New York: McKay, 1960.

Capote, Truman. "The Art of Fiction XVII: Truman Capote." Interview by Pati Hill. *Paris Review* 16 (Spring–Summer 1957): 35–51. Reprinted in *Truman Capote: Conversations,* ed. M. Thomas Inge (Jackson: University Press of Mississippi, 1987).

———. "Handcarved Coffins: A Nonfiction Account of an American Crime." In *Music for Chameleons,* 67–146. New York: Random, 1980.

———. *In Cold Blood: A True Account of a Multiple Murder and Its Consequences.* New York: Random, 1965.

Cash, Jean W. *Flannery O'Connor: A Life.* Knoxville: University of Tennessee Press, 2002.

Christensen, Peter G. "Major Works and Themes." In Waldmeir and Waldmeir, *Critical Response,* 221–29.

Clarke, Gerald. *Capote: A Biography.* New York: Simon and Schuster, 1988.

Creeger, George R. *Animals in Exile: Imagery and Theme in Capote's "In Cold Blood."* Monday Evening Papers 12. Middletown, Conn.: Center for Advanced Studies, Wesleyan University, 1967.

De Bellis, Jack. "Visions and Revisions: Truman Capote's *In Cold Blood.*" *Journal of Modern Literature* 7 (1979): 519–36.

Dyson, J. Peter. "Cats, Crime, and Punishment: *The Mikado*'s Pitti-Sing in 'A Good Man Is Hard to Find.'" *English Studies in Canada* 14 (1988): 436–52. Reprinted in Asals, *Good Man,* 139–63.

Friedman, Melvin J. "Towards an Aesthetic: Truman Capote's Other Voices." In Malin, *Capote's "In Cold Blood,"* 164–76.

Galloway, David. "Why the Chickens Came Home to Roost in Holcomb, Kansas: Truman Capote's *In Cold Blood.*" In Malin, *Capote's "In Cold Blood,"* 154–76.

Garson, Helen S. *Truman Capote: A Study of the Short Fiction.* Twayne's Studies in Short Fiction 36. New York: Twayne, 1992.

Gentry, Marshall Bruce. *Flannery O'Connor's Religion of the Grotesque.* Jackson: University Press of Mississippi, 1986.

Gordon, Caroline, and Allen Tate. "Commentary on Capote and O'Connor." In *The House of Fiction: An Anthology of the Short Story with Commentary,* 2nd ed., edited by Caroline Gordon and Allen Tate, 382–86. New York: Scribner's, 1960.

Grobel, Lawrence. *Conversations with Capote.* New York: NAL, 1985.

Guest, David. *Sentenced to Death: The American Novel and Capital Punishment.* Jackson: University Press of Mississippi, 1997.

Hendin, Josephine. *The World of Flannery O'Connor.* Bloomington: Indiana University Press, 1970.

Hersey, John. "The Legend of the License." *Yale Review* 70 (1980): 1–25.

Hicks, Jack. "'Fire, Fire, Fire Flowing like a River, River, River': History and Postmodernism in Truman Capote's *Handcarved Coffins*." In *History and Post-War Writing*, edited by Theo D'haen and Hans Bertens, 171–84. Atlanta: Rodopi, 1990. Reprinted in Waldmeir and Waldmeir, *Critical Response*, 167–77.

Malin, Irving, ed. *Truman Capote's "In Cold Blood": A Critical Handbook*. Belmont, Calif.: Wadsworth, 1968.

Nance, William L. *The Worlds of Truman Capote*. New York: Stein, 1970.

Plimpton, George. *Truman Capote: In Which Various Friends, Enemies, Acquaintances, and Detractors Recall His Turbulent Career*. New York: Talese-Doubleday, 1997.

Siegle, Robert. "Capote's *Handcarved Coffins* and the Nonfiction Novel." *Contemporary Literature* 35, no. 3 (1984): 437–51.

Spivey, Ted R. *Flannery O'Connor: The Woman, the Thinker, the Visionary*. Macon, Ga.: Mercer University Press, 1995.

Tuttle, Jon. "Glimpses of 'A Good Man' in Capote's *In Cold Blood*." *ANQ* 1 (October 1988): 144–46. Reprinted in Waldmeir and Waldmeir, *Critical Response*, 193–95.

Villon, François. *The Complete Works of François Villon*. Translated by Anthony Bonner. New York: McKay, 1960.

Waldmeir, John C. "Religion and Style in *The Dogs Bark* and *Music for Chameleons*." In Waldmeir and Waldmeir, *Critical Response*, 155–66.

Waldmeir, Joseph J., and John C. Waldmeir, eds. *The Critical Response to Truman Capote*. Critical Responses to Arts and Letters. Westport, Conn.: Greenwood, 1999.

Zaidman, Laura Mandell. "The Evolution of a Good Woman." *Flannery O'Connor Bulletin* 26–27 (1998–2000): 43–51.

"Then I discovered the Germans"

O'Connor's Encounter with Guardini and
German Thinkers of the Interwar Period

W. A. Sessions

On September 15, 1955, Flannery O'Connor wrote a letter to Andrew Lytle. He had been her teacher at Iowa, an early supporter, one of the original Agrarians, and a close friend of Allen Tate and his former wife Caroline Gordon, Flannery's special mentor. Lytle was also the longtime editor of the *Sewanee Review* and, as she knew, a strong Anglo-Catholic. The central paragraph of the letter to him posits a remarkable self-definition by O'Connor at age thirty: "I want to thank you for the letter you sent Harcourt, Brace last spring. What you said in it is what I see in the stories myself but what nobody who reviews them cares to see. To my way of thinking, the only thing that keeps me from being a regional writer is being a Catholic and the only thing that keeps me from being a Catholic writer (in the narrow sense) is being a Southerner; but the religious element is largely ignored and I was glad to have it pointed out" (*HB* 104).

In a letter two years later (July 16, 1957) to her novelist friend Cecil Dawkins, a woman who was also a southerner born a Catholic, Flannery declares, "Catholicity has given me my perspective on the South and probably gives you yours" (*HB* 230). On this point O'Connor is a little more delicate because, as she was aware, her correspondent was preparing to leave the church. She too is repelled, O'Connor writes Dawkins, by Catholics who "operate by the slide rule" so that "the Church for them is not the body of Christ but the poor man's insurance system." In fact, Flannery writes, "Faith has to take in all the other possibilities it can." Such a program of discovery is a means to greater faith, but like any process of self-discovery, the process is lonely. "Anyway," she concludes, "to discover the Church, you have to set out by yourself." Then, as if in an act of what Thomas Aquinas would call practical charity, she enumerates for her lapsing friend the books she now reads "to discover the Church" in her isolation at Andalusia, particularly those by European theologians and philosophers and fiction writers. As she remarks to Dawkins, she had moved in this reading from contemporary French novelists and French philosophers to new terrain: "And then I discovered the Germans." She names three instances of her own German intertextuality, or reading, the most influential and most discussed in her letters and reviews being the theologian, philosopher, and literary critic Romano Guardini. As with so many of her letters, especially when belief in the church is part of the context, she ends the letter to Dawkins with a sharp, even judgmental, reminder: "In any case, discovering the Church is apt to be a slow procedure but it can only take place if you have a free mind and no vested interest in disbelief" (*HB* 231).

By a series of accidents, my own interest in the writings of the German theologian Guardini crossed Flannery's—and then coincided with her readings of other German theologians or philosophers, whom I was to either study myself or actually hear lecture when I studied at the University of Freiburg during 1957 and 1958. Throughout that year Flannery would write to me and inquire about the contacts I was making. She would ask specific questions about writers or thinkers whose work she admired and was learning from. It became an extension of the kind of exchange of ideas and books we had begun in Georgia the year before, when I first met her.

In the spring of 1956 Flannery O'Connor wrote me praising my review of *The Lord*, the newly translated English version of the 1937 *Der Herr* by the German Catholic theologian Romano Guardini. I had recently written the review for the *Bulletin*, our Catholic diocesan paper (hardly more than a printed report for the then few Catholics in Georgia but a place, so Flannery would announce with glee, where "we can get free books"). As she wrote "A," or Betty Hester, who would soon be our mutual friend: "Enclosure from Mr. Wilyum Sessions. . . . I sent him the article and a note expressing equal admiration of his *Bulletin* review."[1] O'Connor also used the occasion of her first letter to invite me to visit her at Andalusia, and I did, on Ascension Day 1956, the first of many visits. During those early years, Guardini and other writers and thinkers from France, Germany, and Italy became favorite subjects for long conversations on Andalusia's wide screened-in front porch or across the long table in the dining room that doubled in those years as living room.

The Guardini connection would in the next year lead to my being given a Fulbright grant to study in Germany, but instead of the University of Munich, where I wanted to study with Guardini, I was sent to study with Heidegger at the University of Freiburg. O'Connor wrote me shortly after my arrival: "Are you going to see Heidegger on his mountain top? Are you going to see Msgr. Guardini, Karl Adam, or Max Picard, or is Max Picard still living? What about Marcel and what about that lady critic that is so good—Claude Edmond Magny?" (*HB* 243–44). I wrote her about the many German, French, and Swiss writers whom I encountered in that special corner of Europe, such as Martin Heidegger; the Swiss Jewish modernist Max Picard, who had become a Catholic and was indeed alive; Yves Congar; and Jean Guitton, two of whose books O'Connor admired, especially the one on the Virgin Mary. I also knew American students who in nearby Basel were attending the lectures of another theologian O'Connor read and admired, the German Calvinist Karl Barth. At a vespers service at the Freiburg Cathedral during Lent 1958, I also heard a homily, about which I wrote O'Connor, by the Swiss priest Hans Urs von Balthasar, now considered by many one of the greatest Catholic theologians of the last century. Recalling these thinkers now, almost fifty years later, has a simple point: Flannery wanted to know about each one and wrote me for firsthand impressions. They could form the living context of her intense daily reading. Isolated at Andalusia, friends might and did provide an enlivening context and a needed distraction for days often spent in pain.

Already by this time O'Connor was showing, as her letters to various friends reveal, her understanding of a range of ideas found in other philosophical and theological masters, from the earlier Anglo-Austrian Friedrich von Hügel to Guardini and Picard, and the pioneering ecumenical priest Karl Adam at the University of Tübingen, and, in her later reading, the Jesuit Karl Rahner from Freiburg. Her letters and conversations also reveal how she understood another German tradition, hardly Christian, that would help her own evolving concepts of history and human choice, represented by Eric Vögelin, who lived in the American South during this period; the Jewish theological writer Martin Buber, a friend of Guardini's, whose "I-Thou" dialectic of religious encounter helped define O'Connor's conception of the prophet; Martin Heidegger himself, for many one of the greatest philosophers of the century, and who had begun his career in the Jesuit novitiate; and, of course, the cultural masters Friedrich Nietzsche, Sigmund Freud, and Carl Jung—especially the latter. Her letters and book reviews affirm just how carefully and profoundly O'Connor did think about the texts of these thinkers that entered her seemingly cloistered life in middle Georgia. As both her fiction and nonfiction demonstrate, her reading of the Germans helped create the intensely parabolic texts in which she transformed quite local realities into universal discourse. It is precisely for interpretation of these complex texts that I want to single out from O'Connor's wide and rather universal reading at least one specific source, namely, Flannery's reading of Romano Guardini. Remarkably, no single published study (not even a dissertation) has dealt with this direct influence or even that of German theologians, except in a general manner.

With the exception of a few studies and books, O'Connor criticism is not noted for examining intellectual contexts for her work. This fact is not surprising for a number of reasons. Even in my own argument, I find a problem that has multiplied itself in O'Connor criticism. So, I want to address this critical ambiguity in my method before I turn to Guardini and his specific texts and their influence on O'Connor's fiction, letters, and essays. I believe looking at the general and specific problems of intertextuality, with some brief critical perspective on my own method, may help focus my argument.

First of all, intertextuality, the process I am analyzing here, in itself guarantees nothing in interpretation. On one level, it poses but one more form of the biographical fallacy, the lie inherent in the critical method of the old historicism at its worst; that is, the mistaken belief that if we know where William Wordsworth and his sister Dorothy went for their walks in the Lake District, we can immediately understand "Tintern Abbey." With source studies, biographical fallacy becomes more treacherous. At the moment this generic fallacy and faulty historicist analysis appears with some frequency in O'Connor studies. To this kind of analysis, including my own, I pose the following question: if we know where O'Connor garnered her ideas of prophecy, choice, and the fundamental horror of the human condition, do we automatically understand O'Connor's dense and violent texts? Can biography per se solve the mystery of those texts? I doubt it. O'Connor herself was quite aware of the dangers of the biographical fallacy, including its use of intertextuality. She is at pains to discuss such problems in *Mystery and Manners*. In fact, her masters —from Ransom to Lytle to Tate and Gordon—had all emerged as Agrarians from an academic and critical reaction to the Vanderbilt school of source studies, embodied, for example, in the still impressive Shakespeare historicism of Walter Clyde Curry. The Agrarians had proclaimed, among other things, the independence of the text itself. At best, one can still say that such reading may lead us to approach the mystery of the text with a little more clarity. In no sense can we say the contextual reading, whether theological, sexual, or Marxist, "explains" the total reality of the text itself. Thus, in O'Connor, neither demonic criticism that is a product of what Paul Ricoeur calls "the hermeneutics of suspicion" nor hagiographical discourse can add up to the singular mystery of her best narratives.

But exactly here is the problem: contextual readings do bring surprises and reversals that may ironically take us back into the text. Setting a context for interpretation out of perspective studies emerging from new historicism, feminism, Marxism, gay studies, and multiculturalism may even take the reader well beyond any author's own understanding of what she wrote. O'Connor did not like interpretations that differed from her own, as I know from her reaction to my comments on *The Violent Bear It Away* and her blistering reply (*HB* 407, 410–11). Furthermore, as biographer, I believe that contextual criticism with appropriate perspectives does bring readers closer to the texts. It can lead to new discoveries of the author's originality and a writer's power to originate whole traditions of literary and cultural history without intending it. The text has, in this sense, its own freedom and being. Who would have thought, for example, that for the celebration of O'Connor's seventy-fifth birthday a young African American woman, with the overtly fictitious name of Guerrilla Girl Alma Thomas, could praise O'Connor, a writer totally "other" from Guerrilla Girl in generation, race, religion, and ideology? Or that Guerrilla Girl could note with great admiration O'Connor's power of "digging from the particular to reach the universal"? Toni Morrison has recognized the impact such surprises in a text may have when she observes, with O'Connor's fiction in mind, "A writer's response to American Africanism often provides a subtext that either sabotages the surface text's expressed intentions or escapes them through a language that mystifies what it cannot bring itself to articulate but still attempts to register."[2] In her structural emphasis on one cultural aspect of a text, *race*, Morrison illustrates a new way to work beyond simplistic ideological or biographical readings. So indeed did Alice Walker, who grew up as a child of black sharecroppers "up the road apiece" from Andalusia. Walker praised O'Connor's universality in a race-ridden society. Indeed, Toni Morrison in her essay also chides "some powerful literary critics" for seeing "no connection between God's grace and Africanist 'othering' in Flannery O'Connor."[3] Both Walker and Morrison appear to understand the essentially parabolic nature of O'Connor's fiction. At least for Morrison it offers a dialectic of the particular "Africanist 'othering,'" which the text cannot escape, and the universal "God's grace," which it cannot escape either. In short, what dramatizes the action of most O'Connor narratives is precisely this dialectic or "tension," to use Allen Tate's critical term, which O'Connor knew well. Her canon thrives on a reciprocating counterpoint between her conscious framing of history as universal (with her own ideological terms) and a local and particular reality that may not be so easily framed. The dialectic between the two—the way the plot turned out—could surprise even Flannery, as she once answered a reader. What I want to show is that Romano Guardini's texts also developed from just such a theory of open and surprising dialectic. His texts provided the young Georgia writer in the 1950s with one more source for the invention and structuring of her own universal narratives. In no sense could his texts "cause" or "explain" O'Connor's fiction. At best, they might help the reader interpret a larger mystery, the stories themselves.

At his eightieth birthday celebration in 1965, the year after O'Connor died, Romano Guardini gave a short address, "Wahrheit und Ironie" (Truth and Irony), in which he described his own dialectic of two identities, his search for truth amid the ironies of his historical existence. As a priest, writer, and philosopher, he had lived in a Germany that had gone from being nineteenth-century Europe's, and therefore the world's, civilization of the future to being a collapsed civilization epitomized by the burning fires and bombed-out ruins of Berlin—the Berlin where Guardini had ministered and taught, even under the Nazis. In 1965 Pope Paul VI had offered Guardini the hat of the Roman cardinal, but in a typical gesture, the German theologian turned it down. It did not befit the ironic twists of his searching life. Born in Verona, Guardini at less than one year of age was brought by his Italian parents to Germany, at that time the world center of new science and technology. His father was both a successful businessman and a diplomat, living in Mainz, where Romano, an official outsider, made his *Abitur* (graduated from high school) and attended discussions with avant-garde Catholic groups reading John Henry Cardinal Newman, Joris-Karl Huysmans, and the radical Léon Bloy, whose work deeply influenced O'Connor. Guardini then studied chemistry and economics at the Universities of Tübingen, Munich, and Berlin. At age twenty, after a crisis of faith, Romano Guardini decided to enter the priesthood. After some years of preparation, he earned his doctorate at the University of Freiburg, refusing to write on what he considered outdated Thomism and opting instead to write on the more fluid and dialectical theology, so he believed, of the Franciscan Saint Bonaventura.

Among the friends he made at Freiburg was Martin Heidegger, with whom Guardini exchanged letters for many years.

At age eighty Guardini had found the right title to sum up his experience of human existence: truth and irony. Against the dialectic that dominated the Thomism of his day and the dialectic of the Hegelian philosophies of his time, including that of Karl Marx, Guardini posed a different dialectic. It too would build on tensions or counterpoints but not moving necessarily into the Hegelian absolute synthesis or harmony. On the contrary, this dialectic existed in a continuous and uneasy relationship between thesis and antithesis, with a synthesis only rarely pointing a way beyond the dialectic. Indeed, Guardini's dialectic starts with a first principle of human history, basic to any argument for him about time. Human life begins with the continuing effects of what Cardinal Newman in his *Apologia Pro Vita Sua* calls the "aboriginal calamity." That is, any absolute in human existence, including the concept of God, is inevitably qualified by irony, ambiguity, and vulnerability, including breakdown. For Guardini, solutions in history could never be inevitable, or absolute, as with Marx and with most modern attempts to "save" history—what O'Connor might have called the Rayber solution. On the contrary, solutions can only exist as probabilities in a broken world. At best, they may exist like the probable "truth" that Aristotle in the *Poetics* says defines the conditional world of the great works of poetry, specifically the representation of the terrible world of Sophocles' *King Oedipus*. Representation does provide harmony but only for the moment of the text. Even in true aesthetic harmony the fact of the terrible world both begins and ends the text. Time is no escape, as O'Connor demonstrates in her most popular and most Sophoclean short story, "A Good Man Is Hard to Find." In this sense, the narrative, the story, or work of art can never transcend itself or its terrible world. O'Connor, for example, can only represent the tensions of that world. No text by itself can redeem a world that originates and continues in "aboriginal calamity," according to Newman in his *Apologia*, a text loved by Guardini and O'Connor (her copy has careful markings). For all three, Newman's "calamity" is the first premise of all human existence, the cause of the inevitable irony and ambiguity that King Oedipus discovered in his own life and, as Newman, Guardini, and O'Connor variously assert, that all human beings discover in their own lives.

In old age Guardini could only confirm from his actually lived life the theory of the dialectic that he had worked out when a young professor at the University of Berlin in the 1920s. This is the theory of *Gegensatz*. The term can be translated, certainly as Guardini meant it, as a thing opposed, an antithesis, a contrast, and a confrontation with the other. It implies a process of interaction, a relationship of living beings in creative tension. The full title of Guardini's 1925 book shows its meaning for him: *Der Gegensatz: Versuche zu einer Philosophie des Lebendig-Konkreten* roughly translates as "The Other: A Study into a Philosophy of Living and Concrete Reality." The starting point then for Guardini's dialectic of existence is not any abstract idea of being but a concretely situated living existence with its special vacillations in everyday life—even on a Georgia farm—between truth and the irony of every human existence.

Two realities therefore dominate human life for Guardini. The truth of this individual self and its being stems from larger absolute truths concentrically surrounding the self, that is, society and finally God. At the other end of the dialectic, this individual self exists in the contradictory ordinary world of choice and ambiguity and historical breakdown, that is, worlds defined by what Guardini calls irony. A dialectic that explains the dual nature of the human being—that is, in the life lived between the two parts of the dialectic—cannot be predetermined. By its nature such interaction of life, starting from the total truth of the self but confronting history, stands open and vulnerable at all times. Choices are conditioned by irony and the overwhelming history surrounding the self.

It is doubtful whether O'Connor knew much of this theory. She did not speak or read German, had almost no Latin, or for that matter any foreign language, except the little bit of French I heard her use in Lourdes in 1958. But she read, and the quality and level of her reading, her searching, her comprehension, and above all her desire did enough. Guardini's concept of a living dialectic provides, I am convinced, a structural context, a backdrop, for certain of her early stories, most obviously "The Displaced Person." The counterpointing style and parabolic depth of that story had rarely been attempted before in southern writing and seldom in other American fiction, although the method had roots in Hawthorne and his disciple Melville. *The Violent Bear It Away* is probably influenced the most by Guardini, especially in its structure. After all, O'Connor wrote the narrative with such deliberation precisely in the years she was discovering Guardini. A good case can also be made for Guardini as a source for the counterpointing technique of all her later fiction. Of course, it is not that O'Connor did not recognize the concrete dialectic of truth and irony in her local worlds, whether Savannah, with its gardens of good and evil, or Milledgeville, calling itself "a bird sanctuary." In such worlds, universals could *only* be known as conditionals. Rather, reading Guardini may have intensified and clarified what the young Georgia writer was observing. I maintain that the result of her reading Guardini is what appears to be a striking difference between O'Connor and both the southern masters William Faulkner and Eudora Welty and her contemporaries William Styron and Reynolds Price.

Guardini's dialectic of truth and irony sprang from his living in the Germany of his time. If O'Connor felt, as she said again and again, that Guardini understood the nature of existence in the modern world, it would be of some advantage to look at his own contradictions of life and existence. They all emanated from the mystery of Germany itself. If Germany was perceived as the great star of European Enlightenment and nineteenth-century tolerance, science, and technology, nowhere did that star shine brighter than in Berlin. Guardini was thirty-eight years old when he was called to a position as a professor at the University of Berlin, in a predominantly Protestant city and with a predominately *Evangelische Fakultät*.[4] From the start he was odd man out, and the Berlin of the Weimar Republic made the irony of his situation even more concrete. There were no cloisters to escape to. Guardini's was not only the Germany of the Protestant giants Bultmann and Barth, it was also the Germany of Martin Buber, a friend who wrote Guardini from Israel in the 1950s. It was a Berlin that included the vibrant papal nuncio, Eugenio Pacelli, who was fluent in the language and culture, and who later, as Pope Pius XII, would give Guardini the title of Papal Monsignor. It was this pope whom Flannery would see in 1958, in those days exalted on his *sedia gestatoria,* and whom she described in a letter to me as the most alive person she had ever seen (*HB* 280). More significantly, however, for Guardini's dialectical theory, Berlin was at this time the city also of Bertolt Brecht, Kurt Weill, Albert Einstein, Werner Heisenberg, Walter Benjamin, Marlene Dietrich, and Hannah Arendt, to name a few. The Weimar culture was modernity itself.

The young professor rose to the occasion. His lectures became famous, given in a voice quiet but powerfully controlled, in a richly modulated *Hochdeutsch.* He fascinated students of all backgrounds as he discussed Pascal, Kierkegaard, Augustine, Dostoevsky, Socrates, and Anselm of Canterbury, topics that became popular books by him, to which he added other texts ranging from his concept of the angel in Dante's *Comedia* to his daring work *Rainer Maria Rilkes Deutung des Daseins* (The Meaning of Being according to Rilke), a work that borrowed from Heidegger and from which Heidegger then appropriated, especially in his writings on Hölderlin. Not surprisingly, among his students in the 1920s were many who became the elite, avant-garde Catholic masters responsible for the changes of Vatican II. Josef Pieper, whom O'Connor read, and Hans Urs von Balthasar were joined by Cardinal Ratzinger (now Pope Benedict XVI) and Karl Rahner, who all lavished praise on Guardini at his eightieth birthday—as did Pope John Paul II, who was shaped by German philosophical and theological traditions, including the texts of Guardini. In this same period, before Guardini himself was expelled from the University of Berlin by the Nazis and then later forbidden to lecture or write, he formed a lasting friendship with Martin Buber, whose "I-Thou" dialectic was crucial to Guardini's own. O'Connor also read Buber, and his dialectic operates within the prophetic cosmology she herself developed.

What is a greater surprise is that in this wide-open Berlin the young professor attracted not only future Catholic intellectuals but also a number of students with no overt religious concerns. Not least of these was Hannah Arendt, a Jewish writer O'Connor profoundly admired, especially Arendt's *Eichmann in Jerusalem*. Moved by the lectures on Augustine that Arendt heard Guardini give at the University of Berlin, the young Berliner went on to Freiburg, where she was a student of Martin Heidegger, and then wrote her doctoral dissertation on Augustine at Heidelberg under the direction of Karl Jaspers. Guardini's open structure to interpretation,[5] which had appealed to his Berlin audience, also held appeal in America after the Second World War. From Thomas Merton to Anne Sexton and to Dorothy Day, Guardini's intellectual imprint appears with its own surprises. It was almost as if his readers knew that behind the written work lay a living concrete existence, itself enmeshed in contradictions and ironies so like their own. If there is one experience in his life that enlightens the modernity of his texts, it is Guardini's presence in the last days of Hitler's Berlin, with the city and culture on fire. Hardly more than a decade later, at a meeting in the divided Berlin, a West German government official of a quite secular background told me in graphic terms of her own terrible experiences during those last days in the burning city as the Russians advanced. At that moment, she said, the importance and hope of Guardini's presence in "the fire" could not be overestimated. It was this Guardini that O'Connor read—the believer—in a burning broken world; a man who lived by a dialectic of truth and irony and, out of it, wrote texts that became probable moments of harmony in divided worlds.

Shortly after O'Connor's illness had forced her into a virtually cloistered life at Andalusia, Guardini appears in her letters. Already by 1954 O'Connor is writing Sally and Robert Fitzgerald that "I am reading everything I can of Romano Guardini's. Have you become acquainted with his work? A book called *The Lord* of his is very fine" (*HB* 74). Only a month after beginning her correspondence with Betty Hester, she writes to the young woman in Atlanta who says she is interested in becoming a Catholic: "I have more to say about the figure of Christ as merely human but this has gone on long enough and I will save it. Have you read Romano Guardini? . . . In my opinion there is nothing like it anywhere, certainly not in this country" (*HB* 99). The next month she is trying to explain her own theological ideas: "I believe that all creation is good but that what has free choice is more completely God's image than what does not have it; also, I define humility differently from you. Msgr. Guardini can explain that" (*HB* 104). In fact, Guardini becomes a leitmotif in O'Connor's letters as she encounters Betty Hester's inchoate theological vocabulary. What O'Connor herself admires in Guardini she thinks Hester will also respond to. Guardini is open to all the ironies of human existence, and to illustrate this, O'Connor writes, "Smugness is the Great Catholic Sin. I find it in myself and don't dislike it any less. One reason Guardini is a relief to read is that he has nothing of it" (*HB* 131).

Knowing Hester's deep love of literature, O'Connor takes another tack when her friend finds Guardini wearing. O'Connor suggests she read "Guardini's monograph on the Grand Inquisitor of *The Brothers Karamazov*" (*HB* 126) or his essay on Prince Myshkin in Dostoevsky's *The Idiot* or other more relevant texts by the German theologian such as *The Church and Modern Man* (*HB* 133). In her copy of Guardini's essay on *The Idiot*—a text that O'Connor explicitly says influenced her invention of Bishop, "the afflicted child" in *The Violent Bear It Away* (see *HB* 191)—O'Connor marks in the margins this Guardini observation: "The existence of Myshkin would seem to be a direct verification of this axiom: the highest values raised to their maximum, but incarnated in an existence which is incapable of affirming itself in this world." Guardini soon disappears from O'Connor's letters to Hester to be replaced by the older, more benign von Hügel, who was not only a layman but an active English Edwardian intellectual who knew the world of Dickens, Conrad, and James. But even with von Hügel, O'Connor failed to reach Hester, who found him as irrelevant as Guardini to her own terrible world. Hester, the writer, responded better to O'Connor's own profound uses of Guardini and his dialectic of truth and irony.

At another time O'Connor wrote Hester defending the use of the negative in art and quoted Guardini to prove her point: "I don't believe that you can ask an artist to be affirmative, any more than you can ask him to be negative. The human condition includes both states in truth and 'art,' according to Msgr. Guardini, 'fastens on one aspect of the world, works through its essence, to some essential thing in it, and presents it in the unreal arena of performance'" (*HB* 173). O'Connor then continues with a credo that goes to the heart of her own method of composition: "I mortally and strongly defend the right of the artist to select a negative aspect of the world to portray and as the world gets more materialistic there will be more such to select from." Then she adds the Guardini dialectic of *Wahrheit und Ironie*: "Of course you are only enabled to see what is black by having light to see it by ... [and] the light you see by may be altogether outside of the work itself. The question is not is this negative or positive but is it believable"—or in Guardini's terms, living and concrete (*HB* 173). For O'Connor the question is, does it work in the story and *as* story?

As this passage indicates, O'Connor developed a strong dialectical sense of style from her reading of Guardini. This sense of style could only proceed from a comprehension that style proceeds always from a special depth within the author. She marked in the margin a particular passage from Guardini's *Meditations before Mass*: "When a man accepts divine truth in the obedience of faith, he is forced to re-think human truth." Thus "performance" in the light of what Guardini calls *Wahrheit* demands a constant vigilance. It demands good craftsmanship, all things in comparative balance, rising from the ability to encounter all the ironies of existence with a real presence within the self and within the text—a real presence, such as that enacted, for O'Connor, in the Orthodox and Catholic Christian liturgies. O'Connor responds to this idea of actualized performance by marking another passage in *Meditations:* "There is a beautiful expression for this in Italian, *'faro atto di presenza,'* to perform the act of *being present*" (italics Guardini's).[6] The mystery of this act of shared performance—the textualization of mystery—is equivalent, so argues Guardini in another passage O'Connor marks, "to that of Moses when he guarded his flocks in the loneliness of Mount Horeb" and suddenly encountered the burning bush and the divine presence of God in the midst of "holy ground." It should therefore be no surprise for us to discover such Guardini analogs in *The Violent Bear It Away*.

In Guardini, O'Connor felt the truth of a real presence in the midst of a world burning like the Berlin he had lived through. Reviewing Guardini's book on the rosary, she notes, "When [Guardini] considers the doctrine or liturgy or practice of the Church, he rethinks these in the light of modern difficulties and preoccupations" (*PG* 16–17). The German theologian makes us feel "that these difficulties are his own, that he does not stand on a height above the modern mind coping with its own agonizing problems but infused with grace." Then, typically, O'Connor takes a theological attitude she finds in Guardini's book and turns it into a very significant comment on what a writing style may be. Guardini, she writes, "considers that the basis for all exaggerations about Mary is her uniqueness but he feels that these exaggerations are useless and harmful"—O'Connor then quotes Guardini—"because the simpler the word expressing a truth, the more tremendous and at the same time the more deeply realized do the facts become." To Guardini's quotation, she adds, "This sums up the effect of his own writing," and one may add, the effect of her own parabolic style and diction. O'Connor then summarizes his "effect" and, in describing it, reveals her own model for writing and reading: Guardini "proceeds slowly and with a simplicity that reveals a depth of meaning to the reader who is likewise willing to be in no hurry" (*PG* 16–17).

Such "depth of meaning" defines not only the kind of reader O'Connor requires but the tendency of her whole style toward a parabolic dimension, toward the persistent use of the aphorism (the genre associated with all religious cultures), and toward an epitomizing ritualistic framing that moves beyond the symbolic realism, for example, of Henry James or the early James Joyce or Caroline Gordon, her literary masters. O'Connor's discovery of the Germans led her, it would seem, to the underscoring of her dialectical style, to her own movement between "Wahrheit und Ironie," a painful dialectic that she had learned early to cope with in the dual tracking of her own experience that defined her at age thirty. If, as I believe, she recognized this double marking of her own existence as dialectical in its "performance" and therefore was capable of producing texts out of that tension of truth and irony, reading Guardini allowed her to devise her own texts. In a way she could "discover" and reconcile what she knew was the bitter irony of her fatal illness.

If what O'Connor read in the isolation of 1950s Georgia gave her courage to endure, Guardini gave her a special hope. The southern woman writer who is also a believer—a minority within a minority within a minority—might, like Guardini, survive in the modern world. She might write texts that represent the dialectic of the modern world, as Guardini saw it and as she understood such tensions from her own experience. By no accident then, her texts of survival are structured like parables, open in both subject and style, blinking at little or nothing. Most astonishing of all, by an irony as strange as any in her short life, O'Connor's texts have moved from their quite local worlds in Georgia into a universal discourse. Elizabeth Bishop had prophesied when Flannery died that her stories would last as long as American literature. The universal appeal of her texts and now of her person has become global, from Japan to Spain, from Israel to Russia, and shows every sign, at least at this moment, of increasing and enduring. The dual tracking, as she describes it to Dawkins and Lytle, has paid off. In fact, today, for a surprisingly large audience, she is considered a hero both as a southern writer and as a religious writer. Toni Morrison has even seen a special dialectic working in O'Connor and has called "brilliant" O'Connor's story "The Artificial Nigger."[7] Chiding "some powerful literary critics" for seeing "no connection between God's grace and Africanist 'othering' in Flannery O'Connor," she contrasts a dialectic of the particular—Africanist "othering"— which the text cannot escape, and the universal—God's grace—which it cannot escape either.[8] For most, however, whatever the background—from the rap artist Guerrilla Girl Alma Thomas to Quentin Tarantino's *Pulp Fiction,* to Jodie Foster in *The Dangerous Lives of Altar Boys,* to Jesuits teaching at Gregorian University in Rome, to consecrated Opus Dei women in Spain, to Bruce Springsteen's *Nebraska,* to David Bowie's recent CD—her texts clearly have offered a direction toward discourse itself in a grotesque, ironic world of ever new "aboriginal calamity." In Guardini, O'Connor had read about dialectical survival in a world of such disasters and, despite the breakdown of her own body, had found endurance from such reading to create. Amazingly, in her life and her fiction, she still offers—and audiences feel— the same hope for survival, for passing by the dragons of a broken world, and most of all, for the making of new texts in that world to represent the "truth" of new life.

Notes

1. With close friends, O'Connor would often enclose letters or parts of a letter from other correspondents. I recently discovered in my own surviving letters from O'Connor a part of a letter Betty Hester sent to her.

2. Toni Morrison, *Playing in the Dark: Whiteness and the Literary Imagination* (Cambridge, Mass.: Harvard University Press, 1992), 66.

3. Ibid., 14.

4. After receiving his doctorate from Freiburg and the publication of his lectures as *Vom Sinn der Kirche* (which immediately became a best-seller), Guardini was "called" by two universities— Bonn and Berlin. He accepted the new Chair of Philosophy of Religion and Catholic *Weltanschauung* in Berlin.

5. This kind of open structure in his interpretations is exactly what still appeals to German theologians like Cardinal Walter Kasper, who now heads an important office at the Vatican.

6. O'Connor reviewed Romano Guardini's *Meditations before Mass* (1955) in the *Bulletin,* November 24, 1956 (*PG* 28).

7. Morrison, *Playing in the Dark,* 68.

8. Ibid., 14.

Seeking Beauty in Darkness

Flannery O'Connor and the French Catholic Renaissance

Sarah Gordon

In Milledgeville, Georgia, where I have spent half my life, there is a revealing story involving the reaction of one of Flannery O'Connor's relatives to the contents of *Wise Blood*. This cousin, reportedly appalled by the bizarre story of Hazel Motes, exclaimed, "Why, I don't know where Mary Flannery got those ideas! She's always associated with *her own kind!*" Another "Milledgevillain," not a relative but a prominent figure, is reputed to have taken her copy of *Wise Blood* and burned it in the backyard. These examples are rather typical of the local reactions to the publication of O'Connor's first novel. Sophisticated readers of today certainly will find such reactions laughable, if not pitiable, but I would suggest that even today there are those who would just as soon not confront O'Connor's *real* folk—the spiritually misshapen and often physically outrageous—and the frequently horrifying situations in which these characters find themselves. Some readers, many of them devout Christians and many of those Catholic, simply see O'Connor's world as ugly, distasteful (if not repugnant), and rather embarrassing. It is as though a Catholic writer has an *obligation* to uplift, to eschew the warty and deformed, to avert her, or his, eyes from the unseemly moment, the tasteless encounter, the literary bloating and scarring that often accompany what secular critics deem "fine fiction."

O'Connor herself had little use for such religious prissiness, such abstract piety, as her letters, essays, and lectures attest. She has written at length, and sometimes quite caustically, about the matter; she writes to Cecil Dawkins in 1960 about the "Pious Style," citing this memorable example: "The worst I ever saw was a writer who said that if the Church was the body of Christ, the blessed Virgin could be thought of as His neck." She promises Dawkins, "I will try to send you something without the Pious Style," continuing that "the only places you can really avoid the Pious Style are in the liturgy and the Bible; and these are the places where the Church herself speaks" (*HB* 369–70). O'Connor underscores the necessity for the Catholic writer to immerse herself in the real—after all, that is the nature of the incarnational art that O'Connor espouses. The writer imitates the descent of Christ into the real world, into history, into the horror, and into humanity in order to demonstrate the possibility of ascent, of resurrection. Furthermore, the reader, according to O'Connor, must be called on to make something of that same descent and ascent; he or she must enter the world of flesh and blood, of religious passion and its aberrant manifestations, of sin and the unlovely in order to see the face of God; as Hopkins wrote, "To the Father through the features of men's faces."

O'Connor was particularly hard on Catholic readers, whose taste in books often revolted her. In a number of her lectures and in the book reviews she wrote for the diocesan *Bulletin,* she took them to task, urging them to toughen up and learn to read on a more sophisticated level—without seeking to find facile inspiration or devotional simplicity in Catholic fiction. In "The Catholic Novelist in the Protestant South," the essence of which essay O'Connor gave as a lecture at the College of St. Teresa in Winona, Minnesota, O'Connor argues that "in the last four or five centuries, Catholics have overemphasized the abstract and consequently impoverished their imaginations and their capacity for prophetic insight" (*MM* 203), defending the use of the grotesque in southern Catholic literature in this way: "The Catholic novelist in the South is forced to follow the spirit into strange places and to recognize it in many forms not totally congenial to him.... I think he will feel a good deal more kinship with backwoods prophets and shouting fundamentalists than he will with those politer elements for whom the supernatural is an embarrassment and for whom religion has become a department of sociology or culture or personality development" (*MM* 207). Speaking, then, to her fellow Catholics, O'Connor stresses the necessity for tough-mindedness in reading habits and an acceptance of the fact that good literature usually must immerse itself in the world of the flesh.

In fact, I am sure that O'Connor would have little patience with those Christian literary critics who want to flatten her narratives to cause them to serve as spiritual allegories, who never engage the often distorted and distasteful, if not hilarious, particulars; those who, in fact, miss the humor and the craziness, often not even mentioning it in their written commentary, in the search for inspiration and the reinforcement of dogma. Only a while ago and in a scholarly forum, I heard an O'Connor cousin express the need for some strong Catholic readings of O'Connor's work. My thought at the time, a thought I have had before about some of the family, was that this person knows little about the history of O'Connor scholarship! Over the years I have found the immediate O'Connor family—with the exception perhaps of Regina O'Connor herself—to be singularly lacking in appreciation of O'Connor's human comedy, infused as it is with exaggeration and an obvious delight in the often hilarious, often horrifying extremes of human behavior. In some cases both family and clergy seem to be bewildered by the pure, unadulterated amusement many experience in reading the stories. How can so many people have such fun with and in many instances be spiritually jarred by Hazel Motes and Joy-Hulga Hopewell? After all, they say, O'Connor's fiction is concerned with ultimate truth, serious issues! Thus, from the family to the Christian community at large, the tendency to look away from the downright zany, often misshapen and unpleasant particulars of O'Connor's fiction is *still* there, forty years after her death. Beyond the Christian, and more specifically Catholic, influences on O'Connor's work, scholars today are exploring other parallels and literary precedents, including the southwestern humorists, cold-war culture, and female anger, that may help explain

O'Connor's fierce style. However enlightening such critical efforts can be, it is to miss the forest for the trees to ignore the Catholic center of O'Connor's work; it is to mistake accident for essence.

Today's Christian readers should recognize that O'Connor's work has spiritual precedent and an aesthetic base in Catholic modernism. Although we surely would never dismiss the strong influence upon her of the medieval church and the tradition of the medieval grotesque—for this we are indebted especially to Gilbert Muller and Anthony Di Renzo—I believe that scholars have paid little attention to the early twentieth-century philosophy and aesthetic initially presented by Henri Bergson and taken up by Jacques Maritain and his wife Raïssa, both converts to Catholicism, and the circle of writers surrounding the Maritains that included poet and polemicist Charles Péguy, Ernest Psichari (the grandson of Ernest Renan, the scriptural scholar who did much to dislodge fundamentalism in his higher criticism of the Bible), the poet Paul Claudel, and the painter Georges Rouault. Typical of most Catholic critics of O'Connor up to the present time, John Desmond in *Risen Sons: Flannery O'Connor's Vision of History* includes a significant tribute to Jacques Maritain's influence on O'Connor's Thomist outlook, while largely ignoring the contributions of the other thinkers and artists in the French Catholic renaissance. Most critics, Catholic or not, tip their hats to the French influence by mentioning Bergson in passing, but to my knowledge no critic has explored in depth the influence of Bergson on Maritain and thus on the ardent Catholic writers associated with Maritain, including Léon Bloy.

Flannery O'Connor's private library contains Bergson's *The Creative Mind: A Study in Metaphysics*, as well as a number of works by and about Jacques Maritain, and works about Léon Bloy, including *Pilgrim of the Absolute*, with selections made by Raïssa Maritain and with an important introduction by Jacques Maritain. It would appear that O'Connor came to know Bloy's work through Jacques Maritain, for Bloy was the spiritual godfather to the Maritains.

In the introduction to François Mauriac's *What I Believe*, Wallace Fowlie distinguishes among two generations of French Catholic writers "whose work has centered about a religious trust and inheritance. Claudel and Péguy were the giants of the first generation. The second generation, writers born in the eighties, includes Jacques Maritain (1882), Charles Du Bos (1882), Mauriac (1885), Georges Bernanos (1888), and Gabriel Marcel (1889)," adding that the work of Mauriac had reached the widest audience (Mauriac xv). This chronological distinction is certainly a workable one; however, I prefer to group these writers in terms of that circle most commonly associated with Jacques and Raïssa Maritain, a grouping that results largely from the compelling account of its development and spiritual activity presented in Raïssa Maritain's *Nos grandes amities*, or *We Have Been Friends Together*, and its sequel, *Adventures in Grace*. The former work contains the candid and moving accounts of the Maritains' conversions, Jacques from a predominantly though nominal Protestant background and Raïssa from Judaism, which followed their studying with Henri Bergson in Paris and their increasingly important relationship with Catholic radical, polemicist, and novelist Léon Bloy—who, as a matter of fact, is not included in either of Wallace Fowlie's groupings.

I want to provide an outline of these French thinkers' kinship with and influence on O'Connor's thought and aesthetic. Because little has yet been done in this approach to O'Connor, I want to number the dots and connect a few of them. In her memoir Raïssa Maritain describes her and Jacques' experience at the Collège de France after Charles Péguy had insisted they attend the lectures of philosopher Henri Bergson. So serious was the Maritains' concern with meaning that, at that time, they decided that if, in their search for an everlasting truth, they found none, they would commit suicide. In Raïssa's words, "We wanted to die by a free act if it were impossible to live according to the truth" (R. Maritain 68). They had heretofore found no solace in scientific positivism or empiricism. Their attendance at the Bergson lectures changed the Maritains' lives. Raïssa writes that the words of Bergson gave them "intellectual joy in restoring metaphysics to its rightful place." She goes on to say, "Bergson assured us that such [transcendental] food was within our reach, that we are capable of truly knowing reality, that through intuition we may attain to the absolute; and we interpreted this as saying that we could truly, absolutely, *know what is*. . . . The important thing, the essential thing was the result: to attain the absolute" (R. Maritain 72).

Excited and challenged by Bergson's idea of *intuition,* which he set up in opposition to total faith in reason, the Maritains found strong support for their own sense of the limitations of scientific positivism in attaining truth. To be sure, Jacques Maritain would later break with Bergson over what he considered the philosopher's failure to go beyond merely criticizing the *misuse* of intelligence or reason. After his own conversion to Catholicism and clearly under the strong influence of Thomas Aquinas, Maritain faulted Bergson for not more fully *embracing* reason as a viable means of moving toward the transcendent. Nevertheless, before the time of their conversion, according to Raïssa's memoir, Bergson showed the two young philosophers "the very possibility of metaphysical work" (R. Maritain 74). For the Maritains, therefore, Bergson opened the door to metaphysical possibility through philosophy; yet, as we shall see, it was the work and the living example of Léon Bloy that actually led the Maritains to conversion.

The influence of Bergson's philosophy on a number of modernist writers and artists has been amply documented, particularly in Paul Douglass's *Bergson, Eliot, and American Literature* (1986), Tom Quirk's *Bergson and American Culture* (1990), and Mary Ann Gillies's *Henri Bergson and British Modernism* (1996). Gillies, in particular, notes that for many of the British modernists, Eliot, Joyce, and Woolf, for example, Bergson's ideas of *intuition* and *la durée* (duration) were extremely compelling. The Maritains were equally seized by these ideas. Raïssa writes, "Bergson forcefully and successfully combated the tendency of the philosophers of his time to reduce everything—even the qualitative, the unique and the incomparable—to number and to space, to quantities which may be measured, superposed and reversed after the fashion of the externality and homogeneity of physico-mathematical relations" (R. Maritain 75). In his concept of *la durée*, which was his "first psycho-metaphysical discovery," Bergson argues that the free act occurs only when "the whole soul is engaged in one of its acts" and that "it is the whole soul . . . which gives rise to the free decision." Although most of our daily actions "are accomplished after the manner of reflexes," in certain cases we make decisions based on a mysterious affinity with "our personal idea of happiness and of honour" (R. Maritain 76–78). These decisions seem "to go beyond the most orderly reasoning and . . . [give] us a feeling of completeness and of justice accomplished, greatly resembl[ing] inspiration, whether [inspiration] belong entirely to ourselves or whether it come from God, because it is in these depths alone that it comes from God, because it is in these depths alone that it can be formed, and that God acts in us" (R. Maritain 78). This "free activity," Raïssa concludes, "is the very life of the spiritual personality, and duration, spirit and life are synonymous." These statements allow us to see clearly the implications of *la durée* for the perception of the possibility of grace—of God's presence *in the moment* and *in us*. Bergson led the Maritains "to foresee that there exists a spiritual realm 'from which descend all spiritual gifts'" (R. Maritain 81). The Maritains had been disturbed by the empiricists' view that "if we cannot measure something and divide it into its constituent elements, we cannot know it." Bergson's insistence that "physical matter was infused with a vital force that brought the matter to life [his *élan vitale*]" enabled the Maritains to see that "vital force" as the presence of God (Gillies 31).

Bergson was also quite forward looking in his ideas about art and what exactly constituted the aesthetic experience. He recognized that "art could be fashioned from things not conventionally thought beautiful" and that we perceivers enter the artist's experience through intuition and can thereby "come to know the essential 'thingness' of the object or experience under scrutiny" (Gillies 20–21). Like Duns Scotus and his literary heir Gerard Manley Hopkins, Bergson implies that the "whatness" or *quidditas* of the thing can be known through a means that transcends reason; for Hopkins and for O'Connor, the faculty that transcends reason is the gift of God's grace—as Hopkins would have it, the "instress" by which we are able to perceive the inscape. I have elsewhere documented Hopkins's influence on O'Connor, especially on "The River," but now I suggest that Bergson via Maritain may have been equally influential. For his part, Jacques Maritain, following Bergson's lead but finding a spiritual route beyond Bergson and through Thomas Aquinas, writes that "it is necessary that we be able to know God in His essence through a gift which transcends all the possibilities of our natural forces" and that the knowledge of God is "superior to reason . . . [but] toward which reason aspires" (qtd. in Herberg 35).

Commending her French mentor, O'Connor writes that Maritain "puts [reason] in the proper perspective, where it serves but not substitutes for revelation" (*PG* 125). In a letter to Betty Hester in 1957, O'Connor urges her to read *Art and Scholasticism*, "the book I cut my aesthetic teeth on" (*HB* 216).

Henri Bergson was also interested in the process of art, that is, in how the artist's sensibility uses the material of the natural world to connect with the viewer or reader. He was strongly convinced that "art, or the aesthetic experience, should startle people out of their daily lives" and that "art [prompts us] to look at the world differently." Art should force us out of our "limited worlds" and serve "as a guide into a new world . . . [turning] us back on ourselves, greatly enriching our inner worlds and prompting us to examine this existence" (Gillies 23). Clearly, for Bergson, the notion that art should "guide us into a new world," turning or "converting" us to a new angle of seeing is dependent upon the artist's presenting the natural world *transformed*, and not necessarily transformed into the traditionally "beautiful." Bergson's idea that art should at the least startle us is posited on the freedom of the artist to *deform* in order to *transform* and is surely kin to O'Connor's frequently quoted justification of her techniques of sensationalism and shock: for the nearly deaf and blind, the artist must use "large and startling figures." The allusion to painting in this statement suggests that, like Maritain's commentary on and defense of the disconcerting elements of modern painting, O'Connor's aesthetic was in large part based on spiritual necessity and urgency. Bergson is certainly not writing out of the commitment to Catholic truth and dogma that will permeate the work of his student and early disciple Jacques Maritain; however, Maritain's "christianizing" or "catholicizing" of Bergson is evident in his adaptation of key Bergsonian ideas in his own work.

Jacques Maritain makes his own use of Bergson's concept of *intuition*, especially in his important work *Creative Intuition in Art and Poetry* (1953), a much used and marked copy of which is in O'Connor's private library. Maritain echoes Bergson's emphasis on the importance of the artistic process, asserting that the Aristotelian radiance conveyed by the great work of art may in fact sometimes be produced through the deformation of the natural. Maritain writes,

> One day, after a walk in the wintertime, Rouault told me he had just discovered, by looking at snow-clad fields in the sunshine, how to paint the white trees of spring. Such a genuine concept of "imitation" affords a ground and justification for the boldest kinds of transposition, transfiguration, deformation, or recasting of natural appearances, in so far as they are a means to make the work manifest intuitively the transparent reality which has been grasped by the artist. (J. Maritain 1965, 165)

However, Maritain goes on to posit that some reference to natural appearances must be present in the artist's work or it cannot be called "intuitive" and thus will "[fall] short of the essence of art." Only through "the instrumentality of natural appearances [can] things reveal some of their secret meanings to the artist's intuition" and can those "secret meanings" be subsequently revealed to the viewer and reader (J. Maritain 1965, 165). Maritain is, of course, concerned particularly with examples of modern painting and poetry; abstractionism and expressionism were especially troubling to many viewers, critics, and Christians at the time. Maritain defends these works as long as they are infused by that creative intuition that finds hidden mystery *in the things of this world*.

In the same vein, O'Connor quotes John Peale Bishop: "You can't say Cezanne painted apples and a table cloth and have said what Cezanne painted" (*MM* 75). Furthermore, in a discussion of the work of Joseph Conrad, O'Connor writes that for Conrad "reality ... was not simply coextensive with the visible" and that Conrad "was interested in rendering justice to the visible universe because it suggested an invisible one" (*MM* 80). For O'Connor grace works "through nature" and depends upon immersion in "a particular society and a particular history" (*CW* 856). Only through immersion in the natural, in the concrete, the everyday, can the artist truly get at the heart of mystery; abstract art, that which has no connection with the natural, usually fails, for this very reason. Deploring the intellectualism present in much abstract modern art, that is to say, its removal from the natural, Maritain writes, "The crucial mistake of abstract art has been to reject—unwittingly—poetic intuition, while rejecting systematically the existential world of Things" (J. Maritain 1965, 160). As O'Connor observes, "The fact is that the materials of the fiction writer are the humblest. Fiction is about everything human and we are made out of dust, and if you scorn getting yourself dusty, then you shouldn't try to write fiction" (*MM* 68). We are here close to the idea of art that suffuses the aesthetic base of Flannery O'Connor's work: what William Lynch calls the idea of art as *incarnation* by which, to return to Maritain's words, the way is "exacting and solitary" and must "[pass] through the sufferings of the spirit" (J. Maritain 1965, 154). For O'Connor, "if the writer believes that our life is and will remain essentially mysterious, if he looks upon us as beings existing in a created order to whose laws we freely respond, then what he sees on the surface will be of interest to him only as he can go through it into the experience of mystery itself. His kind of fiction will always be pushing its own limits outward toward the limits of mystery." With her own brand of opposition to empiricism, O'Connor concludes, "Such a writer will be interested in what we don't understand rather than in what we do" (*MM* 41–42).

Maritain's adaptation of Bergson in this way emphasizes the necessary spiritual base of art and its essential need to be rooted in the here and now, both philosopher and theologian underlining their strong distrust of abstract thinking associated with reductive empiricism. That empiricism depends in its very definition on an exploration of the material world—measuring, weighing, and codifying it—is obvious; the empiricist's immersion in the material world, however, is not to be compared with the incarnational artist's necessary descent into the natural, and even the grotesque, in order to ascend and *transcend* it. Maritain's adaptation of Bergson finds powerful resonance in O'Connor's work. Moreover, I suspect that Flannery O'Connor's notion of the "moment of grace" derives, at least indirectly, from Bergson's notion of *la durée*. Both Eliot's *Four Quartets* ("the moment in the rose garden," "the still point of the turning world") and Joyce's concept of epiphany were major influences on O'Connor's fiction. Her moment of grace suggests precisely what the Maritains drew from their initial exposure to Bergson's ideas: the possibility of the infusion of divine grace into that moment of "free" decision making, the moment at which "God acts in us." Thus for the grandmother in "A Good Man Is Hard to Find," for Sheppard in "The Lame Shall Enter First," and for Mrs. Turpin in "Revelation," there is the possibility *in the moment* for openness to, and reception of, the divine. To be so open and so receptive is to be given, in Raïssa Maritain's words, "a feeling of completeness and . . . justice accomplished . . . a certainty that God acts in us" (R. Maritain 78). O'Connor needed no instruction in the possibility of individual acceptance of divine grace; I only suggest that, through her reading of Jacques Maritain, through the Bergsonian influence on Eliot's idea of the "still point," and through the Joycean notion of epiphany, O'Connor found confirmation of—if not the basis for—the spiritual aesthetic of the moment of grace.

In December 1959 O'Connor expressed her spiritual aesthetic to John Hawkes, who had accused her of being "of the devil's party": "More than in the Devil I am interested in the indication of Grace, the moment when you know that Grace has been offered and accepted—such as the moment when the Grandmother realizes The Misfit is one of her own children. These moments are prepared for (by me anyway) by the intensity of the evil circumstances. It is the violation in the woods that brings home to Tarwater the real nature of his rejection" (*HB* 367–68). The New Critics' warning about intentional fallacy to the contrary notwithstanding, O'Connor's statement clearly links her to the Bergsonian idea of *la durée* as it comes to her via Maritain, Eliot, and Joyce. We note that O'Connor posits that even in the most desperate and sordid of moments, "the intensity of evil circumstances"—the grandmother's last minutes, Tarwater's rape by the homosexual stranger—grace presents itself. In another letter to Hawkes of April 1960, O'Connor continues the discussion of grace:

> Grace, to the Catholic way of thinking, can and does use as its medium the imperfect, purely human, and even hypocritical. Cutting yourself off from Grace is a very decided matter, requiring a real choice, act of will, and affecting the very ground of the soul. The Misfit is touched by the Grace that comes through the old lady when she recognizes him as her child, as she has been touched by the Grace that comes through him in his particular suffering. His shooting her is a recoil, a horror at her humanness, but after he has

done it and cleaned his glasses, the Grace has worked in him and he pronounces his judgment: she would have been a good woman if *he* had been there every moment of her life. True enough. In the Protestant view, I think Grace and nature don't have much to do with each other. The old lady, because of her hypocrisy and humanness and banality, couldn't be a medium for Grace. In the sense that I see things the other way, I'm a Catholic writer. (*HB* 389–90)

For O'Connor, as for Jacques Maritain, grace is possible to human beings only *through* and *within* nature. The sentimental and the pornographic are failures on either side of this mystery: sentimentality errs because of its refusal to enter the natural world, and pornography errs because it never leaves the natural behind. O'Connor writes, "We lost our innocence in the Fall, and our return to it is through the Redemption which was brought about by Christ's death and our slow participation in it" (*MM* 148). That slow participation is our life's journey sanctified by the acceptance of God's grace, sometimes in a moment's leap of faith. In that context, it is interesting that Mauriac, a later Catholic writer but not directly associated with the Bloy/Maritain circle, uses the phrase "moment of grace" in his 1963 testimony, *What I Believe*. A copy of this book is in O'Connor's private library. Mauriac was a writer whose fiction O'Connor read devotedly and recommended to her friends. In *What I Believe*, Mauriac writes, "it was in the darkness of night that I found [Christ], and not every time I wished to find Him. These are moments of grace" (Mauriac 34). Thus, from Bergson through Maritain, Eliot, Joyce, and Mauriac comes a version of the idea of *la durée*; all of these writers, with the exception of Joyce, appear to view the moment of grace as the experience that Raïssa Maritain describes as the moment when God is present, among the sweaty and murderous, among the fraught and the obsessed.

As important as Bergson's emphasis on intuition and duration was to the development of Maritain's and O'Connor's spiritual and aesthetic philosophy, Maritain made his most significant contribution to O'Connor's thought in his emphasis on the importance of human reason. In this way, Maritain challenges his early mentor Bergson and argues that reason is a constructive, not a destructive, force. In fact, O'Connor, in a review for the diocesan *Bulletin* of Maritain's *The Range of Reason*, reminds us that "Maritain's has been one of the major voices in modern philosophy to reassert the primacy of reason" (*PG* 124). However, for Maritain to have the spiritual base from which to break with Bergson and embrace Catholicism, he and Raïssa had to have their souls turned by a real, contemporary example of God's grace in human flesh. Largely through their intimate witnessing of the life and teachings of the scandalous Léon Bloy, the Maritains came to faith. Léon Bloy's radical, if not tempestuous, ideas and his exemplary life of poverty and identity with the poor served as the evidence to the Maritains of grace in the world. One might presumptuously conclude that witnessing the life and profound spirituality of Léon Bloy was decidedly a moment of grace in the Maritains' life journey.

In a letter to Betty Hester in August 1955, O'Connor acknowledged reading Léon Bloy in graduate school (*HB* 98). In 1956 O'Connor writes to her spiritual adviser Father McCown, "I have read almost everything that Bloy, Bernanos, and Mauriac have written" (*HB* 130). Then, in 1957, addressing Cecil Dawkins's skepticism about miracles, O'Connor writes to her lapsed Catholic friend: "Miracles seem in fact to be the great embarrassment to the modern mind, a king of scandal. If the miracles could be explained away and Christ reduced to the status of a teacher, domesticated and fallible, then there'd be no problem. Anyway, to discover the Church you have to set out by yourself. The French Catholic novelists were a help to me in this—Bloy, Bernanos, Mauriac. In philosophy, Gilson, Maritain, and Gabriel Marcel, an Existentialist" (*HB* 231). Scholars of O'Connor's works have repeatedly acknowledged the possible influence of both Bernanos and Mauriac, for O'Connor held in high regard both Bernanos's *The Diary of a Country Priest* and Mauriac's novels, as each explored the conflict between good and evil. These two writers are still read today in some Christian circles. However, the name of Léon Bloy is now virtually unknown, except in certain intellectual Catholic circles.

Léon Bloy's life was characterized by a fierce sense of mission in living among the poor, denunciation of injustice, and most of all, extraordinary devotion to the Roman Catholic Church. Raïssa Maritain's account of Bloy's forceful, indeed outrageous, personality is illuminating. The Maritains encountered his work before encountering the man. Having read a very enthusiastic review of Bloy's *La femme pauvre*, the Maritains decided to read the novel, and "for the first time" they found themselves "before the reality of Christianity." Although the couple had some reservations about Bloy's "endless endeavors to note minute ugliness or mediocrity, that fixed predilection for violence and force, the perpetual hyperbole," they concluded that the novel was "saved by a shining sincerity, an unswerving uprightness, a genuine, deep, inexhaustible lyricism, by the exquisite tenderness of a heart made to love absolutely, to cling entirely to what it loved" (R. Maritain 88). By today's standards, *The Woman Who Was Poor* is not shocking in its presentation of ugliness, violence, and force. It is actually the story of the making of a saint, Clothilde Marechal, as she is spiritually educated *out of* the world of her mother's prostitution and pandering and *into* beatitude. The novel is a forum in which Clothilde is taught about the church by a painter named Gacougnol, a writer named Marchenoir, and an illuminator named Leopold. These three important male minds discuss modern art, Christian art and whether there can be such a thing, and the fact that their contemporaries, other artists and painters, were turning away from the Roman Catholic Church. The young woman, innocent and pious, is eager for learning and enlightenment. Her life of poverty and suffering, like that of Bloy himself, is the making of her sainthood, or so Bloy suggests. The novel is, of course, formulaic Christian fiction in the sense that the female protagonist is the blank tablet, virginal and accepting, on which the doctrines of the church are written. She is thus led by her patriarchal teachers into her roles as, first, obedient lover of Christ and the church; second, devoted and exemplary wife and mother; and, third, the woman of the poor who is saintly in her devotion to Christ and to his reflection in the lives of the poor among whom she lives. Perhaps O'Connor was not as moved by the novel as she was by the life and example of Léon Bloy himself. The novel, after all, is only a means to a message, and quite obviously so. A writer as sophisticated as O'Connor would have had serious reservations about the novel's literary value.

Bloy, through his narrator, presents a sharp warning to his readers: "Take it all round, in fact, and those gracious readers might do even better by not opening the present volume at all, for it is itself a long digression on the evil of living, the infernal misfortune of existence, hogs lacking any snout to root for tit-bits, in a society without God" (Bloy 125). The narrator adds that any "worthy people who ... look upon the infinite as trifling irrelevance to whet the appetite" should not read a certain chapter. In other words, Bloy freely admits that he is not writing for the squeamish or for those who take matters of salvation lightly. Moreover, he is not writing to please literary standards of the establishment; though at times artful, the novel is too often the spontaneous overflow of a passionate spirituality. For the contemporary reader, the narrator's description of the roles appropriate to woman leaves much to be desired; for him, "only two modes of existence" are available to women, "beatitude" and "pleasure" (Bloy 127). Thus, while Clothilde initially may seem to have some potential as a spiritual center for the novel, Bloy makes her one-dimensional, symbolic of the struggles to which fallen flesh is heir. It is not surprising, then, to find Bloy's narrator celebrating the Middle Ages, "that radiant fountain-head" whence cometh right attitudes toward the Creator and his creation. Concerning the novel's ending, Bloy writes that the end will "come soon enough, to rouse pity or horror in those horried sentimentalists who are interested in love-stories" (Bloy 125–26). The narrator or Bloy thus makes it clearly evident that this narrative will use violent and shocking means to turn its readers' heads right.

Even though Clothilde manifests a steadiness of soul and a goodness that Bloy means for us to see as exemplary, the strongest and most interesting characters in the novel are male: Gacougnol, the painter who suddenly dies, a character perhaps modeled on Rouault; Leopold, the illuminator whose intensity usually renders him speechless and who sends to his friends three-word messages along with "a network tracery of arabesques, of impossible foliage, of inextricable scrollwork, of eccentrically tinted monstrous faces" (Bloy 152–53), not unlike the tattoos on Parker's back; and Marchenoir, the outspoken absolutist who argues that "art has nothing to do with the essence of the Church," that "such a thing as Christian art is bound to be impossible," and that he himself is not an artist but, instead, "a Pilgrim of the Holy Sepulchre." Marchenoir attacks science with special vehemence: "Before the rise of scientific moronism, the very children knew that the Sepulchre of the Saviour is the Centre of the Universe, the pivot and heart of all worlds.... The inconceivable immensities of the heavens have no other use, save to mark the position of an old stone where Jesus slept for three days" (Bloy 203). In addition to Marchenoir's attack on scientism, his devotion to the church and his conviction that to be a pilgrim of the spirit is the most important vocation on earth clearly made their impression on the Maritains and, I believe, on Flannery O'Connor.

There are even significant moments in Bloy's novel that the twenty-first-century reader can see echoed in O'Connor's work and experience. For example, in one of Clothilde's prayers to the Virgin, which Bloy quotes in full, there are these lines: "I remember that while I slept You used to take me by the hand and lead me to an adorable land where the lions and the nightingales languished in deadly sadness. You would tell me that it was the Lost Garden, and Your great tears, that were like light, were so heavy that they crushed me as they fell upon me. Yet that used to console me, and I used to wake up feeling that I lived" (Bloy 146). We are reminded of O'Connor's association of the Virgin and sleep in her letter of October 20, 1955, to Betty Hester: "I have come to think of sleep as metaphorically connected with the mother of God. Hopkins said she was the air we breathe, but I have come to realize her most in the gift of going to sleep. Life without her would be equivalent to me of life without sleep and as she contained Christ for a time, she seems to contain our life in sleep for a time so that we are able to wake up in peace" (*HB* 112). Another tantalizing note from Bloy's novel that finds resonance in O'Connor is Clothilde's reading of *Lives of the Saints* and her fascination with Saint Perpetua, whose story we immediately connect with O'Connor's "A Temple of the Holy Ghost." Similarly, Clothilde, like the child in "A Temple," is fascinated by the saints "who shed their blood, who endured horrible tortures" (Bloy 221). O'Connor's child protagonist, of course, wants to be a saint, though she doubts her own ability to become one; instead, she thinks that "she could be a martyr if they killed her quick" (*CW* 204).

O'Connor read and absorbed Bloy in graduate school, especially *La femme pauvre*. Whether O'Connor read either Raïssa Maritain's *We Have Been Friends Together* or her *Adventures in Grace* is not clear. What we do know is that for a time O'Connor was apparently fascinated with Bloy's work and life. In her own private library are *Léon Bloy: A Study in Impatience* by Albert Béguin (1947) and *Pilgrim of the Absolute*, a Bloy reader with selections by Raïssa Maritain and an introduction by Jacques Maritain. In the introduction to his study, Béguin asserts that Bloy "gave back to art its true value as knowledge—and no longer a magic Promethean knowledge but a confession of faith, prayer and truth." Describing Bloy as "one of those who had the clearest vision of the dreadful night descending upon the earth," Béguin maintains that Bloy was "one of the most robustly positive of writers in this age of negation," although for forty years, Bloy "proclaimed that an abyss was about to open beneath the feet of mankind" (Béguin 1–2). Béguin continues, "He called down the wrath of God upon the paltry convictions and the precarious equilibrium of a complacent society which put its trust in science and bourgeois values, seeking the kind of tranquillity that comes from silencing one's soul and forgetting God." These words could certainly be a description of what O'Connor does in her fiction, though perhaps without quite the ferocity of Bloy. Béguin also notes the following statements by Bloy, which stand as summaries of the profound simplicity and intensity of his work, his belief, and his life: "There is nothing true but what is absolute. . . . Except God, everything is indifferent to me. . . . Nothing is necessary, nothing, nothing, nothing, except God. . . . I am first and foremost a worshipper, and I have always considered myself lower than the beasts whenever I have set out to act otherwise than from love and through the promptings of love" (qtd. in Béguin 6–7). Bloy, the "Pilgrim of the Absolute," possessed a face "full of humility and transparent joy," according to Béguin, who cites Bloy's statement made in 1900: "I thirst to be looked upon as a poor man, very lonely and full of love. You do not know my weakness or my ignorance, my downright abjectness or my fiendish sadness, and you know nothing of the joy that is in the depths of my soul."

Béguin attributes to Bloy not only Maritain's conversion but also the impetus for the Catholic revival in France. Béguin writes that if "Péguy, Claudel, Bernanos, Mauriac . . . were not his disciples, he at least prepared the way for them." Bloy began his career as a painter and a vehement unbeliever. His conversion, in 1870, was an event that resulted in large measure from his friendships with "various priests" (Béguin 13–15). Later he met and had a passionate relationship with a prostitute, Anne-Marie Roule, with whom he experienced great sexual passion. Bloy converted Roule to Catholicism, after which she began seeing visions and heard "celestial utterances" that she communicated to Bloy, who alluded to them frequently. Finally, out of her mind, Roule was committed to an asylum, where she died in 1907. Anyone who has looked carefully at the drafts of *Wise Blood* will find there an amazing similarity between unpublished versions of the character of Sabbath Lily Hawkes and Anne-Marie Roule, both of whom were visionaries who had to be locked up—Anne Marie by the mental health establishment and Sabbath Lily, the *wife* of Hazel Motes in the drafts, by Hazel himself. In 1886 *Le désespéré*, Bloy's first great novel, was published. In 1890 Bloy married Jeanne Molbeck, the daughter of a Danish poet, who brought him much peace; a few months before the marriage, in fact, she had converted to Catholicism. Bloy and his wife were frequently visited by and were extremely close to Jacques and Raïssa Maritain, who were his godchildren and "his favorites" among the circle of friends (Béguin 20).

With the publication in 1897 of *La femme pauvre*, Bloy's philosophy and outlook were clear. The book was Bloy's masterpiece, serving as the catalyst to conversion for the Maritains and others. As Jacques Maritain writes in his introduction to Léon Bloy's *Pilgrim of the Absolute* (1947), Bloy possessed "the privileges of the Christian and those of the Poet" and "a profound and intuitive soul." Furthermore,

Bloy possessed, according to Maritain, "a most genuinely Christian sense of the absolute requirements of the Lord," although, he adds, with Bloy "the feeling of mystery, so pure in itself, so lofty in Bloy, sometimes translates itself by means of lightning flashes and a darkness which are too material." Significantly, Maritain's defense or rationale of Bloy's subject matter and technique sounds as though it could be a defense (even O'Connor's own defense cited earlier) of O'Connor's shock tactics: Bloy, Maritain argues, was writing to "men who most of the time live in the senses, and who need to be led to the intelligible by means of the tangible" (J. Maritain 1947, 9–10). Thus "Bloy liked to repeat that he wrote not for the righteous—neither for the perfect, nor for those who are progressing, nor for those who are beginning —but for the sleeping ones who needed his suffering and his outbursts, for publicans and for scoundrels."

Maritain is so clearly convinced of the rightness of Bloy's mission that he writes, "Blessed were ... his fits of violence—which alone were capable of shattering the brass doors that kept those souls imprisoned," adding that "Bloy's frequent reference to excrement, which has scandalised some people, was nothing but his own rather unusual means for insulting the pomp and display in which we complacently rest." Bloy is both prophet and poet, according to Maritain, and such souls as his, "elected to speak in the name of a great number of people dead or suffering are not free to decline their obligation." Because of Bloy's fierce commitment to the lives of the poor, among whose number he and his family were counted, he was intent upon opening "the eyes of many a strayed person who foolishly believed the Church of Christ occupies itself more with safeguarding the possessions of the rich than with consoling the poor" (J. Maritain 1947, 14–15). O'Connor's concept of our radical poverty is closely akin to this, although she was certainly not centrally concerned with social and political reform. O'Connor's repeated focus on poor and provincial southerners is a dramatic way of rendering our radical poverty as fallen human beings.

Léon Bloy's radical subject matter and outlook were not, as should be clear by now, part of a literary pose or the rantings of a madman. *La femme pauvre* is completely consonant with Bloy's *lived* theology—his horror at earthly injustice, his profound concern with the suffering of the poor, especially children, and his sharp denunciation of both materialism and empiricism. In a letter to his friend George Landry, the twenty-seven-year-old Bloy wrote, "In his poor heart man has places which do not yet exist, and suffering enters in order to bring them to life" (qtd. in Béguin 25). Suffering is our human lot, and through it we have the opportunity of becoming opened up to God's presence and thus to become authentically God's children. We can be, then, receptive to the moment of grace. Surely the most quoted of Bloy's statements—the memorable last sentence in *La femme pauvre*—is the best and most concise summary of his beliefs: "There is only one sadness; it is the sadness of not being saints." Of course the attainment of sainthood is impossible for most of us. We are sinners since the Fall, and even our best endeavors fall short of perfection. Even our language is fallen and misses the mark. In fact, the inadequacy of language is constantly underscored in Bloy's work, as it is in Maritain's and O'Connor's. However, Béguin notes that, for Bloy, language, fallen tool though it be, is needed "to detect the presence of mystery, not in order to say what it is but to say where it dwells—which is everywhere" (Béguin 10), very much the idea we find not only in Eliot's *Four Quartets* but also in O'Connor's fictional turning inside out clichéd and familiar words and expressions in order to reinvest them—perhaps to *invest* them for the first time—with spiritual meaning.

Jacques Maritain's introduction to *Pilgrim of the Absolute* is obviously written in part to explain Bloy's radicalism, his outspoken and courageous, if not totally off-putting, approach to matters theological. Clearly while the Maritains themselves were catalyzed to conversion by Bloy and the living example of his radicalism, Jacques Maritain realized that others might have difficulty in accepting Bloy, just as, we might note, readers—many of them Catholic and many even close to her—have been upset by the unorthodox and strange approach of O'Connor's work. Maritain offers this defense of Bloy; I suggest it might equally well be a defense of O'Connor:

> I understand quite well that for certain minds, fortunate in having been spared the dizziness of any abyss, whether from its brink or from its depth, the case of Léon Bloy is a singularly obscure puzzle. But I must repeat: there are perishing souls who seek beauty in darkness, and on whom quiet apologetics would be without avail. Nor would pure theology act on them, for their reason is too weakened by error.... Bloy, in shouting out his disgust at all lukewarmness, in shouting on rooftops his thirst for the absolute, inspires these famished ones with a presentiment of the glory of God. (J. Maritain 1947, 17–18)

I suggest that Bloy's contemporary and friend Georges Rouault, who was also very much a part of the Maritain circle, though a listener rather than a talker, essentially espoused the same aesthetic as Bloy. Oddly enough Bloy himself expressed serious objections to the very paintings by Rouault that suggest Bloy's own aesthetic! Rouault is known for the paintings of his so-called middle period of clown heads, heads of Christ, and a series of compelling scenes of Christ's life called *Miserere*, published in 1948. Jacques Maritain greatly admired Rouault's work and praised it publicly; Maritain went as far as saying in *Art and Scholasticism* that "the ideal of a Christian artist ... is Rouault" (Getlein 11). O'Connor was certainly familiar with the work of Rouault; indeed her copy of Romano Guardini's *The Lord* features a full-color cover of one of Rouault's Christ paintings. Clearly O'Connor's large and startling figures are analogous to—if not influenced by—Rouault's broad strokes and simple outlines, the deliberately distorted bodies, and the wide, wounded eyes of his Christs and his clowns. There is in Rouault's thinking a real and ironic similarity between the world's derision of the clown, forced to fake buoyancy and laughter, and the world's scorn for Christ.

In discussing and defending much of modern painting, Jacques Maritain writes of the need for modern artists to know the history of painting and then to move beyond it. Knowledge of the tradition that he or she is breaking is essential before the painter presents "natural forms [that] are deformed and transposed, transfigured and recast," and the artist must look for what Maritain calls "the illuminating image" (J. Maritain 1965, 166–67) by which the presence of mystery will be conveyed to the viewer. In the stark and often distorted figures of Christ and of the clowns, Rouault found such "illuminating images." The painter had worked on the *Miserere* series for years before World War II but did not publish the work until after the war, when these all-too-human figures of Christ were particularly resonant to a war-weary and debilitated Europe, hungry to find meaning in suffering. As commentators Frank and Mary Getlein observe, the *Miserere* paintings achieved an "almost sculptural quality" and are "witness to hours of painting, meditating on Christ in the world and in men's hearts, repainting, adding, covering up, adding again, looking, thinking, until the surface becomes a thick wall . . . the accumulated records of years of spiritual thought" (Getlein 23).

Georges Rouault had met Léon Bloy in 1903 and was "fascinated" by him, finding in Bloy's work, especially in *La femme pauvre,* "a different Paris." Through Bloy's eyes in this novel, Rouault "saw the down-and-outs of the city lounging around the streets. He saw the unthinking cruelty of the courts to the poor. . . . He saw particularly the pathetic efforts of marginal entertainers—jugglers, clowns, acrobats—to bring a moment's cheer to others out of the misery of their own lives. He looked at the Paris around him and saw the Paris of Léon Bloy. For a travelogue through this limbo, again, a new pictorial language was needed" (Getlein 10–11). In painting too, the "language" needed to be turned inside out. Bloy, Maritain, Rouault, Flannery O'Connor, and Walker Percy agree: unless Christian art and literature are reinvented, the language itself "converted," viewers and readers will not be moved. Rouault thus reinvented his painterly language. Ironically, Rouault's "new pictorial language" was not pleasing to Léon Bloy, who had inspired it. Bloy writes in his journal in 1905, after visiting Rouault's studio, "It's a sorry sight. He's seeking a new path, what a pity! This artist apparently capable of painting the angels now does nothing else but the most shocking and vindictive caricatures. Bourgeois foulness has wrought so violent and horrified a reaction in him that his art seems to have received the deathblow" (qtd. in Getlein 13). Evidently Bloy did not allow the painter the same liberty he claimed for himself as a Catholic writer; although Bloy appears to have objected only to Rouault's broad, exaggerated style and not to his subject matter. Parallels with the squeamish responses to O'Connor's work, certainly in the early days and even among some readers today, are evident.

In spite of such disagreement, so deeply felt in the case of Bloy's reaction to Rouault's work, this group of French Catholic intellectuals and the fiercely passionate climate surrounding them in late nineteenth- and early twentieth-century France set a precedent of spiritual creativity and thought that was, at the least, bound to have been reassuring to Flannery O'Connor. In this community of artists, each was intent on illuminating the possibilities of salvation and those moments of grace in and to the world. Initially sparked by the philosophy of Henri Bergson, Jacques and Raïssa Maritain turned to—and were "turned" by—the living example of radical poverty in Léon Bloy, who, as we have seen, was the spiritual center of the Catholic revival in France. O'Connor was surely comforted and inspired by this loving community of theology, literature, and the arts. She undoubtedly was affirmed in her own aesthetic, by which she intended—like Bloy and Rouault—to pour cold water in our faces and to push us out of our chairs in order that we might understand and experience God's grace.

Works Cited

Béguin, Albert. *Léon Bloy: A Study in Impatience*. New York: Sheed and Ward, 1947. O'Connor's copy is in the Flannery O'Connor Collection, Russell Library, Georgia College and State University, Milledgeville.

Bloy, Léon. *The Woman Who Was Poor*. Translated by I. J. Collins. New York: Sheed and Ward, 1939.

Douglass, Paul. *Bergson, Eliot, and American Literature*. Lexington: University Press of Kentucky, 1986.

Getlein, Frank, and Dorothy Getlein. *Georges Rouault's Miserere*. Milwaukee, Wis.: Bruce, 1964.

Gillies, Mary Ann. *Henri Bergson and British Modernism*. Montreal: McGill-Queen's University Press, 1996.

Herberg, Will, ed. *Four Existentialist Theologians: A Reader from the Works of Jacques Maritain, Nicolas Berdyaev, Martin Buber, and Paul Tillich*. Garden City, N.Y.: Doubleday, 1958. O'Connor's copy is in the Flannery O'Connor Collection, Russell Library, Georgia College and State University, Milledgeville.

Maritain, Jacques. *Creative Intuition in Art and Poetry*. 1953. Reprint, Cleveland: World Publishing / Meridian, 1965.

———. Introduction to *Pilgrim of the Absolute*, by Léon Bloy. Selection by Raïssa Maritain. Translated by John Coleman and Harry Lorin Binsse. New York: Pantheon, 1947. O'Connor's copy is in the Flannery O'Connor Collection, Russell Library, Georgia College and State University, Milledgeville.

Maritain, Raïssa. *"We Have Been Friends Together" and "Adventures in Grace."* Garden City, N.Y.: Doubleday/Image, 1961.

Mauriac, François. *What I Believe*. Translated and with an introduction by Wallace Fowlie. New York: Farrar, Straus, 1963.

Quirk, Tom. *Bergson and American Culture: The Worlds of Willa Cather and Wallace Stevens*. Chapel Hill: University of North Carolina Press, 1990.

The Church-Historical Origin of O'Connor's Blood Symbolism

Inger Thörnqvist

Scholars have different views on the origin of O'Connor's blood symbolism. Stanley Edgar Hyman thinks that O'Connor's venture of writing is inseparable from her Catholicism and that the symbolic concept of *blood* in her fiction is congenial with "the mystic-ascetic tradition of St. John of the Cross" (Hyman 37). In contrast, Spivey contends that O'Connor, in the manner of D. H. Lawrence, uses blood to depict the irrational and unconscious mind, and he cannot find in her fiction any "sky-pointed" symbols. He contends, "For her the Virgin Mary never appears" (Spivey 103). I am aware that there are several other O'Connor scholars, like Spivey, who will not agree with me, but I believe that O'Connor's use of blood as a symbol is grounded in her readings of early church history, in which blood is the medium of divine signals.[1] As such it owes a great deal to the church fathers and the early Christian saints.

In her letter to Spivey of March 16, 1960, O'Connor says, "Those desert fathers interest me very much" (*HB* 382). Zuber shows that in her review of Robert Payne's *The Holy Fire* (1957) O'Connor claims, "These early Fathers probably contributed as much to the development of Christian thought as Augustine and Jerome, and certainly Dionysius the Areopagite, as the author himself declares, influenced mystical theology in the West as much as any Western Father" (PG 40). Kinney's record of her readings confirms that she read several works on the history of the early Christian church.[2] Ralph C. Wood, in his article "The Catholic Faith of Flannery O'Connor's Protestant Characters: A Critique and Vindication," notes that Hazel Motes embodies O'Connor's view of humanity by carrying the sign of faultlessness even after the Fall. He states, "Hazel Motes is the single character in whom O'Connor's Augustinian theology is most fully realized. He is a vivid embodiment of her conviction that—even after the Fall—humanity possesses an indelible divine imprint, a homing instinct for God that makes the heart restless until it finds its peace in His will. The blood drawn from Immanuel's veins pours into all the rivers that course the world. It flows also in Hazel's vascular system, making his blood divinely wise even when he would be humanly foolish" (Wood 22).

In his patristic compilation, Samuel Rubenson notes that in early Christian times one did not view an ascetic life as a means to earn a heavenly afterlife but as evidence that the earthly body carries the possibility of eternal life. The suffering ascetic became a living indication of Christ in the world (Rubenson 34). Obviously O'Connor favored this kind of devotion. In the above-mentioned letter to Spivey, O'Connor explains that she likes the allusion to self-sacrificial suffering in the title of her novel *The Violent Bear It Away*. She writes that the title calls to mind "the violence of love, of giving more than the law demands, of an asceticism like John the Baptist's, but in the face of which even John is less than the least in the kingdom—all this is overlooked" (*HB* 382).

In *The Violent Bear It Away* O'Connor clearly reflects this inner divine pull to sacrifice oneself for Christ by showing that even the atheist Rayber experiences this stern demand as an "undertow in his blood dragging him backwards to what he knew to be madness" (*VBIA* 114). Furthermore, Rayber fears that Francis, his close relative, has inherited this irresistible force that is "hidden in the line of blood that touched them, flowing from some ancient source, some desert prophet or pole-sitter, until, its power unabated, it appeared in the old man and him and, he surmised, in the boy. Those it touched were condemned to fight it constantly or to be ruled by it" (*VBIA* 114).³ Consequently, O'Connor shows that the most fervent craving for divine knowledge is irrevocably implanted in the blood of the chosen as both the crucial privilege and the curse of their prophetical vocation. Accordingly, in *The Violent Bear It Away* the backwoods prophet Mason is certain that Francis's prophetical vocation comes about because "good blood knows the Lord and there ain't a thing he can do about having it. There ain't a way in the world he can get rid of it" (*VBIA* 59). Maybe O'Connor's inspiration for this prophetical marginality comes from Matthew 23:30–35, where Christ reproaches the Pharisees for shedding the blood of the old prophets. Hypocritically, the Pharisees pay reverence to the old prophets, alleging that they would not have persecuted and killed the prophets as their ancestors did if they had been living in that time. In verse 35, Christ predicts a bloody day of vengeance for these hypocrites: "That upon you may come all the righteous blood shed upon the earth, from the blood of righteous Abel unto the blood of Zacharias son of Barachias, whom ye slew between the temple and the altar" (Matt. 23:35; KJV throughout).

O'Connor wrote to Alfred Corn on August 12, 1962, that, contrary to the teachings of the Catholic Church, the Protestant faith "teaches that God does not judge those acts that are not free, and that he does not predestine any soul to hell—for his glory or any other reason" (*HB* 488). The blood symbol O'Connor uses is implicitly the antimetaphor of the predestination doctrine: many in O'Connor's fiction have divine blood, though they do not interpret its signals correctly. Enoch in *Wise Blood* is such an example.

The apologist Justin in his *Dialogue with Trypho* explains the historical revelation of the divine by Christ as predetermined by the operations of the Logos. Accordingly, Justin talks about the *seeds* of the Logos, σπέρματα του λόγου, that induce knowledge in the mind from the Logos. Grillmeier refers to Justin's belief that "these σπέρματα are a participation in the *Logos* by the human spirit. They derive from the activity of the *Logos*, which therefore sows knowledge in the human reason in this way" (Grillmeier 92). The Christian Platonic concept of Logos plays a role in O'Connor's thought. She uses a Stoic image from middle Platonism in order to describe the operations of the Logos as latently present as the Christ-word in all people when she writes to Betty Hester on September 30, 1955, quoting John 1:9, that Justin teaches that the Logos is "enlightening every man who comes into the world" (*HB* 107). In the same breath she alleges that Simone Weil would have shared Justin's opinion about the Logos. Here O'Connor probably refers to Justin's philosophical understanding of Logos as the sparkle of knowledge that resides within every soul. She fictionalizes this concept of Logos as a latent power of nonrational spiritual discernment in Enoch's bicameral mind: "Enoch's brain was divided into two parts. The part in communication with his blood did the figuring but it never said anything in words. The other part was stocked up with all kinds of words and phrases. While the first part was figuring how to get Hazel Motes through the FROSTY BOTTLE and the ZOO, the second inquired, 'Where'd you git thisyer fine car? You ought to paint you some signs on the outside it, like "Step-in, baby"'" (*WB* 87–88). Enoch faces the true nature of his own blood the moment he sees it shed by Hazel's attack on him: "He put his fingers to his forehead and then held them in front of his eyes. They were streaked with red. He turned his head and saw a drop of blood on the ground and as he looked at it, he thought it widened like a little spring. . . . Very faintly he could hear his blood beating, his secret blood, in the center of the city" (*WB* 100).

Similarly, O'Connor demonstrates that Francis, when listening in an Old Testament–sounding prophetical warning of God's judgment, perceives this admonition as "silent as seeds opening one at a time in his blood" (*VBIA* 242). In all likelihood, O'Connor here has in mind the parable of the tiny "grain of mustard" in Matthew 13:31–32. Correspondingly, she communicates to the reader that the scriptural words in their passage through the blood become substantial as "seeds." Grillmeier notes a specific connotation of *seeds* in Justin's description of the experience of divine possession in the Hebrew world, claiming that Justin presupposes that everybody has a share of "the divine seed," although the prophets of the Old Testament possessed it to an exceptional degree (Grillmeier 92–93). However, Justin emphasizes that Christ had the highest indwelling of Logos in a human being. I think that in "The Enduring Chill" O'Connor shows that the divine intuition in human blood is a distinctly physical phenomenon. She gives you an idea that Asbury worries about the possibility that his blood could be besmirched (*CS* 377). And she notably implies that Asbury's blood contains a holy essence by having Dr. Block "humming a hymn" and reflecting that blood "don't lie," as he presses the needle in (*CS* 367). Moreover, Asbury reflects that Dr. Block "was, by definition, the enemy of death and he looked now as if he knew he was battling the real thing" (*CS* 372).

F. L. Cross shows that Cyril of Jerusalem, in his *Fourth Mystagogical Catechism*, quotes 2 Peter 1:4 to emphasize that all Christians, by sharing Christ's body and blood in the Eucharist, have become "partakers of the divine nature" (Cyril 68). In 2 Peter 1:4 we read that Christ, through the bread and wine of the Communion, has given all believers the guarantee that they might "be made of the same body and the same blood with Him. Thus we come to bear Christ in us, because His Body and Blood are diffused through our members" (Cyril 68). At the beginning of *The Martyrdom of Perpetua and Felicitas,* the narrator, in accordance with 1 Corinthians 7:17 and Romans 12:3, declares that "the same Spirit has been sent to distribute all his gifts to all, as the Lord apportions to everyone" (Musurillo 107).

The crucifix, the bloody expression of Christ's redemptive suffering for humankind, plays an important role in O'Connor's blood symbolism in "A Temple of the Holy Ghost," where O'Connor depicts a child, who daydreams of becoming a saint, enduring as little pain as possible (*CS* 243). However, the child's faith grows when she learns that suffering is a necessary plight for winning saintly glory. Thus, after having taken the Communion, the crucifix that is worn by a nun accidentally thumps the child in the face (*CS* 248). In a letter to Betty Hester dated December 16, 1955, O'Connor refers to this crucifix as "the ultimate all-inclusive symbol of love" and also says that in "A Temple of the Holy Ghost" purity means "an acceptance of what God wills for us" and "an acceptance of the Crucifixion, Christ's and our own" (*HB* 124). Furthermore, the child sees the Eucharistic transubstantiation, symbolized by the sun, a God symbol, take shape in the Communion bread that appears like "a huge red ball like an elevated Host drenched in blood" that leaves a line like "a red clay road" over the woods at sunset.[4] Here O'Connor, implicitly refuting the Protestant rejection of transubstantiation, possibly alludes to a vision beheld by the medieval saint Gertrude of Helfta and described in her work *Legatus Divinae Pietatis,* in which Gertrude sees "the Lord dipping the host in the heart of God the Father and bringing it out again colored red as if stained with blood" (Gertrude 29).[5] The hermaphrodite's great symbolic importance in the story is evident in O'Connor's letter to Hester of February 21, 1957, in which she rejects the opinion of "B," who writes that the hermaphrodite is "a lie" (*HB* 202). The child realizes the divine depth of the hermaphrodite's acceptance of the way God made it when, on her way home, she overhears the driver's gratitude for having had the opportunity to see the hermaphrodite at the fair, before the Protestant authorities closed it (*CS* 248). By accepting its freakish body as God's will, the hermaphrodite echoes the complete submission to God that characterized Gertrude's life. After these events the child realizes that she too has to accept suffering by humbly succumbing to God's will. O'Connor explains the story in a December 16, 1955, letter to Hester by saying that she believes that "the Host is actually the body and blood of Christ, not a symbol," and that Hester can acquire a greater sense of the story by considering "the mystery of the Eucharist in it" (*HB* 124).

The church fathers' writings richly exemplify the early Christian view of divine blood as exceptional. In his collection of texts by Pseudo-Dionysius, Paul Rorem shows that in *The Divine Names* this author describes Christ's essence as atypical of the natural order, since "he was formed from a virgin's blood" (Rorem 65).[6] Hence, he conceptualizes the Virgin's blood as a partly divine essence. The tale of Polycarp's martyrdom reveals how the first Christian community believed that the divine defense against evil dwells within the Christian's blood. In his compilation of martyrdom stories, Herbert Musurillo shows that *The Martyrdom of St. Polycarp* provides evidence that blood in early Christian history was associated with faith. We are told that when the fire at the stake did not consume Polycarp, the executioner stabbed him with a knife, which resulted in such a great eruption of blood that it actually extinguished the fire. The spectators understood that the large quantity of blood that flowed from his body was evidence of his election by God (Musurillo 15). In verse 15 of *The Martyrdom of Saints Perpetua and Felicitas*, Felicitas's sacrificed blood is described as "holy" and "innocent" (Musurillo 123).

O'Connor depicts her characters' blood as completely *private* and as fundamentally *irrational*. In "The Enduring Chill" she illustrates the personal sensation of possessing divine blood by Asbury's irritation with the blood test that invades "the privacy of his blood" (*CS* 373). In *The Violent Bear It Away*, by showing Rayber's vain attempts to dissuade Francis from obeying Mason's command to baptize Bishop, O'Connor implies that the irrationality of divine wisdom is ingrained in his blood: "You have that order lodged in your head like a boulder blocking your path" (*VBIA* 193). She demonstrates both the nonrationality and the individuality of the divine blood in "The Life You Save May Be Your Own" through Mr. Shiftlet's irritation with the female bureaucrat's ignorance regarding his divine blood, as she reduces his wedding ceremony to nothing more than a reflex action of "paper work and blood tests" (*CS* 153).

O'Connor even portrays the natural world as involved in the shedding of redemptive blood. In this sense she is in sympathy with the apologist Irenaeus. Grillmeier claims that Irenaeus, when he defends Christian faith against the gnostic idea that the Creator is disconnected from the created world and from the redemption of humankind, draws on the conventional idea of a universal *oikonomia*. According to this concept, the whole universe and nature participate in the process of redemption by Christ. He explains, "Irenaeus preserves the christocentricity of this traditional concept, but extends it so that it has universal scope" (Grillmeier 101).

O'Connor reflects this understanding of the omnipresence of God's salvation in the tormented natural landscape in "A View of the Woods," where she seems to suggest parallels between Christ's redemptive bloodshed and the human exploitation of the earth by describing the holes in the soil that the caterpillar has dug as the "red pit" and the "red hole" (*CS* 335). She informs Betty Hester, in a letter dated December 28, 1956, that the woods in this story are a Christ symbol (*HB* 190). She symbolizes Christ's presence in the woods by describing the trees as being "raised in a pool of red light." It also appears as if a person was "wounded behind the woods and the trees were bathed in blood" (*CS* 348). O'Connor illustrates a universal yearning for redemption by the terror of the landscape's being sacrificed for the human evil of economic profiteering. This affliction she also depicts by "the red corrugated lake" (*CS* 335). In "The River" she depicts a river, which according to the preacher-healer Bevel brings redemption, as the red river of Christ's blood in which you can be baptized and healed and that flows "to the Kingdom of Christ" (*CS* 166). He admonishes people to lay down their burden in "the rich red river of Jesus' Blood," that contains soul-saving "Faith," "Life," and "Love" (*CS* 165). In this display of the holy blood that concretely permeates nature, O'Connor agrees with the early church's Latin liturgy. Anders Piltz finds that this liturgy presented natural phenomena as embodiments of Christ. This metaphysical picture occurs in the hymnal *Illuminans Altissimus,* where the scene at first seems to be from Virgil's *Aeneid.* Here it is mentioned that "the spirit"—since the beginning of time—maintains heaven, earth and sea, moon, and the stars from within. A world soul mingles with this enormity and gives birth to human beings and other organic life, such as animals. This spiritual energy is a heavenly fire, but the material world encloses it and forces it downward. Ambrose of Milan gives this scene a Christian reinterpretation by altering the text to say that Christ is the one who lights the stars in space, while he also is truth and peace on earth (Piltz 41).[7]

To contrast with the metaphor of blood as the medium connecting humanity and God, O'Connor uses a reverse semiotics: anemia indicates atheism. Thus she uses a semiotics of atheism in *The Violent Bear It Away* by describing Francis's blood as chilled, so his face looks "dry and old," when he realizes that Rayber's ungodliness has sneaked into him "like the current of death in his blood" (*VBIA* 194). Similarly, in "The Lame Shall Enter First," O'Connor reveals Sheppard's unconscious feelings of guilt for his lack of Christian love through the fact that his face is "drained of color" (*CS* 481). In *Wise Blood* she also indicates that divine salvation cannot exist in a bloodless and lifeless organism by showing that Hazel's divine blood seems to push him to reject the bloodless mummy that Enoch offers him as the new Christ (*WB* 187–88). Subsequently, she reveals that he actually does not want to embrace the belief in a bloodless Christ, although he preaches about such a Christ (*WB* 141). Occasionally, however, Hazel reveals that he actually believes in the corruption of both soul and body and the redemption of these only through divine blood. His conscience tells him that to abide in sin is indeed a deeply destructive state. He is often reminded of his own participation in the fallen state of humankind and that, since the time of his grandfather's preaching, Christ has pursued him. During his flight from the Christ-image that troubles his mind, a road sign announces the message "WOE TO THE BLASPHEMER AND WHOREMONGER! WILL HELL SWALLOW YOU UP?" (*WB* 75). Hazel reflects, "There's no person a whoremonger, who wasn't something worse first. . . . That's not the sin, nor blasphemy. The sin came before them" (*WB*

76). Contrary to the modern gnostic presupposition, he finds that sin has its roots in original sin.

According to Bart D. Ehrman, Justin in his *Dialogue with Trypho*, chapter 30, teaches the exclusiveness of doctrinal knowledge and prophetical gift.[8] He stresses that these gifts are a grace bestowed only upon those who devote themselves to Christ. Divine dogma was considered low and ungodly because people "were not illuminated by grace to understand that these same doctrines have called your people, mired in sin and sick of a spiritual disease, to conversion and spiritual repentance; nor did they understand that prophecy, which was given to mankind after the death of Moses, is eternal" (Ehrman 111). I believe that O'Connor wants to demonstrate that divine blood inflicts an alienation from the world and a troubled participation in the prophetical line of succession. Thus, she shows that Francis's blood is part of a continuous line of prophets that starts with Abel, the first human being who was slain in cold blood (*VBIA* 242). Furthermore, the alienation of divine blood from natural law becomes evident in that Rayber, even though he is an atheist, feels uneasy about being the other when he sees that Francis, the agent of this fatal baptism, in his blood feels a togetherness with Bishop "by some necessity of nerve that excluded him" (*VBIA* 196).

The letters of Saint Paul show the early Christians having a collective self-image as a community blessed in Christ. To be *in Christ*, ἐν Χριστῷ, according to 1 Corinthians 1:2 means to be "sanctified in Christ" or in Philippians 1:1 to be "all the saints in Christ." Musurillo shows that at Perpetua's martyrdom, as described in *The Martyrdom of Saints Perpetua and Felicitas*, Felicitas is aware of being divinely sustained from within through a symbiotic relationship between her own suffering and Christ's forbearance (Musurillo 106–31). In the hour of her childbirth, Perpetua affirms that the pain she endures now is of another kind than the suffering she will bear later, at her martyrdom, in the name of Christ. She affirms that "another will be inside me who will suffer for me, just as I shall be suffering for him" (Musurillo 123–25).

O'Connor displays the presence of divine blood in the human body in "A View of the Woods," where Mr. Fortune's divine blood foments a merciless self-understanding, when, after having killed his granddaughter, he feels his heart expand by the transition of divine blood through his heart (*CS* 355–56). Similarly in "Revelation," O'Connor symbolizes Mrs. Turpin's impending redemption with blood: the book that was thrown at her raises a mark on her face that ranges in color from pink to red. Moreover, employing the fish, an ancient Christ symbol, O'Connor tells us that the marks on Mrs. Turpin's skin look like "pink fish bones" (*CS* 501). Unmistakably, the presence in the doctor's office of "cotton wads with little blood spots on them" also signals Mrs. Turpin's coming revelation (*CS* 489). Finally, at the high point of her torturous self-recognition, Mrs. Turpin sees a "red glow" spreading over the hogs, which "appeared to pant with a secret life" (*CS* 508). Similarly in "The Displaced Person," human blood forebodes the Transfiguration as Father Flynn blushes, reddens, when he approaches the peacock, which is the symbol of Transfiguration (*CS* 198).

Blood as an apocalyptic sign turns up in different guises in O'Connor's stories. In *The Violent Bear It Away*, it appears in Mason's expectation that the sun will "burst in blood and fire" at the Last Judgment (*VBIA* 5). This image appears in the prediction in Acts 2:19–21 about the appearance of blood signs in the sky during the last days. In "Greenleaf," as the sun gradually approaches the earth through "thin red and purple bars" looking like a "swollen red ball," divine judgment transforms the sun into "a bullet" (*CS* 328–29). I discern three symbols in this story that signal the impending divine doom: *red* indicates the presence of Christ's redeeming blood, *purple* signifies repentance and could possibly be associated with the liturgical color for Lent, and the *bullet* stands for divine doom.

In "Sermon 62" Bernard of Clairvaux compares the *wall* to the physical side of Christ's salvation of the soul—that is, the church—in its being perforated by "clefts" through which the saving blood of Christ pours out over the soul (Bernard 246). Bernard states that the wall keeps the "the crannies, the many and varied resting-places and mansions which are in her [the church] Father's house (John 14:2), in which he lodges his children according to the deserts of each!" Bernard also predicts the posthumous healing of the church by comparing this to a celestial restoration of the wall, "to perfection and wholeness" (Bernard 246).

In "The Partridge Festival" the "red brick" of the infirmary wall, behind which Singleton is kept in custody, probably symbolizes the institution's significance as the scene of Calhoun's and Elizabeth's impending redemption (*CS* 441). In "A Temple of the Holy Ghost," O'Connor, in all likelihood, symbolizes an aspect of monastic life by Mount St. Scholastica's red walls (*CS* 247). If O'Connor indicates that the wall carries such an allusion, it may symbolize a promise of the coming rectification of God's creation in Heaven, since in a monastery one prepares oneself for holy perfection and in a penitentiary one contemplates and regrets one's sinfulness. Hence, the wall serves as a symbol of the growth of salvation on earth.

Samuel Rubenson informs us that in the early first century the Greek word *martys* denoted those who, by sacrificing their lives, confirmed their testimony to Christ and the resurrection. Contemporary hagiographical tales give us a picture of the martyrs performing a vicarious atonement between humanity and God that cleared the road to salvation for many Christians (Rubenson 11). I think that the Confederate soldiers after the Civil War were thought of similarly, as martyrs, in the South. In "The Fiction Writer and His Country," O'Connor claims that a story's quality should be judged according to its concentration on Christian endurance. She expresses her belief that it is impossible to avoid suffering, and she quotes from the church father Cyril of Jerusalem to support her belief:[9] "The dragon sits by the side of the road, watching those who pass. Beware lest he devour you. We go to the Father of Souls, but it is necessary to pass by the dragon" (*MM* 35). This presentation of Cyril of Jerusalem's catechism is a personal exegesis of the sixteenth paragraph of his "Procatechism" that expands upon 1 Peter 5:8 and Hebrews 12:9, which tell us about the serpent that lies in wait for those saved by Christ, who must pass it before they can come into the Kingdom of God (Cyril 50).

Evidently the close connection between the Christlike suffering and the Christ-imitating life is typical of the church fathers. Ehrman demonstrates that the author of *The Epistle of Barnabas* emphasizes the revitalizing effect of Christ's blood.[10] Chapter 7 of the letter explains that the Lord suffered in order to give men life by the blood of his wounds (Ehrman 98–106). Grillmeier writes that in early Christianity the Jews and the Greeks disregarded the image of the bleeding Christ that was highly treasured by the church (Grillmeier 71). In "The Catholic Novelist in the Protestant South," O'Connor defends this bleeding Christ-image, siding with the early church's apologia of the suffering and bleeding Christ, when she criticizes the aversion that "the politer elements," those who think they have superior esthetic judgment, display for the tormented expressions of the holy (*MM* 207).

According to her letter to Betty Hester of July 25, 1959, O'Connor finds that true sainthood exists outside the Catholic Church and suggests that "there is doubtless unwritten sacred history like uncanonized saints" (*HB* 343). These thoughts seem compatible with her remark in "Some Aspects of the Grotesque in Southern Fiction" that a "Christ-haunted" feeling persistently annoys the southern mind (*MM* 45). Her conviction that "uncanonized saints" and "unwritten sacred history" exist, along with her impression that the South is "Christ-haunted," coincides with her empathic fictional picture of the southern backwoods prophet as well as with the adoration of the Civil War soldier by the South. Wilson, stressing that national sainthood was an idea endemic to the postbellum South, mentions the mythologizing of Confederate general Robert E. Lee to Christlike proportions in the sermons of preachers (Wilson 48–49).

Judith Perkins points out that the church fathers Justin, Ignatius of Antioch, and Irenaeus associated prophetic calling with suffering (Perkins 37–38).[11] Obviously, in *The Violent Bear It Away*, O'Connor illustrates this connection by applying her semiotics of blood to the burden of the prophetical vocation. Accordingly, Francis fears that he is physically unable to break free from his lineage of prophetic blood, and he fears he will be exhausted by "hunger like the old man, the bottom split out of his stomach so that nothing would heal or fill it but the bread of life" (*VBIA* 21). O'Connor bases this semiotics of a hunger for God on the promise in Matthew 5:6 of gratification to those who "hunger and thirst after righteousness." In their collection of Gregory of Nyssa's works, Drobner and Viciano show that the Cappadocian church father claims that the Christlike human longing for the holy is not entirely metaphorical but is "a true passion," a God-blessed physical hunger, which originates in Christ's voluntary participation in human hunger and thirst on earth (Gregory 153). Pseudo-Dionysius employs "food" in a similar way in *The Divine Names:* "I believe that by solid food is depicted a perfection and sameness of an intellectual and stable order, by virtue of which and during the exercise of a knowledge which is stable, powerful, unique, and indivisible, the divine things are shared with the intelligent workings of sense perception. It is in this way that Paul, himself a recipient of wisdom, imparted truly solid food" (Pseudo-Dionysius 286).

Perkins informs us that "like martyrs, the prophets functioned in the Christian context as a 'type' for suffering" (Perkins 38). Thus, Justin describes himself in his conversion story as inspired by the suffering of the Old Testament prophets.[12] Likewise, Ignatius of Antioch, in his letter to Magnesius, associates a prophet's greatness with his ability to bear pain. In *The Violent Bear It Away* O'Connor depicts prophetical suffering as an inherited addiction to a Christlike victimization by Francis's identification with the prophetical calling, which he feels as a craving, "building from the blood of Abel to his own, rising and engulfing him" (*VBIA* 242). Through this portrayal she wants the reader to associate with all the martyrs and prophets throughout Christian history, who are alienated in the profane world but familiar with God's Kingdom, the "violent country."

Ehrman explains that Tertullian concludes that the nucleus of Christian spiritual strength is ingrained in human blood and that this germ grows within the Christian during times of persecution. Tertullian therefore calls the blood of Christians "seed" (Ehrman 75–82). According to Perkins, Tertullian writes that when persecuted, the Christian feels honored, and when he is sentenced, he is grateful (Perkins 24). Ehrman shows us a similar spirit in *The Letter of Ignatius to the Romans,* in which Ignatius declares that "the greatness of Christianity lies in its being hated by the world, not in being convincing to it" (Ehrman 29). In *The Martyrdom of Perpetua and Felicitas* the narrator says about the courage of the martyrs, "These new manifestations of virtue will bear witness to one and the same Spirit who still operates" (Musurillo 131). Obviously, the same readiness to fight to the death for one's convictions existed during the Civil War. Wilson notes that in times of trouble the battle against evil tends to generate a firm faith. He says that during the Civil War the South was firmly convinced that God was on its side (Wilson 58).

In "The Lame Shall Enter First," the juvenile delinquent Rufus's name—Rufus is Latin for red—suggests his role as a catalyst in the disclosure of the underlying selfishness of Sheppard's humanitarian ambitions. In this story O'Connor seems to symbolize her vision of a Christlike atonement by an African American for white sin with the black maid's "red rain-coat" (*CS* 454). Furthermore, by employing an established symbol for Christ, the *rose,* I believe that O'Connor suggests black pain is Christlike by portraying the black maid's mouth as "a large rose that had darkened and wilted" (*CS* 454). In "Judgment Day," "Why Do the Heathen Rage?," and "A Circle in the Fire," I believe that O'Connor signals a kind of martyrdom by the redness of a black man's eyes (*CS* 538, 484, 176).

I find a reverse semiotics of martyrdom in O'Connor's depiction of the ruthless betrayers of the innocent. Thus, she portrays the betrayal of Christ in terms of the biblical accounts about the blood curse over the witnesses, betrayers, and killers of Christ by alluding to the passage in Matthew 27:25, where the betrayers require that Barabbas be released instead of Christ, crying out, "His blood be on us, and on our children." Accordingly, in "The Comforts of Home," the moment at which Thomas betrays "Star," when his hands look as if they have been immersed in "a pool of blood," seems to be a prototypical reflection of this Matthew text (*CS* 403).

Eusebius of Cæsarea, in his work *The History of the Church*, reports that the soldier martyr Dorotheus and his associates, who fought in the name of the Lord during the early Christian centuries, demonstrated an unyielding resistance and courage by shedding their blood.[13] In book 8 of his exposé of the historical church, Eusebius tells us that the courtiers of the Emperor in Nicomedia, martyr soldiers of the church, saw persecution as a blessing for their faith and thus willingly sacrificed their lives to demonstrate that they valued Christ more than material possessions. An equally determined Christian commitment is noted by Perkins in *The Letter of Ignatius to the Romans* (6:1), in which its author claims that "it is 'better for me to die' to Jesus Christ than to rule the ends of the earth" (Perkins 190).

To fictionalize this ideal of the early Christian martyrs probably felt natural to O'Connor, who lived surrounded by the southern myth of the Confederate soldier. O'Connor's story "Why Do the Heathen Rage?" conspicuously reflects her acquaintance with the early Christian martyr soldiers. I think that Wilson finds a similar idea in the myth of the Confederate soldiers' fight against the Yankees. Southern Protestant ministers saw the Southern soldiers as "sublime" since "they fought a war of principle, a war whose lesson was that one should follow conscience despite the risks of defeat" (Wilson 41). Wilson compares the sentimental southern adoration of the Civil War soldier between 1865 and 1920 to Christ worship. Indeed, the soldiers were referred to in Protestant preaching "as parables of Christian conduct" (Wilson 39). In O'Connor's story, Walter's mother, who worries about her son's lack of determination, finally discovers that he has been reading a book that quotes a fourth-century letter in which Jerome scolds Heliodorus for having left the ascetic desert life.[14] Jerome was not only an erudite biblical scholar but also an energetic critic of the contemporary spiritual lethargy and decay among the clergy. Walter has underlined the following in a letter, written in the desert of Chalcis 374 A.D. O'Connor herself read Jerome, according to Kinney, and marked this quote:

> Love should be full of anger. Since you have already spurned my request, perhaps you will listen to admonishment. What business have you in your father's house, O you effeminate soldier? Where are your ramparts and trenches, where is the winter spent at the front lines? Listen! the battle trumpet blares from

heaven and see how our General marches fully armed, coming amid the clouds to conquer the whole world. Out of the mouth of our King emerges a double-edged sword that cuts down everything in the way. Arising finally from your nap, do you come to the battlefield! Abandon the shade and seek the sun. (Jerome 3)

On the page facing the quote in her copy of *The Satirical Letters of St. Jerome*, O'Connor has made the following note, showing her admiration of the rigor of ascetic rule: "I like the rule that corrects the emotion" (Kinney 74). I sense that O'Connor, by quoting Jerome's admonition to be spiritually courageous and militant, commends the kind of stamina that she treasured. O'Connor criticizes the spiritual vacuity of modern times by contrasting it to the ideal of the Confederate soldier and the early Christian ascetic and martyr. The building of the Reconstruction South and the creation of the first Christian empire under Constantine in the fourth century resemble each other in that they both demanded a readiness to suffer for the principle the new ideological order was based on.

The southern antihero is evident not only in O'Connor's depiction of Walter in "Why Do the Heathen Rage?" but also in "A Late Encounter with the Enemy." According to Harry Klevar, O'Connor was inspired to write this story after seeing an announcement in the *Union Recorder* on August 23, 1951, that read, "General William J. Bush will don a dashing new Confederate uniform and squire his wife to her graduation tomorrow from the Georgia State College for Women, in the largest single summers graduating class in GSCW history" (Klevar 123). O'Connor transformed the husband in the newspaper report (who did not die attending the ceremony), into the grandfather who unexpectedly meets a disgraceful death, not in the war, but in his wheelchair on the college campus near the Coca-Cola machine. O'Connor satirizes General Sash's lifelong gnostic obsession with an imagined glorious past, which has blinded him to the historical implications of salvation. In the end, an encounter with his own real history puts an end to his gnostic longing for immortality through fame and makes him see reality as it has come to pass (*CS* 143).

I find that the blood symbolism in O'Connor's fiction has its origin in early Christian imagery and thought, in which blood is the medium of divine signals. Her descriptions of characters who experienced God's presence as an urge in their blood for divine knowledge were probably inspired by the church fathers and by early Christian saints such as Jerome, Justin the Martyr, Irenaeus, Bernard of Clairvaux, Gertrude of Helfta and others.

Justin the Martyr's teaching of the Logos as the omnipresent principle by which God enters the human mind corresponds well with O'Connor's depiction of Francis in *The Violent Bear It Away*, who hosts this silent—yet clearly perceptible—

presence of God as seeds flowing through his blood, ceaselessly reminding him of his vocation. It tells him that he is one in a line of many prophets through the ages; nevertheless, blood works here as an anti-symbol for predestination, since Francis has the chance to reject what it conveys to him. Wise blood, though not always experienced as such, appears in all kinds of O'Connor characters, not just in those called as prophets. Thus, Mr. Shiftlet in "The Life You Save May Be Your Own" is irritated by the bureaucratic treatment he receives at his wedding, when the true nature of his blood is not recognized, and comments, "What do they know about my blood?"

Justin also describes the prophetical gift as indelibly tied to Christ and to the eternal wisdom that is given through succession. O'Connor sees a bloodline that starts with Abel and passes through the generations of prophets in Christian history until it ends up flowing through the veins of Francis. Mr. Fortune experiences divine blood in the hour of his redemption as his heart expands with the flow of divine blood.

O'Connor's description of an unconscious discernment in Enoch's blood, by which one part of his brain does not work rationally but comes to conclusions anyway, seems to refer to Justin's understanding of the Logos as the sparkle of knowledge in every human soul: "Enoch's brain was divided in two parts. The part in communication with his blood did the figuring but it never said anything in words" (*WB* 87). These ideas about the power of blood to protect against evil and to guarantee a good relationship with God are present in the story of the martyr Polycarp, whose blood flowed out and quelled the flames his persecutors had set for him.

The urgings of the blood seem also to play a crucial role in "The Enduring Chill," where Asbury's blood is understood by the doctor as real and as worth praising in a hymn. Asbury himself has failed to understand this and is weak and faithless. O'Connor also uses a reverse semiotics of blood, where anemia indicates atheism, as with Rayber in *The Violent Bear It Away* who, when he recognizes his own lifelong atheism, feels drained of blood and old, and realizes that atheism has been like death itself to his blood. Sheppard's lack of faith in "The Lame Shall Enter First" is evident when his face loses its color. In *Wise Blood* O'Connor shows that the same Hazel who rejects a Christ with blood, when confronted with a bloodless mummy, does not accept this proffered Jesus.

The story "A Temple of the Holy Ghost" evolves around the concept of Communion participation with the elements of wine and bread being the real presence of the blood and body of Christ. The child becomes aware that God requires us to suffer for sanctity, as is shown by the child's vision of God dipping the Communion host in blood, a vision also described by Gertrude of Helfta. The unnatural character of Christ is explained by Pseudo-Dionysius in *The Divine Names* as his being of a partly divine essence by virtue of being formed from a virgin's blood. Saint Felicitas claims that her ability to endure her martyrdom is due to her awareness that Christ is present within her and will help her to endure her physical pain.

In "A View of the Woods," where O'Connor compares the redemptive bloodshed of Christ with the ruthless exploitation of nature in the name of modern progress, the influence of Irenaeus's idea of the participation of the entire universe in the redemptive process becomes evident. In the woods, which according to O'Connor symbolize Christ, red holes are dug in the soil as nature is invaded by human profiteering. The woods shed blood in their vicarious atonement for human sin: the light over the woods makes them seem bathed in blood, and a person seems to lie hidden, wounded behind them. The lake is also described as red. A similar Irenaean picture of nature as everywhere participating in redemption appears in "The River," where the healing and saving river that flows to the Kingdom, according to the preacher-healer, is the blood of Christ.

There are several occasions where blood serves as a symbol for the Apocalypse in O'Connor's fiction. A direct reference to the biblical Apocalypse is made in *The Violent Bear It Away* with the mention of Doomsday, when the sky will become blood red. In other stories, such as "Greenleaf," the sun is described as red or blood red when redemption has taken place or will occur. In "Revelation" a red glow from the sky spreads out over the hogs in the pen when Mrs. Turpin has her final revelation.

Substantiating her view of suffering as necessary for salvation, O'Connor explicitly refers to the text by Cyril of Jerusalem, where he tells us that it is necessary for the believer to pass the dragon that lies in wait and threatens the Christian's way to heaven. Her conviction that there are "uncanonized saints" and her impression that the South is "Christ-haunted" coincide with an adoration of the Southern Civil War soldier. In *The Violent Bear It Away* she depicts the essential characteristic of her prophet's faith as a hunger. This description is congenial with Pseudo-Dionysius's view that faith is a real, physical sensation. Pseudo-Dionysius talks about divine wisdom in terms of pure food.

In the works of Ignatius of Antioch and Justin and in Eusebius's church history, the resistance against an un-Christian faith and the willingness to suffer for one's conviction are crucial. Willingness to suffer for a perceived just cause was also the spirit behind the Civil War soldiers. O'Connor admires the endurance of the first Christian martyrs and places it in direct contrast to modern laxity. The letter from Jerome that Walter reads in "Why Do the Heathen Rage?" mirrors this ideal of courage, which values spiritual strength over earthly supremacy. Here O'Connor implicitly links the ideological foundation of the Constantinian Empire and the Reconstruction South.

In summary, O'Connor is congenial with the church fathers in the use of blood as a symbol in the following ways:

1. The Word disseminates the prophetical vocation by seeds in the blood. An irresistible, physical, divine craving in the prophet's blood, originating in Christ's suffering, connects the generations in a continuous, unbreakable line of prophetical vocation.

2. An irresistible force in the blood connects the divine with the human and warns its carrier of evil.
3. Blood must be sacrificed for Christ and the resurrection, as in the early Christian ideal of the martyr.
4. The whole natural world is involved in the redemption by Christ.
5. The real presence of divine blood is found in the Eucharist.
6. Apocalyptic signs of blood are found in the sun.

Notes

1. Among those who would side with Spivey, see Suzanne Morrow Paulson, "Apocalypse of Self, Resurrection of the Double: Flannery O'Connor's *The Violent Bear It Away*," in *Flannery O'Connor: New Perspectives*, ed. Sura P. Rath and Mary Neff Shaw, 121–38 (Athens: University of Georgia Press, 1996); Paulson, *Flannery O'Connor: A Study of the Short Fiction* (Boston: Twayne-Hall, 1988); Jefferson Humphries, *The Otherness Within: Gnostic Readings in Marcel Proust, Flannery O'Connor, and François Villon* (Baton Rouge: Louisiana State University Press, 1983); Josephine Hendin, *The World of Flannery O'Connor* (Bloomington: Indiana University Press, 1970).

2. E.g., Alban Butler, *The Lives of the Fathers, Martyrs, and Other Principal Saints*, 4 vols. (Baltimore: Metropolitan, 1845). For further information, see Kinney, *Flannery O'Connor's Library*, 52–53, 73–74.

3. The pole-sitter alluded to was probably Simeon Stylites (390–459), also called "the Elder," the first Christian ascetic, who did penitence by constantly sitting on a pillar. For more information, see *The HarperCollins Encyclopedia*, 1191–92.

4. It is interesting to reflect on whether O'Connor's frequent fictionalization of visions may be at least partly rooted within her own experience. Systemic lupus erythematosus can disturb the performance of the brain, which may cause a disturbance in the perception of reality, so that the personal reality becomes identical with being under the influence of a hallucinogenic or a psychotic state of mind. See Podvoll, *The Seduction of Madness*, 146.

5. Gertrude of Helfta (1256–1301?) was a medieval visionary who had a conversion experience at the age of twenty-five and lived thereafter in humble submission to God's will.

6. Pseudo-Dionysius was a Christian Platonic theologian, also called "Denys the Areopagite," of the fifth and early sixth centuries. His *The Divine Names* greatly influenced later theologians. For further information about him, see *The HarperCollins Encyclopedia*, 408–9; for further information about his work, see Rorem, *Pseudo-Dionysius: A Commentary*, 167–69.

7. Ambrose (c. 339–97) was a bishop of Milan and a doctor of the church. He introduced much of Eastern Christian theology to the Latin tradition (*The HarperCollins Encyclopedia*, 39).

8. Justin, an apologist and martyr, died c. 165. For further information, see *The HarperCollins Encyclopedia*, 728.

9. Cyril (c. 315–c. 386) was a bishop of Jerusalem. For more information, see *The HarperCollins Encyclopedia*, 389.

10. *The Epistle of Barnabas* was the work of an anonymous Christian in the late first or early second century. For further information, see *The HarperCollins Encyclopedia*, 139.

11. Ignatius of Antioch (c. 35–107), bishop and apostolic father, who wrote seven letters that became pivotal in the formation of Christian faith. For further information, see *The HarperCollins Encyclopedia*, 652.

12. Justin studied different philosophies but became a Christian. He debated with Trypho in *Dialogue with Trypho the Jew* (*The HarperCollins Encyclopedia*, 689–90). Also, see note 8 above.

13. Eusebius of Cæsarea (260–339/340) was the first chronicler and compiler of church documents. For further information, see *The HarperCollins Encyclopedia*, 490.

14. The church father Jerome (c. 340–420) was the greatest biblical scholar of his age. He devoted himself to a severe ascetic life. For further information about him, see *The HarperCollins Encyclopedia*, 689–90. Heliodorus was a priest, who in the second century followed Jerome from Aquileia to the Near East to be a hermit but later returned to Italy, where he became bishop of Altinum. Jerome warns him in his letter against the temptations of the world. For further information, see Doyé, *Heilige und Selige*, 492–93.

Works Cited

Bernard of Clairvaux. *Bernard of Clairvaux: Selected Works*. Translated by G. R. Evans. New York: Paulist Press, 1987.

Cyril of Jerusalem. *St. Cyril of Jerusalem's Lectures on the Christian Sacraments: The Procatechesis and the Five Mystagogical Catecheses*. Edited by F. L. Cross. London: S.P.C.K, 1951.

Doyé, Franz von Sales, ed. *Heilige und Selige der römisch-katholischen Kirche: Deren Erkennungszeichen, Patronate und lebensgeschichtliche Bemerkungen*. Vol. 1. Leipzig: Vier Quellen, 1929.

Ehrman, Bart D. *After the New Testament: A Reader in Early Christianity*. New York: Oxford University Press, 1999.

Eusebius Pamphilus. *Ecclesiastical History: Translated from the Original with an Introduction by Christian Frederick Cruse and an Historical View of the Council of Nice by Isaac Boyle*. Grand Rapids, Mich.: Baker Book House, 1955.

Gertrude of Helfta. *The Herald of Divine Love*. Edited and translated by Margaret Winkworth. New York: Paulist Press, 1993.

Gregory of Nyssa. *Gregory of Nyssa, Homilies on the Beatitudes: An English Version with Commentary and Supporting Studies*. Proceedings of the Eighth International Colloquium on Gregory of Nyssa, Paderborn, September 14–18, 1998. Edited by Hubertus R. Drobner and Albert Viciano. Leiden: Brill, 2000.

Grillmeier, Aloys. *Christ in Christian Tradition: From the Apostolic Age to Chalcedon*. 2nd ed. Vol. 1. Translated by John Bowden. London: Mowbrays, 1975.

The HarperCollins Encyclopedia of Catholicism. Edited by Richard P. McBrien et al. New York: HarperCollins, 1995.

Hyman, Stanley Edgar. *Flannery O'Connor*. Minneapolis: University of Minnesota Press, 1966.

Jerome. *The Satirical Letters of St. Jerome*. Translated and introduced by Paul Carroll. Chicago: Gateway Editions, 1956.

Kinney, Arthur F. *Flannery O'Connor's Library: Resources of Being*. Athens: University of Georgia Press, 1985.

Klevar, Harvey. "Image and Imagination: Flannery O'Connor's Front Page Fiction." *Journal of Modern Literature* 4, no. 1 (1974): 121–32.

Musurillo, Herbert, ed. *The Acts of the Christian Martyrs*. Oxford: Clarendon Press, 1972.

Perkins, Judith. *The Suffering Self: Pain and Narrative Representation in the Early Christian Era*. London and New York: Routledge, 1995.

Piltz, Anders. "Mellan dogm och dikt: Den äldsta latinska hymndiktningen som kyrkohistorisk källa." *Kyrkohistorisk Årsskrift* 101 (2001): 37–45.

Podvoll, Edward M. *The Seduction of Madness: Revolutionary Insights into the World of Psychosis and a Compassionate Approach to Recovery at Home*. New York: HarperCollins, 1990.

Pseudo-Dionysius. *Pseudo-Dionysius: The Complete Works*. Edited by Paul Rorem et al. Translated by Colm Luibheid. New York: Paulist Press, 1987.

Rorem, Paul. *Pseudo-Dionysius: A Commentary on the Texts and an Introduction to Their Influence*. New York: Oxford University Press, 1993.

Rubenson, Samuel, ed. *Svenskt patristiskt bibliotek*. Vol. 2, *Martyrer och helgon*. Skellefteå: Artos, 2000.

Spivey, Ted R. *Flannery O'Connor: The Woman, the Thinker, the Visionary*. Macon, Ga.: Mercer University Press, 1995.

Wilson, Charles Reagan. *Baptized in Blood: The Religion of the Lost Cause, 1865–1920*. Athens: University of Georgia Press, 1980.

Wood, Ralph C. "The Catholic Faith of Flannery O'Connor's Protestant Characters: A Critique and Vindication." *Flannery O'Connor Bulletin* 13 (1984): 15–25.

"The very heart of mystery"

Theophany in O'Connor's Stories

Jack Dillard Ashley

> Then like a monumental statue coming to life, she bent her head slowly and gazed, as if through the very heart of mystery, down into the pig parlor at the hogs.
>
> Flannery O'Connor, "Revelation"

> Who breaks a butterfly upon a wheel?
>
> Alexander Pope, "Epistle to Dr. Arbuthnot"

"What in the world is theophany?" a friend asked. She was tutoring a student in a religion class in which the topic was to discuss theophany in the book of Genesis. I drew a blank, though I had a hunch. Upon searching, however, I found little information on the subject. The root of the word I recognized as an appearance, a showing, a revelation, a manifestation, perhaps vestige, an evidence. The prefix, of course, is God or a god. A standard dictionary definition is a manifestation or appearance of God or a god to man, as in the use by Henry Hart Milman in 1854—"The universe is but a sublime Theophany, a visible manifestation of God"—which the *Oxford English Dictionary* cites. It further defines the term as "a manifestation or appearance of God or a god to man" in "forms of time and space and the sphere of physical nature" (11:276).

Theophany clearly is kin to other terms of theological and religious signification. Epiphany, for instance, is a manifestation or appearance of some divine or supernatural being (*OED* 3:243). A modern definition of epiphany, courtesy of *The Random House College Dictionary* (1991), is "a sudden perception of or insight into reality or the essential meaning of something often indicated by some simple commonplace occurrence." This signification is a literary commonplace following upon the use of the term by James Joyce who, according to Richard Ellman, "borrows from Christianity the term 'epiphany' to describe the thing of beauty in its most vivid manifestation" (Joyce 1964, 143). Among numerous critical writings, Joyce's only definition of the term is that of Stephen Daedalus: "a sudden spiritual manifestation, whether in the vulgarity of speech or of gesture or in a memorable phase of the mind itself" (Joyce 1965, 3). According to Robert Scholes, "In the theory of art he was working on as a young man, he employed the term 'epiphany' to refer to moments in which things or people in the world revealed their true character or essence" (Joyce 1969, 253). For Joyce, "An epiphany was life observed, caught in a kind of camera eye which reproduced a significant moment without comment. An epiphany could not be constructed, only recorded" (Joyce 1965, 4).

A third term of kindred derivation is hierophany, literally a manifestation or appearance of the holy, sacred, priestly, sacerdotal. Religious symbols or sanctuaries are classified as hierophanies and exist for the sake of the experience of the sacred and divine (*Encyclopedic Dictionary of Religion,* 1666). Hierophanic, the adjective, thus denotes sacred mysteries, persons, objects, symbols; it is the mysterious, the priestly, and the sacerdotal. O'Connor employed a related term in "Revelation"; Ruby Turpin in the pig parlor raised her arm "in a gesture hieratic and profound" (*CS* 508).

Here I wish to posit three generalizations. First, theophany as a term, event, and concept is richly associated with the Old Testament, while epiphany is associated with the New; the content of theophany is Hebraic, while that of epiphany is Christian. Second, theophany occurs in the macrocosm and is often formed of macrocosmic phenomena, while epiphany is microcosmic noumena or mystery. Third, theophany typically arouses the emotions of terror, awe, reverence, and sorrow, while epiphany leads to light, illumination, recognition, and elevation of reason. It is useful in the context of these generalizations to introduce the datum related to me by my colleague Jerry Hackett, professor of medieval philosophy at the University of South Carolina.

As a conceptual term, *theophania* was first used by John Scotus Erigena (c. 810– c. 877) in the second and third parts of *Periphyseon: On the Division of Nature* (c. 860). Erigena describes four divisions of nature: (1) nature that creates and is not created; (2) nature that creates and is created; (3) nature that does not create and is created; and (4) nature that does not create and is not created. The first and fourth divisions are God beginning and end, source and fulfillment. The second division is that of intelligible forms, while the important third is that of sensible forms or theophanies. The four constitute a descending and reascending Neoplatonic emanation. Of the intelligible and sensible forms of divisions two and three, Frederick Copleston comments, they "constitute, not only a 'participation' of the divine goodness, but also the divine self-manifestation or theophany" (Copleston 123). Copleston quotes from *On the Division of Nature,* section three, fourth paragraph, a vivid and paradoxical definition of theophany: "the appearance of the non-appearing, the manifestation of the hidden, the affirmation of the negated, the comprehension of the incomprehensible, the speaking of the ineffable, the approach of the unapproachable, the understanding of the unintelligible, the body of the incorporeal; the essence of the super-essential, the form of the formless" (Copleston 123–24). Copleston offers a final summary of theophany: "Just as the human mind, itself invisible, becomes visible or manifest in words and gestures, so the invisible and incomprehensible God reveals Himself in nature, which is, therefore, a true theophany ... creation is a theophany, a revelation of the divine goodness, which is itself incomprehensible, invisible and hidden" (Copleston 124).

The Bible, especially the Old Testament, abounds in theophanies. *The New Catholic Encyclopedia* comments, "Actually the very fabric of the *OT* is woven of repeated self-revelations of God to Israel, often through theophanies" (Burtchaell 14:69). In form there are two sorts of theophany: one is lyric, hymnic, oracular, orphic with theophanic imagery, while the other is narrational, anecdotal, sequential, episodic, with theophanic events. The song of Deborah in Judges 5:4–5 is lyrical and oracular: "the earth trembled and the heavens dropped, the clouds also dropped water. The mountains melted from before the Lord" (KJV throughout). The canticle in chapter 3 of Habakkuk and the majestic opening of Nahum are instances of the lyrical, oracular, orphic theophany: "The Lord hath his way in the whirlwind and in the storm and the clouds are the dust of his feet. He rebuketh the sea, and maketh it dry, and dried up all the rivers.... The mountains quake at him, and the hills melt, and the earth is burned at his presence ... his fury is poured out like fire, and the rocks are thrown down by him ... with an overrunning flood he will make an utter end of the place thereof, and darkness shall pursue his enemies" (Nah. 1:3–8).

Like Nahum's majestic theophanic hymn, the Psalms are frequently orphic as in 18, 77, and 97 with images of fire, lightning, smoke, darkness, earthquakes, clouds, thunder, hills melting like wax, smoke in the nostrils of God, fire out of his mouth. So are the gloomy songs of major prophets Jeremiah and Isaiah: "Thou shalt be visited of the Lord of Hosts with thunder and with earthquake and great noise, with storm and tempest, and the flame of devouring fire" (Isa. 29:6). Judith's hymn foretells "woe to the nations that rise against my people. God will send fire and worms into their flesh" (Jth. 16:17).

There are many instances in the Old Testament of the second formal sort, the episodic, narrational, anecdotal, sequential theophany, which is usually made and shaped of the four elements. A strong east wind embodying the element air heralds the parting and closing of the Red Sea in Exodus 14, and God speaks to Job out of a whirlwind (Job 38:1). The element of earth is evident in the many instances of earthquake and is especially vivid as God's means of punishing Korah, Dathan, and Abiram for presumption: "the ground clave asunder that was under them: and the earth opened her mouth, and swallowed them up.... They, and all that appertained to them, went down alive into the pit, and the earth closed upon them.... And all Israel that were round about them fled at the cry of them: for they said, lest the earth swallow us up also" (Num. 16:31–34).

Theophany frequently comes in earthquakes, as in Joel 2:10: "The earth shall quake before them; the heavens shall tremble" and at Christ's crucifixion in Matthew 27:51: "the earth did quake, and the rocks rent." Theophany by water is evident in the great flood of Genesis 7:11: "all the fountains of the deep were broken up, and the windows of heaven were opened." The opening and disastrous closing of the Red Sea in Exodus 14 embody theophany by water. The element most prominent in theophany is fire. God speaks to Moses out of the burning bush in Exodus 3 and protects the three prophets in the furnace in Daniel 3. In 1 Kings 18:38, Elijah's offering is consumed by God's fire: "Then the fire of the Lord fell; and consumed the burnt sacrifice, and the wood, and the stones, and the dust and licked up the water that was in the trench." Sodom and Gomorrah in Genesis 19 are dispatched by God's fire and brimstone. But of all biblical theophanies, the great one, so-called in the New American Bible, is Mount Sinai in Exodus 19:16–18: "there were thunders and lightnings, and a thick cloud upon the mount. . . . And Mount Sinai was altogether in a smoke, because the Lord descended upon it in fire; and the smoke thereof ascended as the smoke of a furnace, and the whole mount quaked greatly." An interesting reversal of three elemental theophanies occurs in 1 Kings 19, in which the Lord is *not* in strong wind, is *not* in earthquake is *not* in fire, but comes to Elijah in a still, small voice.

One New Testament theophany, excluding the Apocalypse, which deserves mention is Pentecost in Acts 2:2–3, when the apostles were in one place and "suddenly there came a sound from heaven as of a rushing mighty wind . . . and there appeared unto them cloven tongues like as of fire." Finally as to theophany in the New Testament, I suggest—not assert—that each of the members of the Trinity has a theophanic elemental association. God the Father is a consuming fire (Heb. 12:29); God the Son comes by water (1 John 5:6); and God the Holy Spirit, the agent of inspiration, is figured in the wind, the *pneuma,* in John 3:8: "The wind bloweth where it listeth . . . so is everyone that is born of the Spirit."

O'Connor, to my knowledge, makes no verbal or interpretive issues of these varieties of God's manifestation theophanic, epiphanic, or hierophanic. It is, however, possible to classify and denominate many of her stories by means of these traditional images. A few of her stories—or at least parts of them—are hierophanic, that is, characterized by sacred priestly, sacerdotal imagery and meaning often iconic or iconographical (see Guroian). In "A Temple of the Holy Ghost" the artful confluence of the sun "like an elevated Host drenched in blood" with the Host shining ivory-colored in the midst of the monstrance (*CS* 248) is the hierophanic final image of the story. In "The Enduring Chill" the repeated reference to a fierce bird with spread wings and an icicle crosswise in its beak waiting to descend is an hierophany and constitutes the brilliant conclusion of the story: "But the Holy Ghost, emblazoned in ice instead of fire, continued, implacable, to descend" (*CS* 382). The most important hierophany in O'Connor's fiction is the icon on Parker's back: "the haloed head of a flat stern Byzantine Christ with all demanding eyes" (*CS* 522).

Some of O'Connor's most important stories are epiphanic, that is they prominently feature a sudden intuitive recognition on the part of a central character. Of these I would single out the impressive instances of "A Good Man," "Greenleaf," and "Everything That Rises Must Converge." As the grandmother's head clears for an instant, she sees The Misfit's face twisted close to her own, and she murmurs, "Why you're one of my babies. You're one of my own children!" (*CS* 132). This epiphany is a stunning instance, though ironic, of Aristotelian *anagnorisis* of blood kinship. In the climax and conclusion of "Greenleaf" Mrs. May has "the look of a person whose sight has been suddenly restored but who finds the light unbearable" (*CS* 333), and there is a hint of Plato's myth of the cave in the description. Julian in recognition of his mother feels a tide of darkness sweeping him back to her, "postponing from moment to moment his entry into the world of guilt and sorrow," deferring, that is, his spiritual birth (*CS* 420).

The current topic, however, is O'Connor's tales and theophany. She makes frequent use of theophanic components as comparisons, metaphors, and similes. Here is a brief survey: Mr. Head "burned with shame" (*CS* 269), and Nelson's face was "burning with shame" (*CS* 262). Later in the story the action of mercy covered Mr. Head's pride "like a flame and consumed it" (*CS* 269–70). Mark Fortune feels "a hot sluggish tide in the air, the kind felt when a tornado is possible" (*CS* 351), and Ruby Turpin's protuberance looks like a miniature tornado cloud (*CS* 505). Star Drake causes a disturbance in Thomas "as if he had seen a tornado" (*CS* 393). At Bailey's death the grandmother "could hear the wind move through the tree tops like a long satisfied insuck of breath" (*CS* 129), and the last film of illusion is torn "as if by a whirlwind" (*CS* 382) from Asbury's eyes. Parker lunges into the midst of his revilers "like a whirlwind on a summer's day" (*CS* 529). The black woman rumbles "like a volcano about to become active" (*CS* 416) in "Everything That Rises." Ruby Turpin is certain that she "is about to be in an earthquake" (*CS* 499), while "A View of the Woods" concludes with the image of "trees marching across water" (*CS* 356, cf. Mark 8:24) and "Everything That Rises" with "a tide of darkness" (*CS* 420). There is vivid imagery of ice and freezing, for instance when Mrs. May looks "in a freezing unbelief" (*CS* 333) and Hulga's eyes are "icy blue . . . the look of someone who has achieved blindness by an act of will and means to keep it" (*CS* 273). Often ice is associated with treason and deceit as in Dante's ninth circle of Hell: Nelson's mind is said to be "frozen around his grandfather's treachery" (*CS* 267), and the eyes of Sulk, Shortley, and Mrs. McIntyre "come together in one look that froze them in collusion forever" (*CS* 234). Finally, there are two statements made by the narrator in "The Lame Shall Enter First" that effectively define theophany: Rufus Johnson appears to Sheppard as "some elemental warping of nature" (*CS* 450), and Sheppard himself is said to be "like a man lashed by some elemental force of nature" (*CS* 447).

O'Connor's fictions are, however, more deeply rooted in the tradition of theophany than mere comparisons or similitudes would indicate. Often plots, especially conclusions, are theophanic. As an example of theophany by air I choose the apocalyptic ending of "The Life You Save May Be Your Own." Tom Shiftlet, deserted by the hitchhiker who jumps from his car, stops and discovers that "a cloud . . . shaped like a turnip, had descended over the sun, and another, worse looking, crouched behind the car" (*CS* 156). Unwisely for him, he prays "Oh Lord! . . . Break forth and wash the slime from this earth!" (*CS* 156). The turnip descends with a guffawing peel of thunder and fantastic raindrops. I interpret the two turnip shaped clouds to be tornado clouds, which Shiftlet is racing into Mobile where he may be whirled in fractured atoms, beyond one circuit or another. A stormy day has become a *dies irae*.

Water is a part of Mr. Shiftlet's theophany, but it is the sole content of Bevel's experience in "The River": "He plunged once and this time the waiting current caught him like a long gentle hand and pulled him swiftly forward and down." The final image is that of Mr. Paradise, who "rose like some ancient water monster" (*CS* 174). In "The Displaced Person" the Shortley family leaves Mrs. McIntyre's place just before dawn as it begins to drizzle. The car moves slowly, "like some overfreighted leaking ark" (*CS* 212–13), evoking the theophany of Noah's flood.

Two striking variants of water theophany occur in original endings that O'Connor changed. The original ending of "Good Country People" was Hulga's final sighting of Manley while sitting in the straw in the dusty sunlight: "She saw his blue figure struggling successfully over the green speckled lake" (*CS* 291). In other words, she saw her savior walking on water, water that isn't even there; the lake is a delusion occasioned by her lack of glasses. But delusion or no, it is a brilliantly ironic echo of a major biblical theophany. O'Connor's editor suggested the two final paragraphs that now exist, in which Mrs. Hopewell and Mrs. Freeman see Manley emerging from the woods. The original ending of "A View of the Woods" was a passage that O'Connor herself struck. After Mark Fortune has slaughtered Mary Fortune and has himself died of a stroke, there comes a rainstorm, and the eye sockets of both corpses are filled with rain, perhaps with tears:

> Pitts by accident found them that evening. He was walking home through the woods about sunset. The rain had stopped but the polished trees were hung with clear drops of water that turned red where the sun touched them; the air was saturated with dampness. He came on them suddenly and shied backward, his foot not a yard from where they lay. For almost a minute he stood still and then, his knees buckling, he squatted down by their side and stared into their eyes, into the pale blue pools of rainwater that the sky had filled. (*HB* 190)

The imagery of eye sockets filling with water from the sky was perhaps too mannered and outré even for O'Connor. Is it perhaps analogous to tears freezing in the eye sockets of the traitors in the ninth circle, that of ice, in Dante's *Inferno*?

The imagery of earth in O'Connor's stories frequently reflects pride of ownership. Characters such as Mrs. Cope in "A Circle in the Fire" and Mrs. Hopewell in "Good Country People" provide instances of such pride. Mrs. McIntyre in "The Displaced Person" is the most articulate of all in declaring her prideful reliance upon her soil, her place: "and all I've got is the dirt under my feet!" (*CS* 203). She will, however, soon be put in her place by the events occasioned by the advent of the Pole, the displaced person. The image of earth as imbued with spiritual content and expressive of divine purpose is most effectively portrayed in "A View of the Woods" in which, as in other stories, earth is regarded by O'Connor's characters as a salable commodity. But from the outset the earth appears to the reader to have noumenal meaning and power, fear in a handful of dust. The yellow earthmover lifts out the dirt, eating a square red hole in what had been a pasture. Mary Fortune watches "the big disembodied gullet gorge itself on the clay, then, with the sound of a deep sustained nausea and a slow mechanical revulsion, turn and spit it up" (CS 335). Mary Fortune warns Mark that the driver may "cut off some of your dirt" (CS 338). Mark likes to think of Mary Fortune as thoroughly of his clay (CS 338), but when she declares that she is "PURE Pitts" (CS 355), Mark bashes her head against a rock. Then he hallucinates that he and the gaunt trees are marching across a lake. There is no one to help him, the place "deserted except for one huge yellow monster . . . gorging itself on clay" (CS 356). By means of this new ending the story both begins and ends with a fantastic monster devouring earth, violating its sanctity and despoiling the earthly handiwork of God.

There is another story in which earth has suggestions of mystery and power though lurid and comical in O'Connor's management. It is "Greenleaf" in the character of Mrs. Greenleaf, the prayer-healer, who is of the earth, earthy. When Mrs. May first witnessed the ritual, the sound of Mrs. Greenleaf was so piercing "she felt as if some violent unleashed force had broken out of the ground and was charging toward her" (CS 316). After praying for Jesus to stab her in the heart, Mrs. Greenleaf "fell back flat in the dirt, a huge human mound, her legs and arms spread out as if she were trying to wrap them around the earth" (CS 317). The Greenleaf bull, Mrs. May's nemesis, is no less a creature of earth as he pawed the ground (CS 311) and ambled down the dirt road (CS 323). Mrs. May "felt the quake in the huge body as it sank, pulling her forward on its head" (CS 334).

The fourth element is fire, which I reserve for ultimate importance in O'Connor's scheme of the elemental. The torching of Mrs. Cope's property is the conclusion of "A Circle in the Fire" with its allusion to the three young prophets of the third chapter of the book of Daniel. The infidel Nebuchadnezzar spoke and said, "Blessed be the God of Shadrach, Meshach, and Abed-nego, who hath sent his angel . . . that they might not serve nor worship any god, except their own God" (Dan. 3:28). O'Connor's conclusion emphasizes "a few wild high shrieks of joy as if the prophets were dancing in the fiery furnace in the circle the angel had cleared for them" (CS 193). The burning bush seen by Moses in Exodus 3 as a theophany of fire is recalled in "Parker's Back" and is a major motivation for both Moses and Parker: "the tractor crashed upside down into the tree and burst into flame. The first things Parker saw were his shoes, quickly being eaten by the fire. . . . He could feel the hot breath of the burning tree on his face" (CS 520). Though not having found her house a burnt wound between two blackened chimneys (CS 502), the conclusion of "Revelation" is the mighty vision informed by fire of the swinging bridge reaching to heaven with echoes of Jacob's ladder of Genesis 28. Ruby saw the purple streak "as a vast swinging bridge extending upward from the earth through a field of living fire," and she could see by the shocked and altered faces of the virtuous that "even their virtues were being burned away" (*CS* 508).

Here are some generalizations that summarize O'Connor and theophany: (1) Her imagination is greatly informed and enriched by events, characters, themes—often theophanies—of the Old Testament. (2) The elements as deployed and portrayed by O'Connor—air, water, earth, fire—are anagoges more medieval than modern and exist finally in her fictions on the level of "the divine life and our participation in it" (*MM* 111). (3) Hers is a demanding spiritual exercise consisting more of awe than love, unless the latter be of the tough sort. Charity hardly enters her devotions or creations and compassion is a word alien to her vocabulary. (4) Beauty and sublimity reside in terror, fear, and trembling, effectively reversing the dictum of Milton's Satan that "terror be in love" (*Paradise Lost*, bk. 9, l. 490). For O'Connor the very heart of mystery lies in God's severe dealing with humankind, the frail microcosm, by means of the mighty elements of the universe, the feral macrocosm. It is the requisition of this verity that prompts the wit and rage between her teeth and from her pen.

Is there a problem of balance and proportion here, a kind of overkill? O'Connor's characters we know to be frail, fragile, diseased, soiled, mean, petty, trivial, and often silly. Her universe in theophanic fashion is feral, brutal, indifferent, vindictive, cruel, dirty, malevolent, often savage, and full of summer's flare and winter's flaw. Its murderous blast would have their bodies bowed, their eyeballs streaming. The poet who sings "the world is ugly and the people are sad" seems on target (Stevens 85). Does O'Connor break butterflies upon wheels? Does she like Pope set out perhaps gratuitously to "flap this bug with gilded wings, / This painted child of dirt that stinks and stings"? (Pope 336). Since all her human beings are children of dirt, "Now standing, now a-squat and never still / But always scratching with [their] dung-filled nails" like Dante's Thaïs (*Inferno*, canto 18, ll. 120–21), is the end product worth the dreadful pother of the elements that perform the flapping? Is tragic Lear worth the storm, a kind of pagan theophany? Can dust be turned into joy? Can O'Connor's maculate humanity ever rise and be borne along "by the love that moves the sun and all the stars" (*Paradiso,* canto 33, l. 148)? Apparently suffering by theophany was worth it for Ruby Turpin, since ordinary phenomena of macrocosm are transformed into the sonorous ecstasy of luminous theocosm: "In the woods around her the invisible cricket choruses had struck up, but what she heard were the voices of the souls climbing upward into the starry field and shouting hallelujah" (*CS* 509).

Works Cited

Burtchaell, J. T. "Theophany." In *New Catholic Encyclopedia,* prepared by an editorial staff at the Catholic University of America, 14:69. New York: McGraw-Hill, 1967–89.

Copleston, Frederick. *A History of Philosophy.* Vol. 2, *Mediaeval Philosophy: Augustine to Scotus.* Westminster, Md.: Newman Press, 1965.

Dante Alighieri. *Inferno.* Translated by Thomas G. Bergin. New York: Grossman Publishers, 1961.

Dante Alighieri. *Paradiso.* Translated by Thomas G. Bergin. New York: Grossman Publishers, 1961.

Encyclopedic Dictionary of Religion. Philadelphia: Sisters of St. Joseph of Philadelphia; Washington, D.C.: Corpus Publications, 1979.

Erigena, John Scotus. *Periphyseon: On the Division of Nature.* Translated by Myra L. Uhlfelder. Indianapolis: Bobbs Merrill. 1976.

Guroian, Vigen. "The Iconographic Fiction of Flannery O'Connor." *Intercollegiate Review* 36, nos. 1–2 (Fall 2000–Spring 2001): 46–55.

Joyce, James. *The Critical Writings of James Joyce.* Edited by Ellsworth Mason and Richard Ellman. New York: Viking Press, 1964.

Joyce, James. *Dubliners.* Edited by Robert Scholes and Walton Litz. New York: Viking Press, 1969.

Joyce, James. *The Workshop of Daedalus.* Edited by Robert Scholes and Richard M. Cain. Evanston, Ill.: Northwestern University Press, 1965.

Milton, John. *The Complete Poetical Works of John Milton.* Vol. 9, *Paradise Lost.* Edited by W. V. Moody. Student's Cambridge Edition. Boston: Houghton Mifflin, 1924.

Pope, Alexander. *Poetical Works.* Edited by Herbert Davis. New York: Oxford University Press, 1978.

Stevens, Wallace. "Gubbinal." In *The Collected Poems of Wallace Stevens,* 85. New York: Alfred Knopf, 1954.

Metaphoric Processes in Flannery O'Connor's Short Fiction

Karl-Heinz Westarp

All language is in the widest sense of the word metaphorical, because whatever signification a word contains has been "carried over" (the Greek word for that is *meta-phérein*) from one form of existence to another, a phenomenon in the real world—physical or mental—has become a linguistic phenomenon, which can be used for communication processes between humans. If the linguistic phenomenon is not precise, communication is made difficult or—in the extreme—impossible. Linguistic precision is therefore a *non-plus-ultra* for the artist who creates new worlds with words.

Metaphoricity works in two diametrically opposed ways in theology as well as in language and poetic creation: in the first, the direction of motion is from spiritual to physical reality; in the second, movement goes in the opposite direction in that the physical reality points, or becomes translucent, to an underlying spiritual reality. This means in the realm of theology that God's spirit is concretized in the creation, the Logos is "enfleshed" in Jesus, a process theologians—with reference to Paul's letter to the Philippians: "God ... emptied himself, ... being born in the likeness of men" (2:6–7)—call "descending Christology." Similarly, in language analysis the mental signifier/signified, according to Saussure, is concretized in the linguistic sign or the word; in poetry inspiration takes the form of a text. In theology metaphoricity in the opposite direction is found in Paul's letter to the Romans (God's "eternal power and deity, has been clearly perceived in the things that have been made" [1:20]); in the search for the divine in created nature, the "inscape of things" as Gerard Manley Hopkins called this search; and in the detection of Christ's divinity in the man Jesus, the "mediator" between God and man, who according to Philippians 2:9 was "exalted," what theologians call "ascending Christology," to bring the spirit of grace to mankind through word and deed. In language analysis, metaphoricity in the second direction means that a word "makes sense," has a meaning in the communicative process. Finally, in poetry it means that the text with its concrete words and images is pried open in the hermeneutic process to reveal its multilayered and polyvalent meanings; the concrete word becomes epiphanic, to use James Joyce's term, or as Flannery O'Connor formulated it: "The longer you look at one object [word], the more of the world you see in it" (*MM* 77).

To see these three areas of two-way metaphoricity with their many parallels as one was O'Connor's ambitious poetic project, as I hope to show. She was such a perfectionist in her attempts to find precise and concrete words and images, for only thus, she was convinced, could she shock her reader into new awareness about the meaning of life. As she wrote to Eileen Hall in 1956: "Art is not anything that goes on 'among' people, not the art of the novel anyway. It is something that one experiences alone and for the purpose of realizing in a fresh way, through the senses, the mystery of existence" (*CW* 988).

For O'Connor the artist, knowledge about the fundamental tenets of Christian faith was a necessity and a lived reality. The books in her library, her letters, and her book reviews amply prove the seriousness she brought to the study of Christian thought. Central is her interest in the Incarnation, and she called fiction "so very much an incarnational art" (*MM* 68). In 1955 she wrote to her friend Betty Hester, "One of the awful things about writing when you are a Christian is that for you the ultimate reality is the Incarnation, the present reality is the Incarnation, the whole reality is the Incarnation, and nobody believes in the Incarnation; that is, nobody in the audience. My audience are the people who think God is dead. At least these are the people I am conscious of writing for" (*CW* 943). Richard Giannone thinks that a "disincarnate faith" offended O'Connor (Gianonne 184). In a letter to Hester O'Connor mentions the church's emphasis on the body (*HB* 100), and in a letter to Cecil Dawkins she states that "the fact of the Word made flesh ... is the fulcrum that lifts my particular stories" (*HB* 227). Opposed to the Manichean separation of "spirit and matter" (*MM* 68), O'Connor held that God's creation was an enfleshing and thus a union of spirit in matter, which for her reached its peak in the Incarnation. Here O'Connor proves to be in keeping not only with the Bible but also with major theologians. Hebrews 11:3 reads, "By faith we understand that the world was created by the word of God, so that what is seen was made out of things which do not appear." This understanding of the Creation is also that of Thomas Aquinas, whose *Summa Theologiae* O'Connor "read for about twenty minutes every night" (*HB* 93), and according to whom God's Word is the origin of all created being: "the inner-Godly Word is the origin of all created being" (Krings 425, my translation).

In her review of Karl Barth's *Evangelical Theology*, O'Connor, in keeping with this understanding of the Creation, made his definition of theology her own: according to Barth theology "is science seeking the knowledge of the Word of God in God's work" (rpd. in Getz 203). This work is brought to completion in Jesus, "born in the likeness of men," in whom "God's active power embodied itself in a visible man" (Price 43). The Gospel according to John formulates this in its prologue: "And the Word became flesh and dwelt among us" (1:14). Karl Rahner, with whose theology O'Connor was familiar through her reading of his *Theology of Death* (*HB* 520), defines the incarnated Logos as "the highest form of God's self-communication," in which "God promises himself to the world" and where Christ "is not only a possible communicator of salvation ... but is Himself this irrevocable and historically manifested communication" and this is "the peak and the center of the divinization of the world" (Rahner 825, 839, my trans.). In these few words Rahner formulates what became known as descending Christology, or the *kenosis* (Phil. 2:7) of God's Word, which becomes an integral part of the world, and ascending Christology, the *hypsoma* (Phil. 2:9) or the exaltation of God's humble servant and with it the "deification" of the world through God's grace. "When spirit penetrates matter, the infinite *I AM* becomes the integer *IS* and transforms the world: 'The Word made flesh has returned to the world its full dimensions' (Asals 72)" (Archer 108). This is how Emily Archer and Frederick Asals formulate the incarnational process and its results, which characterize O'Connor's works. As I see it, O'Connor became through her life and work what Teilhard de Chardin had called for in the passage from *The Divine Milieu* that O'Connor had quoted in her review of the book: a Catholic who is "passionately vowed by conviction and not by convention to spreading the hopes of the Incarnation" (rpd. in Getz 162). The enfleshed "word of God is living and active" (Heb. 4:12) and "comes to be expressed in the word of the apostles" (Scheffczyk 1404, my trans.). The enfleshed Word becomes word again in the good tidings or the "gospel," or as in the title of Jean Levie's book, which O'Connor reviewed in 1963, *The Bible, Word of God in Words of Men*, which is why Augustine thought of the Incarnation as an "inverbation" (Scheffczyk 1406).

For O'Connor the sacraments were the most prominent incarnational signs of the power of God's sanctifying grace. In a sacrament physical signs—such as water in baptism—accompanied by words—"in the name of the Father and of the Son and of the Holy Spirit" (Matt. 28:19)—bring about the redemption of the person baptized. O'Connor is looking for similar "pregnant" signs in the concrete world in which the depth of ultimate reality can radiate. But she is aware that she writes for an audience who thinks God is dead and who does not believe in the Incarnation, so she has to define "something by defining what it is not" (Angle 160). Herein lies one of the reasons for O'Connor's often horrifyingly "grotesque" situations, her freaks, her modern metaphysical conceits. According to Emily Archer, O'Connor's is "a sacramental world," in which "groomed pigs, idiot children, and peacocks all have the capacity to 'pant with a secret life'" (Archer 101). "To see straight" (*HB* 131), to look at the concrete reality of the world "in order to find at its depths the image of its source, the image of ultimate reality" (*MM* 157) was quintessential for O'Connor's metaphorical understanding of the sacraments.

Irwin Howard Streight has called O'Connor's language "incarnational" (Streight 233), and Max Edelman Boren thinks that "if there is a key to understanding her writing, it is through the 'word made flesh'.... The Incarnation is used by O'Connor as a literary device for rendering profound significance; she finds the divine in material, physical language.... It is a material, fleshy language, deformed and mutating, that creates a 'texture of existence'" and "a unique text as deeply profound as it is concrete" (Boren 124, 126). For her any work as a writer had to start "where all human knowledge begins—with the senses" (*MM* 155). The senses transfer impressions of the concrete—"inspired"—world, to the human brain, where they are linked with words that, according to John Locke, are "sensible marks of ideas, and the ideas they stand for are their proper and immediate signification" (qtd. in Selden 108). Words must be concrete and precise, otherwise they cannot be "translucent, with shadowed depths beyond each word," as O'Connor formulated it in an interview (Betts 112). Critics have used a number of epithets to characterize O'Connor's prose. It is "pellucid, controlled, and unadventurous" for one (Bawer 320), while Melody Graulich calls it "concrete, earthy, ironic language, so unlike the ethereal, high-minded, abstract diction commonly associated with religious writers. Her language is O'Connor's strength.... Through distortion, indirection, 'gaps,' negations, and ambiguous language, O'Connor finds the way" (Graulich 83).

O'Connor saw herself in line with literary predecessors such as Eliot, who created "metaphors of displacement or estrangement that make way for the 'revelation' of a new world" (Kessler 20), or Joyce, who called "a sudden spiritual manifestation, whether in the vulgarity of speech or of gesture" an *epiphany* (Joyce 211), which in a typically paradoxical O'Connor formulation "may be a matter of recognizing the Holy Ghost in fiction by the way he chooses to conceal himself" (*HB* 130). She was also familiar with Gerard Manley Hopkins's concept of *inscape* (*HB* 517). According to Marion Montgomery, "from the witness of her letters, one sees that the whole world shines for her with that presence which Gerard Manley Hopkins pursues as the inscape of the particular, discrete creatures of this world" (Montgomery 459). It seems to me that Hopkins's inscape precisely covers the way in which O'Connor sees reality and uses words to describe it. In Hopkins's celebration of the sensuous, the concrete, the particular—his "instress of the inscapes," both of things and of words—all of these motifs converge. The concept that O'Connor herself uses for the translucency of her prose is *radiance*, which seems to combine Joyce's epiphany and Hopkins's inscape. In her essay "Catholic Novelists and Their Readers," she states that writers should pay "strict attention to the order, proportion, and radiance of what they are making" (*MM* 189). Radiance will only be obtained through the correct use of concrete language.

Two linguistically oriented scholars have drawn attention to two features in O'Connor's language that help us understand her metaphoricity. The French semiotician Michael Riffaterre has coined the sociolinguistic concept of the *hypogram*—literally "that which is written underneath"—which Irwin Howard Streight successfully applies to an analysis O'Connor's prose. Riffaterre calls his model "hypogrammatical because a deictic sign points to a latent text, to a hypogram underneath the text, ... and from this the text draws its significance" (Streight 13). In his article "A Good Hypogram Is Not Hard to Find," Streight exemplifies copiously how the concept of the hypogram can illuminate O'Connor's metaphoric language. "A hypogram is an absent presence; in a sacral sense, it allows for and effects the generative force of the Word upon the word. For O'Connor, who I contend uses language 'incarnationally,' the hypogram abides in the heaven of the 'added dimension'

(*MM* 150) that she spoke of as being manifest in her stories, from which the Word/word as Logos (meaning) has come down to the lexical and semantic terrain of the text": for example, "the animated sun is a signal for the O'Connor reader that some epiphanic encounter is about to take place" (Streight 233). The other linguistic feature is O'Connor's frequent use of the copula *as if*. Edward Kessler has drawn attention to its importance as an anagogical pointer in O'Connor's fiction. He adduces a number of examples where he sees a metaphoric duplicity in this feature. The particle "as," characteristic of the simile, expresses a similarity between tenor and vehicle, whereas the "as if" undermines this similarity. Kessler says that "metaphor as lie—the bringing together of two incongruous entities *as if* they were one— remains the poet's only means of pointing toward the true. . . . Simile can intensify our awareness of the given world, but it does not, like O'Connor's *as if*, yoke together unambiguous declarative sentences with metaphoric uncertainty" (Kessler 9, 21). "The *as if* offers imaginative access to the unknown, a bridge between veristic resemblances and the ultimate substance of all O'Connor's fiction: apocalyptic power, that which for convenience we call mystery" (Kessler 111). No matter which of the above approaches we use or which concept we apply in an attempt to come to grips with O'Connor's linguistic metaphoricity, all of them make it clear that she presents in her prose a surface reality characterized by precision of detail, which is enjoyable in itself because of its artistic perfection, but that this surface invites the reader to look beyond, to look for its roots.

Awareness of metaphoricity, of the metadiscourse enfleshed in the surface discourse of the text, is always present in O'Connor's view of the artist and art and in her way of performing and perfecting her art. For O'Connor the vocation of *artist* demanded full-time dedication, and she was cognizant of the artist's special obligation: "The writer is one who operates at a peculiar crossroads where time and place and eternity somehow meet. [The writer's] problem is to find that location" (*MM* 59). In this characterization it is already clear that O'Connor knew she had to be fully aware of the concrete life experiences that within themselves contain the radical dimension of otherness. She described herself as having "one of those food-chopper brains that nothing comes out of the way it went in" (*CW* 918), a formulation close to Coleridge's definition of the artistic imagination, which "dissolves, dissipates, in order to re-create" (qtd. in Selden 145). O'Connor was convinced that the artist had to be at one with the created world in order to be able to reveal the Creator behind it. She admonished herself, "The artist himself always has to remember that what he is rearranging *is* nature, and that he has to know it and be able to describe it accurately in order to have the authority to rearrange it all" (*MM* 98), which resembles Paul LaCroix's idea that nature is only a dictionary from which the artist creates his work. The constant awareness of the duplicity of purpose in writing was important for O'Connor: precision in the description of all aspects of nature and society, but always also stressing the fact that "the main purpose of the fiction writer is with mystery as it is incarnated in human life" (*MM* 176) together with the obligation never to overstep one's limits as an artist. "What-is is all [the writer] has to do with; the concrete is his medium; and he will realize eventually that fiction can transcend its limitations only by staying within them" (*MM* 146). O'Connor's multiple concerns as an artist are summed up by Marion Montgomery: she had to pay "strict attention to a multiple burden as artist, to the tedious labor of words and to the limitation of human understanding in the presence of mystery" (Montgomery 59).

For O'Connor the *artwork* was not only demanding for the writer. If she had enfleshed a vision properly, the experiencing of the work would call for a continuous exertion by the reader: "A story is good when you continue to see more and more in it, and when it continues to escape you. In fiction two and two is always more than four" (*MM* 10). What is true for the artist, that she needs to pay attention to precision and detail in experience and the expression thereof, is also true for the reader, who has to pay careful attention to all the details of the text, though he will never get to "the end." The reader must understand that "fiction must always be an incarnational art, and as such it must work completely by analogy, through outward signs of the inward" (Fickett 49).

In order to elevate art to its incarnational status, O'Connor knew that she had to pay careful attention to concrete sense impressions, to translate these into precise wording, and to use unfamiliar, often distorted images to lead the reader through manners to the experience of the depth dimension of mystery. She knew that fiction "operates through the senses. . . . No reader who doesn't actually experience, who isn't made to feel, the story is going to believe anything the fiction writer merely tells him" (*MM* 91). The "concrete details of life . . . make actual the mystery of our position on earth" (*MM* 68). "Whatever the novelist sees in the way of truth must first take on the form of his art and must become embodied in the concrete and human. . . . Every mystery that reaches the human mind . . . does so by way of the senses" (*MM* 175). "Weltanschauung," which according to Friedrich Schleiermacher, who coined this concept, means to "to see, to cognize the universe *in its sensuous detail*" (qtd. in Selden 199), started for O'Connor with sense impressions, and she considered that as being of special importance to the artist. When she spoke to young writers, she admonished them to start with the rendering of sense impressions and stay away from abstractions or mere telling. "The beginning of human knowledge is through the senses, and the fiction writer begins where human perception begins. He appeals through the senses, and you cannot appeal to the senses with abstractions. . . . [T]he world of the fiction writer is full of matter, and this is what the beginning fiction writers are very loath to create. They are concerned primarily with unfleshed ideas and emotions" (*MM* 67). She considered it a major part of her task as a novelist "to make everything, even an ultimate concern, as solid, as concrete, as specific as possible" (*MM* 155) and "to portray reality as it manifests itself in our concrete, sensual life" (*MM* 170).

For O'Connor art was necessarily realistic art, because "the artist penetrates the concrete world in order to find at its depths the image of its source, the image of ultimate reality" (*MM* 157). Throughout her career O'Connor was an ardent reader, always concerned with improving her art. She admired other authors for the perfection of their literary performances. About a scene in her friend Caroline Gordon Tate's short story "Summer Dust," she wrote to Betty Hester that Tate is "great on getting things there so concretely that they can't possibly escape—note how that horse goes through that gate, the sun on the neck and then on the girl's leg and then she turns and watches it slide off his rump. That is real masterly doing" (*HB* 187). She praised Katherine Anne Porter for her "ability to make things actual. [She] can create the sweating stinking life out of anything, the purely animal" (*HB* 481). O'Connor also admired Joseph Conrad, whose "aim as an artist was to render the highest possible justice to the visible universe." She added about her own art that for her "the visible universe is a reflection of the invisible universe" (*HB* 128). Andrea Hollander Budy, who admired O'Connor's "ability to envision, to locate her stories, detail by detail, and to deliver her characters *through* those details," comments that O'Connor was in a constant learning process to improve her work that "its language must be alert, its images fresh and honest, and its concise particulars, which may seem almost accidentally included, must deliver—with a chill of recognition—the enduring world" (Budy 70).

The sheer physicality of language was of paramount importance to O'Connor because language "should reinforce our sense of the supernatural by grounding it in concrete, observable reality" (*MM* 148). She was annoyed when critics reprehended her for her shockingly concrete pictures, which they thought to be "perverse." She defended herself, saying, "Isn't it arbitrary to call these images such as the cat-faced baby and the old woman that looked like a cedar fence post and the grandfather who went around with Jesus hidden in his head like a stinger—perverse? They are right, accurate, so why perverse?" (*HB* 470) She was convinced that in a world where the author has to shout to the deaf and draw startling pictures for those blind to depth perception she had to resort to unconventional and distorted images that "connect or combine or embody two points; one is a point in the concrete, and the other is a point not visible to the naked eye, but believed in by him firmly" (*MM* 42). In her desire to reach out to the reader and make him see, she chose extreme formulations, but she also used clichés in new ways. In line with Søren Kierkegaard, whose *Fear and Trembling* she had read (*HB* 273), O'Connor thought the seamy side of things would open up into an experience of the sublime, and she used distortion or depictions of the negative sides of human behavior as "the only way to make people see" (*CW* 932). In her search for concrete images for her stories, O'Connor did not shy away from the use of bloodshed and violence. She found "that violence is strangely capable of returning my characters to reality and preparing them to accept their moment of grace" (*MM* 112). "Grace, to the Catholic way of thinking, can and does use as its medium the imperfect, purely human, and even hypocritical" (*HB* 389). Criticism has by now come around to seeing O'Connor's use of violence no longer as "gratuitous . . . it is essential as a device to move the reader toward something else, something that could be seen as the embodiment of the story's mystery" (Whitt 11).

As a poet O'Connor had detected a kindred intelligence in Teilhard de Chardin. In her review of his book *The Phenomenon of Man*, she wrote, "His is a scientific expression of what the poet attempts to do: penetrate matter until spirit is revealed in it" (rpd. in Getz 180). It was her main goal as a fiction writer to present mystery "as it is incarnated in human life" (*MM* 176), in concrete situations, often taken from the horrors of real life. What the writer "sees on the surface will be of interest to him only as he can go through it into an experience of mystery itself. . . . Such a writer will be interested in what we don't understand rather than in what we do" (*MM* 41–42). O'Connor is here in accord with the insight of the Danish anatomist and geologist Niels Stensen (Nicolaus Steno, 1638–86): "Pulchra sunt quæ videuntur, pulchriora quæ sciuntur, longe pulcherrima, quæ ignorantur" (Beautiful is what we see, more beautiful what we know, by far the most beautiful what we do not know). O'Connor has given us a number of striking examples of characters, settings, and images, which are entirely plausible on a surface level and continue to be so, while they at the same time constantly grow in depth, which renders them unforgettable. A sign, according to Longinus, of true greatness in literature, which "gives abundant food for thought: it is irksome, nay, impossible, to resist its effect: the memory of it is stubborn and indelible" (qtd. in Selden 153).

Already in "The Geranium," her first published story, O'Connor presents us with striking images of isolated, uprooted metropolitan life with people boiling out of trains "like vegetables in soup" and with a "cracked flower pot" and a geranium with "its roots in the air" (*CW* 705, 712, 713). In O'Connor's first novel, Hazel Motes, isolated in Taulkinham, looking up saw that "the black sky was underpinned with long silver streaks that looked like scaffolding and depth upon depth behind it were thousands of stars that all seemed to be moving very slowly as if they were about some vast construction work that involved the whole order of the universe and would take all time to complete" (*CW* 19). His counterpart, Enoch Emery, in desperate need of human contact, finally finds refuge in the subhuman shape of a gorilla. Unforgettable are The Misfit, Mr. Shiftlet, Ruby, Nelson and Mr. Head, General Sash, Hulga Hopewell, and Mrs. Shortley, to mention just a few of the protagonists in O'Connor's first collection of short stories. In connection with them we are presented with response-provoking images: The "crooked cross" of Mr. Shiftlet, who in the end "with his stump sticking out the window . . . raced the galloping shower into

Mobile" (*CW* 173, 183). Nelson and Mr. Head face final failure of self-complacency in the figure of the "artificial nigger," as if "faced with some great mystery, some monument to another's victory that brought them together in their common defeat" (*CW* 230). Mrs. Freeman's facial expressions—"neutral," "forward and reverse" (*CW* 263)—are as descriptive of her character as is Hulga's wooden leg and the content of the Bible salesman's two Bibles. Mrs. Shortley, "the giant wife of the countryside" (*CW* 285), is not able "to see" until her moment of death, when "her eyes like blue-painted glass, seemed to contemplate for the first time the tremendous frontiers of her true country" (*CW* 305). Central in O'Connor's second novel is the battle between young Tarwater and Rayber with the imagery of baptismal water and Tarwater's burning hunger and thirst for the bread of life: "His hunger was so great that he could have eaten all the loaves and fishes after they were multiplied" (*CW* 478). Perhaps even more memorable and striking are some major characters of O'Connor's second collection of stories: Julian, Mrs. May, Mary Pitts and Mr. Fortune, Asbury, Rufus Johnson and Sheppard, Mrs. Turpin, and Parker and Sarah Ruth. They too come alive in the imagination by means of striking images that catch the reader's attention through their easily recognizable ordinariness but also keep him searching for deeper meanings. As in all metaphor, the known is used to hint at the unknown, the surface becomes translucent and reveals the underlying mystery.

Though O'Connor never wanted to overstep the boundaries of the artist out of deep respect for mystery, her constant attempt to create precision and by it depth or a "consubstantiality of all things under God" (Trowbridge 82) was motivated by her wish to disclose in her characters "the mystery that [she] saw residing in the concrete" (Baker 85) for the benefit of her readers. She believed that "man has fallen and that he is only perfectible by God's grace, not by his own unaided efforts" (*HB* 302). But she was also aware that "all human nature vigorously resists grace because grace changes us and the change is painful" (*CW* 1084). She wrote to Betty Hester, "Part of the difficulty of all this is that you write for an audience who doesn't know what grace is and don't recognize it when they see it. All my stories are about the action of grace on a character who is not very willing to support it, but most people think of these stories as hard, hopeless, brutal, etc." (*CW* 1067). But the characters are prepared for the moment of grace, O'Connor says, "by the intensity of the evil circumstances" (*CW* 1119). As Bruce Bawer sums up O'Connor's treatment of her characters: "O'Connor's barbs can sting. Yet her point is manifestly not to hold these characters up to ridicule, but rather to offer each of them as an example of a flawed and troubled human soul on its way to an epiphany" (Bawer 317) or "an awakening to all of reality as grace" (Kilcourse 37).

Approaches to O'Connor's work are legion, and there seems to be no end of friends and foes, who either love her work or hate it. It seems to me that my attempt to show the importance of metaphor in connection with her work provides a new way to approach her fiction, starting with a close reading of the linguistic surface, but then focusing on the different layers of metaphor also in her presentation of character, and finally leading to an understanding of postlapsarian man. Precision of expression being O'Connor's unrelentingly sought-for artistic goal, she was convinced that in achieving this she would open our eyes to the depth dimensions, the mystery, and the roots of our existence. Metaphor by definition bridges the gap between the known and the unknown; it can therefore be seen as *the* key to an ever-new fascination with O'Connor's work.

Works Cited

Angle, Kimberley Greene. "Flannery O'Connor's Literary Art: Spiritual Portraits in Negative Space." *Flannery O'Connor Bulletin* 23 (1994–95): 158–74.

Archer, Emily. "Naming in the Neighborhood of Being: O'Connor and Percy on Naming." *Studies in the Literary Imagination* 20, no. 2 (1987): 97–108.

Asals, Frederick. *Flannery O'Connor: The Imagination of Extremity*. Athens: University of Georgia Press, 1982.

Baker, J. Robert. "Flannery O'Connor's Four-Fold Method of Allegory." *Flannery O'Connor Bulletin* 21 (1992): 84–96.

Bawer, Bruce. "Under the Aspect of Eternity: The Fiction of Flannery O'Connor." In *The Aspect of Eternity*, 309–20. Saint Paul, Minn.: Greywolf Press, 1993.

Betts, Doris. "Talking to Flannery." In *Flannery O'Connor: In Celebration of Genius*, edited by Sarah Gordon, 109–15. Athens, Ga.: Hill Street Press, 2000.

Boren, Max Edelman. "Flannery O'Connor, Laughter and the Word Made Flesh." *Studies in American Fiction* 26, no 1 (1998): 115–28.

Budy, Andrea Hollander. "An Enduring Chill." In *Flannery O'Connor: In Celebration of Genius*, edited by Sarah Gordon, 67–70. Athens, Ga.: Hill Street Press, 2000.

Fickett, Harold, and Douglas R. Gilbert. *Flannery O'Connor: Images of Grace*. Grand Rapids, Mich.: Eerdmans, 1986.

Getz, Lorine M., ed. *Flannery O'Connor, Literary Theologian*. Lewiston, N.Y.: Mellen Press, 1999.

Giannone, Richard. "Warfare and Solitude: O'Connor's Prophet and the Word in the Desert." In *Flannery O'Connor and the Christian Mystery*, edited by John J. Murphy et al., 160–89. Provo, Utah: Brigham Young University Press, 1997.

Graulich, Melody. "'They Ain't Nothing but Words': Flannery O'Connor's *Wise Blood*." *Flannery O'Connor Bulletin* 7 (1978): 64–83.

Joyce, James. *Stephen Hero*. New York: New Directions, 1963.

Kessler, Edward. *Flannery O'Connor and the Language of Apocalypse*. Princeton, N.J.: Princeton University Press, 1986.

Kilcourse, George. "'Parker's Back': 'Not Totally Congenial' Icons of Christ." In *Flannery O'Connor and the Christian Mystery*, edited by John J. Murphy et al., 35–46. Provo, Utah: Brigham Young University Press, 1997.

Krings, H. "Wort, I." In *Handbuch Theologischer Grundbegriffe*, edited by Heinrich Fries, 4:406–17. Munich: DTV, 1970.

Montgomery, Marion. *Why Flannery O'Connor Stayed Home*. La Salle, Ill.: Sherwood Sugden, 1981.

Price, Reynolds. "The Gospel according to Saint John." In *Incarnation: Contemporary Writers on the New Testament*, edited by Alfred Corn, 38–72. New York: Viking, 1990.

Rahner, Karl. "Inkarnation." In *Sacramentum Mundi,* edited by Karl Rahner et al., 2:824–40. Freiburg: Herder, 1968,
Riffaterre, Michael. "Hermeneutic Models." *Poetry Today* 4, no. 1 (1983): 7–16.
Scheffczyk, Leo. "Wort Gottes." In *Sacramentum Mundi,* edited by Karl Rahner et al., 4:1402–13. Freiburg: Herder, 1968.
Selden, Raman, ed. *The Theory of Criticism.* London: Longman, 1988.
Streight, Irwin Howard. "A Good Hypogram Is Not Hard to Find." In *Flannery O'Connor and the Christian Mystery,* edited by John J. Murphy et al., 231–41. Provo, Utah: Brigham Young University Press, 1997.
Trowbridge, Clinton W. "The Comic Sense of Flannery O'Connor: Literalist of the Imagination." *Flannery O'Connor Bulletin* 12 (1983): 77–92.
Whitt, Margaret Earley. *Understanding Flannery O'Connor.* Columbia: University of South Carolina Press, 1997.

Fiction's Echo of Revelation

Flannery O'Connor's Challenge as Thomistic Maker

Marion Montgomery

Everybody who has read *Wise Blood* thinks I'm a hillbilly nihilist, whereas I would like to create the impression . . . that I'm a hillbilly Thomist.

Flannery O'Connor, Letter to Robie Macauley, May 18, 1955

Catholic or Protestant, [the believing writer] is equally unhappy. He feels like Lancelot in search of the Holy Grail who finds himself at the end of his quest at a Tupperware party.

Walker Percy, "How to be an American Novelist in Spite of Being Southern and Catholic"

It is with something of his playful indirection that I chose the epigraph from Walker Percy to begin this revisiting of Flannery O'Connor in her home country. Both Percy and O'Connor share a sense of being challenged as writers because both are southern and Catholic at a point in cultural history when to be either is likely to be suspect, requiring of them as novelists an indirection in respect to their beliefs in their fictions. It is an indirection always appropriate to the making of fiction according to the necessities of art, even of pagan art when it is good in itself as art. But it is as well a strategy suited to them as poets who find themselves residents in an unbelieving world. Neither is reluctant to be direct about his or her belief as a Christian, of course. As for their sharing a double jeopardy in being both southern and Catholic, however, they differ in an important circumstance to their journeying the unbelieving world, each as *homo viator*—as persons on their separate but companionable ways. Unlike Percy, Flannery O'Connor seems to have faced this challenging double jeopardy to her gifts as a possible writer from about the time she was baptized in infancy. Percy, on the other hand, had to work hard to discover the difficulties. He is, by comparison, late in coming to terms with his "southerness," as he is also late in his conversion to the Roman Church.

We may discover yet another difference. Though both recognize the common jeopardy to them as fiction writers, Percy's term "unhappy" hardly seems apt of Flannery O'Connor. Given Percy's playful wit when he was in social circumstances —lectures and the like, especially when before the variety of audiences as may be remembered by many of us—it may seem something of a surprise that he would think of himself as unhappy. It is not likely that his audience at the University of Southwestern Louisiana, where he said this, would have put much weight on the word *unhappy*, so delightfully playful their guest, though deeply serious in his argument for that occasion. We discover by asides and private remarks from time to time that nevertheless he would rather be at home in Covington, even though, as on this occasion, he is speaking to an audience largely southern, though not also largely Catholic. He proves genial and mannerly, whether in Louisiana or New York or Illinois, perhaps especially so to audiences outside the South, who are at times largely Catholic but on other occasions are neither southern nor Catholic. This is enough to make him long for Covington.

Percy is almost always mannerly, even if on occasion not necessarily genial. With Flannery O'Connor it seems most often otherwise. In similar public appearances, she is likely to be reserved, cautious—even timid. Until some silly question is put to her, at which time she may respond in a most prickly manner. But she knows the virtues of manners, remarking famously that bad manners are better than no manners at all. Speaking at a Southern Writers' Conference at my own university, and to would-be writers for the most part, she was very blunt in warning: "I have a very high opinion of the art of fiction and a very low opinion of what is called the 'average' reader," of whom she encountered many along her way. One suspects she may also here mean average writers who are romantically engaging a dream of becoming writers, a calling she sees as a spiritual and intellectual labor most demanding of personal risk. As that conference dragged on with its "workshops" (as I remember it), she excused herself. She had to get back to Andalusia before dark to feed the chickens, she said.

I think it true enough to suggest that while Percy was more social when necessity required it of him, he was as a person nevertheless in degree more unhappy than she, public manners sometimes suggesting the contrary. Flannery O'Connor is seemingly reserved and cautious in any country other than perhaps that abutting Andalusia, her mother's farm in central Georgia. Sometimes not even a comfortable presence there was possible. There was an increasing stream of random visitors awash on the premises. She was given to a comic wit Percy appreciated, at home or away—used sometimes as a manner of self-protection, though on occasion turned into incisive judgment. She did not always suffer fools gladly, even on her front porch. Her wit may be caustically tempered to sharpness then, as when she responds to a correspondent from a university asking her searching questions about one of her stories. She responds shortly about his academic manner of treating a story like "a frog in a bottle." It was not always easy for her to be charitable, though she knew herself obligated to be so. Let us say she was especially tried by naive responses to her work, but most especially so when such naiveté came across to her as sophisticated nonsense—that is, as it may be disguised in academic clothing. Most especially caustic at times when it came across at her on the front porch at Andalusia, borne at her by an unexpected stranger. Not that she could not be somewhat gentle with the spiritually naive. But gentleness was sometimes trying for her.

There is an anecdote concerning what we might take as her attempt to be generous-spirited to an old naive friend. The friend had come home from Greenwich Village, way up there in New York City, all excited by what she had seen and heard and done. Thus enlightened, she was home for a visit and came out to Andalusia to share her adventures with Flannery, whom she supposed entrapped by the provincial South. Calling on her old acquaintance and friend out at the farm, the two of them talked and rocked on the front porch, the friend recounting high adventure among poets and artists. The visitor at last fell silent for a spell, the two of them still rocking. Then, looking out over the pines and pastures, peacocks and chickens pecking about the yard—perhaps even seeing the jackass O'Connor had bought for her mother as a Mother's Day present—she exclaimed, "Oh, Flannery! If only I could take you out of all this!" And Flannery rocked a minute before responding in her nasal voice, "Out of all *what*?"

There is another story, shared by a mutual friend and complementary of this challenging visitation upon Flannery by a friend—New York imported to central Georgia. This mutual friend arrived by bus from southern Georgia for a visit. She was let out at the dirt road leading up to Andalusia only to find Flannery meeting her half way down the road, hobbling on her crutches, to share an encounter of an act of country charity the day before. She could not wait to share it. A man, visiting Miss Regina, Flannery's mother, on farm business, was walking and talking with Mrs. O'Connor when he realized that Flannery was trailing along behind them on her crutches. The visitor felt obligated to include her, poor cripple that she was. He stopped, reached down at his feet, and caught up one of Flannery's chickens. Then he threw it high up in the air, and the chicken, squawking and fluttering, managed to land safely a few yards away. Turning to Flannery like a considerate uncle, he said, "It don't take much to give a chicken a good time." Charity toward small things like a chicken, shared charitably with a hobbling girl—to impress her mother no doubt. A mother, incidentally, who was a rich burden to Flannery as writer, though Flannery recognized herself as well to be a burden on her mother's patience. It is not easy to run an orderly farm with a poet-daughter hobbling along, attuned like Dante on his pilgrimage to collect incidents and phrases to consequential comic dramas of fallen man. It could not have been easy for Regina to accommodate to Flannery, an indirect acknowledgment of which perhaps is in that story, "The Enduring Chill," in which Asbury is a deliberate irritant to his mother, who loves him anyway. Flannery, of course, recognized depths more remote than the comic surface in such encounter, concerned as she was with her obligation to her calling as a "prophet of distances." Something more profoundly afoot than might be recognized by someone treating one of her stories like a "frog in a bottle" or sealed safely in a piece of academic Tupperware, the research paper container professionally sterilized for a journal.

It is nevertheless impossible to escape the Tupperware party, she discovered, even on her own front porch at Andalusia. But that too was a lesson Flannery seems to have been born knowing: in Greenwich Village or in Milledgeville or even out at the farm, human nature fallen is human nature, whatever its spectacle of color. As she became more and more known for her fictions, the challenge of intrusion became exacerbated, though it also proved rich provender, amenable matter, to the making of fictions, as any clever Dante discovers. Whenever and wherever, she knew very well she could not escape those who see the world with *provincial* eyes, *provincial* being a concept understood quite differently by Flannery O'Connor on her front porch than by many of her visitors—whether a stranger from parts unknown like Mr. Shiftlet or an old acquaintance returned from the big city bearing imported light. Especially, she suspected, someone venturing South from a northern place or a southern venturer to the North now come home with tales of a fabulous Greenwich Village, a more romantic place than allowable in central Georgia at Andalusia. And O'Connor would know an essay on provincialism by an old acquaintance, Allen Tate. Provincialism, Tate says in it, is an attitude that "is limited in time but not in space." It is "a state of mind in which regional men lose their origin in the past and its continuity into the present, and begin every day as if there had been no yesterday" (Tate 542). Northerner or southerner—either may prove to be provincial.

For both Tate and O'Connor, no solution is whole that does not embrace the material and legal order within a spiritual vision. *Programs* and *rulings* in the name of the *common good* are but temporary—temporal—solutions always in decay, requiring an acknowledgment of the spiritual dimension to any viable hope for the common good. Otherwise provincialism obtains. Such provincialism is to be seen, Tate says, in contrast to "the classical-Christian world, based upon regional consciousness, which held that honor, truth, imagination, human dignity, and limited acquisitiveness, could alone justify a social order, however rich and efficient it may be. We have become largely provincials," Tate adds, and so we "do not live anywhere," having committed ourselves "to seeing *with*, not *through*, the eye" (Tate 546). That O'Connor recognizes what Tate calls *provincialism* as the modernist mode of deportment to creation is indicated in her address to a sometimes popular condition of mind much celebrated in fiction and poetry in her day. Hers was the century that seemed almost to pride itself as the "Age of Alienation." Of that malady of spirit, embraced as if a virtue of mind, O'Connor says in "The Catholic Novelist in the Protestant South": "Alienation was once a diagnosis, but in much of the fiction of our time it has become an ideal. The modern hero is an outsider. His experience is rootless. He can go anywhere. He belongs nowhere. Being alien to nothing, he ends up being alienated from any kind of community based on common tastes and interests. The borders of his country are the sides of his skull" (*MM* 199). Such is the dead end waiting the provincial, the modernist, spirit.

Tate's words were written at the end of World War II, just before he entered the church in which Flannery O'Connor was at home from her cradle. (Anyone who has raised children knows what an ambiguous phrase—this *at home*—proves to be, churched or not.) It was the Maritains who sponsored him. And it had been Jacques Maritain, long before, who had written a small book summoning Western artists to the virtues of Thomism in recovering a proper deportment to their making. Maritain's *Art and Scholasticism,* the second edition of it, coincided in 1927 with the appearance of T. S. Eliot's "Ash-Wednesday." And already by the 1920s, Tate and Eliot had become friends. Caroline Gordon, Tate's wife and a close friend of the Maritains, was later to become an insistent mentor to Flannery O'Connor—whether Flannery wanted or not. There occurred, this is to say, a continuity in some Western letters of the Thomistic aesthetics signaled by Maritain's little book. That book became a touchstone to a small but vital diaspora of artists. It was centrally important to Eric Gill, who published its first English edition as *The Philosophy of Art* at Ditchling in 1923, the year after Eliot's *Waste Land*. It was important to David Jones, whose *Anathemata* (1952) has yet to be recognized as the considerable poem it is, rivaling at least Pound's *Cantos*. Maritain's small book was important to G. K. Chesterton and that circle remembered as the Distributists and to some of the Fugitive-Agrarians, partly through T. S. Eliot. It was important to Eliot, who translated and published in his *Criterion* some of Maritain's work. And of course, it was important to Walker Percy and Flannery O'Connor as representative of that strange phenomenon: southern Catholic writers of fiction.

Maritain's *Art and Scholasticism* was of special importance to Flannery O'Connor, coming to her with recommendation from several respected quarters. Out of it, and from Saint Thomas Aquinas's own words, which she read almost nightly, she came to understand as poet the importance of the local to her art, but more importantly she had confirmed her own intuitive recognition of the importance of seeing *through* the eye, rather than *with* it, as if making the eye merely an instrument of intentionality in service to the art of making. That is, to see through the eye is to surrender in communion with the thing seen. She, unlike Eliot at her age, could never have thought of "myth," for instance, as "simply a way of controlling, of ordering" art, as Eliot says concerning Joyce's use of myth in *Ulysses* (Eliot 177). For her, the eye is not an instrument to be used as a technological convenience evolved by accident in the flesh, serving the intellect as if detached from personal communion with reality here and now through the flesh. In that distortion and in the interest of intellect detaching itself from reality to serve art, one thus chooses "not to live anywhere." The choice will then become to flit along the surface of creation, being careful not to become entangled in any place. The mere spectacle of reality becomes sufficient unto the moment of the self-awareness of the artist, who thus mistakes himself as primary over his obligation to the good of the thing he makes, his story or poem.

If the particularities of things speak more than spectacle, we are unavoidably in the presence of a mystery about *being* itself. And a prudential deportment in the presence of a mystery unresolved requires a responsible deportment to things in response to their recognizable particularities. *This* thing is not simply *a* thing in a reductionism to a generalized concept, become abstract formulation through our intellectual deportment. It is *this thing in itself.* Prudence responds properly to a dignity inherent to it because it exists as the thing it is. Our manner of deportment may lack reason's formulations, such as this one of mine here underway, but we recognize intuitively a responsibility to the dignity of the thing though willfulness may reject that responsibility. By the very rejection, we nevertheless affirm the dignity inherent to the existing thing. This is the moment of intellectual response out of which grows the history of philosophy itself as so variously manifest in what Yeats called "monuments of unaging intellect." Not only the Thomism, which is our—and O'Connor's—concern, but the philosophy of Socrates' nemesis, the Sophists, or the Stoics, or the positivistic materialist of our age, and on and on.

As for the maker of stories, this point of departure in a manner of response to recognized existences here and now is crucial to the relation of *action* to *spectacle* as addressed by art. And so for the artist, *manner* of response to a *thing* as actual, whatever the thing responded to, becomes *matter* to his making. It becomes centrally important to art in a making with signs, with words, as O'Connor is very much aware. There is a phrase of hers made into a celebrated title to her speculations on this matter, her *Mystery and Manners.* It is most apt as a title, given the nature of her reflections. She sees that since *human nature* in action, revealed through spectacle and articulated by signs, is the matter proper to drama, this action becomes the theme in the matrix of O'Connor's speculation about the mystery spoken by things in themselves to her opened eyes and ears. It is through *manners* that as *persons* we respond to *things,* and that is the essence of drama. (On this point, Aquinas reminds us that art is not an imitation of nature per se but an imitation of the action of nature—an important distinction in that it relates art to the possible or probable rather than to the actual, which is the province of history as opposed to art.) That response is always made in *a* place and at *a* time, always *here* and *now,* though it will in a next moment be remembered as *then* and *there.* Art is of necessity local. Manners, meaning the *manner* of a person toward things known here and now, will prove larger by implication than merely a matter of history's accidents, a matter of mere spectacle remembered. This is to suggest that manners are larger than, though conspicuous at, the level of spectacle, for the *ground* of spectacle itself as encountered in things here and now is larger than the mere history of things as known and remembered. (That is why William Butler Yeats's comfort in "monuments of unaging intellect" proves at last inadequate, his confidence in art's rescue of the artist through such monuments being a very ancient romantic illusion.)

We conclude that manners speak a communal deportment defined by spectacle in the cultural matrix of this place at which we stand within this place's "history." But it is *manner* in respect to the particular person so standing that is central—his manner in response to things existing now, though also to be remembered as existing *then* (that is, as "history"), whether the *then* be but yesterday or centuries ago. For the things to which we respond exist always anterior to our response. Manners, this is to say, have to do with tradition and the responsibility of *this* person here and now to the sorting of his tradition *as measured by the truth of things known*. That is a lesson O'Connor takes from Thomas Aquinas, leading her to declare that so important are manners for her, that bad manners are better than no manners at all. That recognition leads her to the virtue of a prudential humility, not often understood by those who are intellectually imprudent and so likely to set humility itself aside.

Of course, we usually think of manners as merely common gestures made within a community out of convenience—as if but traffic signs to avoid social accidents—or as evolved by a particular community through a common consent over time, the consent now become mere habit—vestigial like our appendix. Among "southern" manners one still celebrated pretty much in this understanding of manners is that of hospitality. But hospitality, for O'Connor and many others, is more anciently viable than presently, as if but a residual presence to a geographical location, history's detritus. Out of a piety of manner toward things in themselves, we anciently supposed we might be entertaining gods or angels unaware. That is a tradition to which O'Connor is attuned, particularly suited as a dramatic matter still available to her, though perhaps only residually present in a dwindling remnant—in "southern" culture, that is, whatever the geographical coordinates. But there is a lingering implication whereby even in bad manners—and perhaps evident elsewhere, even in Atlanta or New York—there is reflected still the history of manner, to be recovered and made acceptable by a community in a place.

We are speaking here, then, of *tradition,* of some version of tradition accepted knowingly or unknowingly and reflected willy-nilly in our manners good or bad. Manners, or their absence, are spawned by intellect out of, or supported by, each person's deportment toward things. And it is notable that our *manner* revealed in our *manners* is evident through signs, received from *a* person, whether signs approving of or rejecting things, including ourselves. By consent through such signs, there may be recognized a community of which *this* person is *member,* however much fallen. The manner may indeed be seen in manners toward things that are not persons. That is a deportment of the person that we may not ordinarily recognize as requiring or implying a *communal* deportment. As Flannery O'Connor is writing her fiction, there is a very popular distinction being made in respect to manner. It comes from Martin Buber, who distinguishes between a manner of communion with things and with people, not an "I-it" but an "I-Thou" communion. And this distinction is in O'Connor's repeated concern for our having separated grace from nature as a gambit in the conquest of nature itself, especially of human nature.

It is indeed a difference we emphasize in O'Connor's fiction. Recall her grandmother in "A Good Man Is Hard to Find," who at the story's close responds in an act of love, a gesture of manner deeper than manners, made *toward* another, in a vulnerable openness hardly usual to her and so surprising. But on careful reflection, we discover it is not really out of character. The gesture is toward The Misfit and accompanied by her exclamation: "Why you're one of my babies. You're one of my own children!" (*CS* 132). It is at once a confession and an expression of love delayed, as we reflect on it within the story's context under our rubrics of *manner* and *manners*. There has been a comical foretelling of this resolving communal gesture, foreshadowing the dire consequences to the grandmother, in a preliminary eruption anticipating her death. The grandmother has smuggled her cat, Pitty Sing, along on this expedition, carefully guarded against detection as a stowaway. One might import here Flannery's own attitude toward cats, she a "bird person," as it might be popularly put, though this biographical point is not necessary given the long history of the cat's association with the occult and its dark practices. When we see Pitty Sing rubbing against The Misfit at the story's end, taken up and cuddled by him, we might suspect here an agent of the devil, cozening even The Misfit. There seems a bind implied from the beginning between the Grandmother and her cat, the Grandmother naive in her deracinated spiritual manner, superficial in her concern for place in relation to orientation in history and nature. She "misses" the comfort of tradition, to which the rest of her family prove not only indifferent but increasingly hostile. A certain irony perhaps attaches then to the Grandmother's attachment to Pitty Sing, as if a bonding impossible to her with her natural and civil family, with her son and his wife and her three grandchildren, all seeming to her foreign to her own desires for some recovery of the comfort of place, though as distant as "east Tennessee."

From the outset we recognize a family in which manner hardly speaks manners, a gathering of misfits one to the other. The grandmother has led the expedition astray in pursuit of a "tradition" that she dreams might be restorative of dignity, first, to herself and, perhaps, to this chaotic family, a tradition long neglected. She is innocent of place, and so they look in the wrong place. Realizing her error, she upsets the valise hiding Pitty Sing. And the cat, snarling and displaced, sinks claws into Bailey's shoulders—Bailey is the driver—causing the wreck. Such are the circumstances, the dramatic context. We may wonder, after the story's end, whether there is a communal relation of the grandmother to the cat, if the cat might enable her to some love hardly evident among these people as confined by a "natural" history as family. Their manners are used to the convenience of selfish isolation, all with their own agendas for this "vacation" as opposed to a "retreat." Alienation is writ small in this family, though large in its suggestiveness as it speaks to an absence of love. There is that small saving gesture of Bailey's wife, protecting the baby as they wreck, but it seems only a fleeting spectacle in the story. Having read the story, we are not likely to be moved by pity for those here slaughtered, except by sentimentality for the infant perhaps. We are especially not moved for those nasty brats—the one named for a Hollywood star and the other for an evangelist to the Georgia colony: June Star and John Wesley. Their collective unmannerliness at least tempts us to an indifference to their fates. Such a response on our part may say something of our own manner toward creation, as again O'Connor is sufficiently aware as the story's maker. She knows her audience well, and sometimes "plays the devil" with it, as we say in Georgia.

Manner is revealed through manners. But most tellingly revealed in manners, one person to another, as in the resolution effected through The Misfit and the grandmother. For though manners imply community consent in *common,* governing the deportment of a person within community at large as signifying participation in a body, it is in the actions of one person to another that manners may be regarded as good or bad at last. One might explore this point at length in O'Connor's dramatic uses of *manners* in story after story. Remember that contest of manners, under the pressures of manipulative chicanery, between Mr. Shiftlet and Mrs. Lucynell Crater in "The Life You Save May Be Your Own." Good or bad manners, either may prove adaptable when a subversion is underway. Mr. Shiftlet displays a piety of manners, with an intent to deceive, against another person, Mrs. Crater, who proves more wily than he does.

Whatever the dramatic deployment of manners in relation to her drama, O'Connor does not lose sight of an important aspect of reality: manners distorted by intent nevertheless speak an acknowledgment of the actuality of the person against whom manners are being deployed. That actuality speaks a context of this present and defines a local arena in which human nature displays itself. It is out of this recognition that O'Connor attempts on one occasion to reassure a contemporary southern writer who has become uncomfortable with her own "southerness." She writes Cecil Dawkins, implying a truth about Dawkins's Alabama by indirection. No place can be all bad in its persons, and certainly not as a place. For herself, speaking of her middle Georgia place at Andalusia, she says, "It is great to be at home in a region, even this one." It is a "home" currently much maligned by a cultural condescension from Atlanta and New York folk, she knows. But after all, everybody has to be somewhere, and no place is ever an Eden recovered to the wandering person by manners good or bad. How ironic to the ears of O'Connor, then, that advertising slogan that Atlanta is a city "too busy to hate."

As for that condescension of one "culture" to another, of Atlanta or New York to rural Georgia out of sensibilities supposed the more refined, O'Connor evens the score somewhat in making Atlanta her Taulkinham in *Wise Blood*. Hazel Motes in that novel, in pressing bad manners to the level of blasphemy, discovers that one can not blaspheme what does not exist, so that his very attempt at impious rejection becomes a proof of the existence of that which he attempted to deny as existing at all, in her words, that "ragged figure" of Christ in the back of his mind. That discovery leaves his new-founded "Church without Christ" a shambles. He has attempted a blasphemous forcing of his intent by reducing the local to random insignificance, but that is not possible even when that local is the corrupted City of Man (Taulkinham), as both Flannery and Saint Augustine might name it. There is something inherent in the local that bites Haze at the nexus of intellect and will in the arena of dramatic action, which is consciousness. That action calls attention to the spiritual implications of the local, even those to be experienced in a Taulkinham née Atlanta, toward which community Haze conducts himself with intellectual condescension.

Not O'Connor, but Motes is that "hillbilly nihilist" she finds herself charged with being. As for her, believing as she does in the inclusive actuality of natural grace, she believes as well in the actuality of the devil as an implicit agent encouraging intellectual man to a nihilistic rejection of the good that is evident in the actual. And whatever is *actual, is* and therefore is *good,* Thomas Aquinas reminds us. She dramatizes the contention of good and evil as joined by Haze's will, within the arena of Haze's soul. In her prefatory note to the 1962 reissue of the novel, she reminds us that "for the author Hazel's integrity lies in his not being able to . . . get rid of the ragged figure who moves from tree to tree in the back of his mind" (*MM* 115). She realizes, observing the reception of *Wise Blood* on its first appearance, that the challenges to her are great, given the disparity between her vision and the spectacle with which her skeptical audience is content, the audience who are largely ignorant of the possibilities of grace. For her, grace is always in contention with the devil within the arena of conscious intellect itself. That is the arena of the *signified,* the dramatic action toward which spectacle itself points, as Aristotle noted. Spectacle derived from context is required to mediate this intellectual action of a character between poet and audience—often the spectacle of violence and often, as she knew, mistaken for the significant action of the intellectual soul. We are not simply intellectual soul, as Plato and Socrates would have it, but intellectual soul *incarnate,* to be perfected in a simple unity as *person,* which means the necessity of orderly accommodation of spectacle. If Plato inclines to reject creation as a drag upon the spirit away from its possible perfection, especially evidenced by our body, Saint Thomas Aquinas argues the body itself is the special medium, a gift in our nature through which grace proves operative upon the intellectual soul through the senses. It is the senses that allow the person a bonding in the local with all creation. The rejection of that bonding is a denial of stewardship. Thus Adam fell, bequeathing a complicating violence—and that violence may either rescue or damn us consequent to Adam's fall, as Flannery's second novel announces in its title, *The Violent Bear It Away*—"It" being the Kingdom of Heaven in the biblical text from Matthew.

In her prefatory note to the reissue of that first novel, *Wise Blood*, she will affirm with confidence her own conviction of the reality of grace to nature, so that nature itself proves mediator, through our senses, to the uncertain will, raising in will a concern for prospects of its rescue to the truth of things. Hers is a vision largely rejected by our world, the world in which she finds herself. Still she affirms her vision, as shocking as it may be to modernist sensibilities: "Free will does not mean one will," she says, "but many wills conflicting in one man. Freedom cannot be conceived simply. It is a mystery and one which a novel, even a comic novel, can only be asked to deepen" (*MM* 115). It is within the limited consciousness of *this* person as an actual intellectual soul incarnate that this dramatic tension of will occurs, the will responding to the devil, on the one hand, and yet sustained by grace, on the other. In this respect for the action of drama, she as maker is Aristotelian, though hers is that Aristotle baptized by Saint Thomas, as it is sometimes said. *Spectacle*, Aristotle argues in his *Poetics*, must be distinguished from *action*, though it is through spectacle engaged by the means of our sensual nature that we may come to recognize action as an immaterial reality, the movement of the will immeasurable by any physics or biology. Action is spoken necessarily by indirection, then: through masks, through the dance, through all the intellectual "play" rising out of human nature to the level of spectacle through intellect as summoning instrument. Intellect is itself an immaterial reality, spoken as a reality by that indirection called spectacle through the body, acknowledged or denied through manners signaling manner. For Flannery O'Connor as dramatist, this proves a challenge that she must address long after that parenthesis of Western intellectual culture bracketed between Sophocles and Dante, that inheritance still spoken of as a "Classical Culture" once informing community. For that is a tradition long since rejected at the time she comes to write.

Art, through the time of Dante, was largely and more commonly understood in relation to this distinction between spectacle and action. O'Connor, however, must attempt to recover to her art some persuasive common ground suited to her dramatic intentions in order to reveal unexpected spiritual action through spectacle as commonly taken. The concrete local—that which is immediate to the senses—has meanwhile been distorted through the cultural circumstances of community through the separation of grace from nature. Community is itself disrupted from the reality of existential reality as actual in itself, as a communion of persons as a body. The challenge is that she must nevertheless use those cultural circumstances gone awry, the dislocation made evident through spectacle—a spectacle that suggests existence is randomly chaotic, whether made nominally collective as "nature" or "person" or "community." She must work toward a recovery of spiritual action as the most significant responsibility to the person who exists here and now in community and in nature at large. What she knows to be missing is any common understanding of the meaning of the cultural circumstances in relation to a vision that may be held more or less in common. The formal understanding possible in relation to myth, for instance, that held common between Sophocles and his audience, gave Sophocles a purchase in revealing action through stylized spectacle. But that common point of departure for art, binding poet and audience, no longer exists.

O'Connor's response to this initial challenge lies in a comic enlargement, given that comic or tragic masks no longer signify any common intellectual consent of an audience to a dramatist. Nor could she, as could Dante, depend upon allegorical complexities of signs to structure a story. O'Connor recognized such a modern allegorical attempt as failing by degree in her favorite American writer, Hawthorne. She favors Hawthorne in that she shares with him a belief that man is fallen and that man by his fallen nature inclines to sinfulness. (I have explored this theme at length in my *Why Hawthorne Was Melancholy.*) She, as a Catholic novelist, "believes that you destroy your freedom by sin," but she also knows that "the modern reader believes ... that you gain it that way" (*MM* 117). How then make believable a gesture or action by a character that reveals his willful action as that of a self-diminution, though "read" as if its opposite, as if self-reduction were the means to absolute freedom? It must be, she says, signaled (signed) by an art in a gesture or action "which is totally right and totally unexpected" in the character (*MM* 111). It must be at once "in character and beyond character," so that it may speak at an analogical level of a spiritual reality beyond any formal allegorical structuring of a story (*MM* 111). To accomplish this is "to suggest both the world and eternity," that level at which occur both "the Divine life and our participation in it" (*MM* 111). That is why she sees the concept of epiphany in relation to her fiction as quite other than as understood by James Joyce, a difference we shall presently explore under the auspices of Saint Thomas Aquinas.

It is to this end that she would be, as prophetic poet, a "realist of distances," though that is an office usually unnoticed or aggressively rejected by her audience (*MM* 44). That means for her the necessity of a realism more profoundly persuasive than the mere naturalism that is ordinarily understood as defining the usual country of the serious novelist. For her the very real spiritual country has been distorted by dogmatic naturalism, making art itself a documentation of a provincialism certified as psychological realism. By that certification, art becomes a prohibitive boundary excluding any passport to the transcendent. And so hers must be a strategy as maker through which she may overcome the reader's own provincial spirit as it flits randomly on the surface of spectacle in a deportment of intellect that allows the person to mistake spectacle as the only significant arena to "realistic" action. How telling then a coincidence of violence, both at the level of spectacle and at the level of Mercy's terror, when Tarwater at once drowns and baptizes Bishop. How puzzling to her audience.

We need only to this point recall the constant use of, and so decay of, the term *tragedy* as we hear it announcing random automobile wrecks on the highway, made the more "newsworthy" when there is a "pile-up." In "The Nature and Aim of Fiction," she attempts some recovery of a degree of common ground more than that of spectacle, of random "pile-ups." First is the necessity to recover the local as a point of departure in recovering viable community. She says that the "longer you look at one object, the more of the world you see in it; and it's well to remember that the serious fiction writer always writes about the whole world, no matter how limited his particular scene" (*MM* 77). We may thus come to remember that, in recovering the gift to our nature of seeing with, not through, the eye, we may yet come to seeing with our intellect as well. We may, this is to say, have moved somewhat toward a recovery of integrity as person, no longer more or less divided like Gaul into intellect, soul, and body. In this respect, Saint Thomas Aquinas argues intellect must be *informed* by the truth of things experienced, his *informed* bearing a literal meaning. His argument suggests a deeper mystery to our experience than the level of the spectacle of things might leave us to conclude. And so, in "The Fiction Writer and His Country," she enlarges: "To know oneself is to know one's region. It is also to know the world, and it is also, paradoxically, a form of exile from that world" (*MM* 35). How different a *person* is from an *object*, when the person as an integrity is recognized as intellectual soul incarnate. For, though a book cannot be at once on the table and off the table, in O'Connor's vision of him, a person may well discover himself in two places at once: in the immediate here and now of *this* place as citizen of nature and local community but also beyond it, in a "country" discovered at last, as permeating this very here and now. That is the abiding mystery within reality whereby grace and nature cohabit, so to speak, though modernist man has labored at that disjunction of grace from nature.

If she finds this truth about human nature explicated rationally by Saint Thomas Aquinas's Scholasticism, his is a rational witness to experience, as she has already known it. Nevertheless, Saint Thomas serves as prophetic philosopher companionable in his witness to that known mystery, lest it be forgotten. Flannery O'Connor knows this to be true by her experience of this place, a place to which her ecstatically romantic friend returns from Greenwich Village wanting to rescue her from, a reality misunderstood as dead, as "provincial." O'Connor could but recognize a further witness to this reality, not in rational explication of experience such as that she reads in Saint Thomas but as witnessed by a specific event in a distant time and country. Dame Julian of Norwich holds a hazelnut on her open palm, and in the small object seen through the eye in an openness of love, she discovers it to be held from collapsing into nothingness, even as she is so held. She shares with that small thing a suspension from nothingness through *connaturality*, Saint Thomas would say. They are sustained in *being* by an all-sustaining love. In that suspense, in a moment of an epiphany, the person makes a discovery, which Josef

Pieper expresses in his small and marvelously cogent book *In Tune with the World: A Theory of Festivity*: "To celebrate a festival means: to live out for some special occasion and in an uncommon manner, the universal assent to the world as a whole" (Pieper 30). The epiphany in such a festive moment is to see the whole world present in a festive offering of that whole world through objects ceremonially raised. The offering may be only a hazelnut on the open palm, or it may be bread and wine offered to be transformed by love. Such an epiphany is most often private, in contrast to communal festivity. In such a private moment, through the eye and through the object, the person discovers the "world as a whole," in Tate's phrase. In Pieper's phrasing, this is to discover that "Existence [*all* of the *world*] as we know it . . . does not just 'adjoin' the realm of Eternity; it is entirely permeated by it" (Pieper 30). That is the experience of mystery Flannery O'Connor has in mind when she says that the longer we look at an object, the more of the world we see in it. It is a recognition that comes early for Flannery O'Connor and continues with her, evident to her always in things themselves. When such things are borrowed to the task of incarnating her fiction, they thereby bear with them an interior light of grace within her made story.

Through that recognition she sees that, as an intellectual creature whose peculiar gift calls her to the making of fictions, hers becomes a demanding responsibility to a gift that allows little leisure for any self-satisfaction grading into pride such as often tempts the artist, either as creator, as opposed to maker, or as intentional savior of mankind by art. Hers is a vocation, a calling, so that she reminds us and herself in "Catholic Novelists and Their Readers": "Vocation is a limiting factor, and the conscientious novelist works at the limits of his power and within what his imagination can apprehend. He does not decide what would be good for the Catholic body and proceed to deliver it" (*MM* 183). Or if he attempts to do so, he is likely to end up writing what she calls on another occasion that "depressing new category" of fiction, "light Catholic summer reading." Or he may end up writing an ideological tract presuming godhead. Not that she fails to see that even bad art may serve God's good ends, for "God can make an indifferent thing, as well as evil itself, an instrument for good" (*MM* 174). To do this, however, "is the business of God and not of the human being." Such is the mystery of evil's dependence upon and eventual service to the good, but it is to be accomplished only through God's intentionality, that is, by grace, not by the artist in assuming power as creator. Meanwhile, as Thomas Aquinas says (*Summa Contra Gentiles*, bk. 3, ch.11), "Moral evil is based on the good rooted in human nature," in contrast to that seeming evil that "springs from the nature" of a thing in itself, a deprivation of the thing's formal actuality such as a blindness of the eye as organ, as opposed to that willed blindness of the eye in denials that human nature is fallen in this person and needing that rescue that grace alone can accomplish. But for her, that is action beyond the story, a mystery that art can only deepen.

Note Flannery O'Connor's response to the question of whether being crippled affected her writing: no, she says, since she writes with her head, not her feet. It is in her recognition of this distinction between the evil possible through willfulness and the evil that "springs from the nature" of things—fires or lions, storms or serpents. Or lupus, that old secret wolf in nature. Hence she will (with what one is tempted to call ironic mischief) adapt even poor art as suited to the effecting of grace, using that poor art, made poorly in a context of moral evil. She will use it as matter to her own better art. Thus we see that complex reality of moral evil and bad art, accomplishing in the actions of her story a rescuing action of grace to Mr. Head and Nelson in "The Artificial Nigger." The action comes through the decaying statue of the "artificial nigger."

Such then is the unwavering presence to her of Revelation, which makes her declare that, as she wrote to Betty Hester, "the present reality is the Incarnation" (*HB* 92). That is the abiding mystery, an abiding presence she encounters when she looks long and deeply into the reality of any actual thing perceived through her incarnate nature. Hence her remark that "the longer you look at one object, the more of the world you see in it," by which seeing one comes "to know" oneself. And that, she also says, proves paradoxical in that it proves as well "a form of exile from the world" in that in the world one journeys toward a proper end. She sees, as does Dame Julian of Norwich, that without that Presence the thing she looks at long and hard would fall to nothingness. It cannot be rescued solely by her own desire that it not fall to nothingness. She is relieved by that certainty, a certainty to which one must return through things themselves along the way, since certainty is not unwavering in fallible human intellect as besieged by the will. Not even the saint always avoids the nagging intrusion of doubt, however intent upon certainty. Even Saint Augustine prays fervently, as did Saint Peter before him after his denial of Christ: "I believe. Help thou my unbelief." This is that Augustinian moment of a contingency in the will to believe, of wills in conflict within one person. Perhaps it is conflict more continuous for Walker Percy than for Flannery O'Connor as persons. But for both, that is the centering action underlying the level of spectacle in their fictions, their made things.

Works Cited

Aquinas, Thomas. *Summa Contra Gentiles (On the Truth of the Catholic Faith)*. Translated by Anton C. Pegis, James F. Anderson, Vernon J. Bourke, and Charles J. O'Neil. 5 vols. 1955–57. Reprint, New York: Doubleday, 1975.

Aristotle. *Poetics*. Edited by Francis Fergusson. New York: Hill and Wang, 1961.

Buber, Martin. *I and Thou*. 1923. New York: Touchstone, 1976.

Eliot, T. S. "*Ulysses*, Order and Myth" (1923). In *Selected Prose of T. S. Eliot*, ed. Frank Kermode, 175–78. New York: Harcourt Brace Jovanovich, 1975.

Maritain, Jacques. "*Art and Scholasticism*" and "*The Frontiers of Poetry*." Translated by Joseph W. Evans. South Bend, Ind.: University of Notre Dame Press, 1974.

———. *On the Use of Philosophy: Three Essays.* Princeton, N.J.: Princeton University Press, 1961.
Montgomery, Marion. *The Prophetic Poet and the Spirit of the Age.* Vol. 3, *Why Hawthorne Was Melancholy.* LaSalle, Ill.: Sherwood Sugden, 1983.
Percy, Walker. "How to Be an American Novelist in Spite of Being Southern and Catholic" (1984). In *Signposts in a Strange Land,* edited by Patrick Samway, S.J., 168–85. New York: Farrar, Straus and Giroux, 1991.
Pieper, Josef. *In Tune with the World: A Theory of Festivity.* 1963. Translated by Richard and Clara Winston. South Bend, Ind.: St. Augustine's Press, 1999.
Tate, Allen. "The New Provincialism" (1945). In *Essays of Four Decades,* 525–46. Chicago: Swallow Press, 1968.

O'Connor's *Everything That Rises Must Converge* and Theories of the Short Story Sequence

Hans H. Skei

Flannery O'Connor's late short stories are superbly handled tales of deprivations and shortcomings, of human folly and man's limitless capacity for stupidity, set in a strikingly beautiful world that her characters either fail to see or feel threatened by. Her fictional world is narrow, at times almost claustrophobic, yet one may hold that space, if not spatial form, is crucial to her short fictional pieces. Rarely do her characters leave rural or small-town Georgia, yet we have the feeling that they are coming home from some sort of exile, be it up north or simply from being alienated in their domestic environment. They are coming home for a final countdown, confrontation, revelation—described in what appear to be ingeniously staged tableaux, where characters act according to some basic laws of human nature, which in combination with sociological and psychological factors, contribute to their downfalls— and their violent deaths more often than not.

We may infer that only a limited number of themes are fictionalized in O'Connor's stories, and that similar if not identical situations, confrontations, character types, and family relationships appear and reappear to the exclusion of everything else. Her deliberate control of narrative voice and her use of narrative omniscience, even in what appear to be personalized narratives or narratives from inside someone's head, add to most texts a deeper meaning than the events of the stories in themselves could possibly convey. With ease and technical brilliance, the texts change points of view, move between time past and present, and apply dialogue when needed; yet the narrative authority is never threatened or in doubt. We may find dialogic tension between characters, worldviews, and attitudes within a given text, but there is a controlled and controlling narrative voice—*in* the text and somehow one step removed and *above* the text—that seems to settle things once and for all within the limits of the story we read. That we still may find that some of the stories have ambiguous endings does not indicate a lack of skill on the part of the writer, but rather underlines her consummate skill as an artist and the complexity of the questions she addresses in her fiction. I am not necessarily thinking in religious terms here, although questions of sin and expiation, redemption, and individual versus communal suffering may be brought up. Perhaps the modern literary short story is bound up with the experience of the sacred or, indeed, the uncanny in situations that are not of the familiar daylight kind. Maybe Charles May is right when he suggests that the modern short story can be seen as yet another attempt "to regain through art what has been lost in religion."[1] What is peculiar about O'Connor's stories is that many characters seem unaware of their predicament, their chance encounters with something larger than themselves, so that the existential or epiphanic experience must be reached by the reader, firmly led by a narrator who knows all too well who the freaks are.

O'Connor made fun of the word "compassion" in her essay on the grotesque in southern fiction (*CW* 813–21), yet beneath the violence and the human folly and suffering, we may still find some grace, some dignity, perhaps even some compassion—one of Faulkner's favorite words—but then, of course, he was writing to uplift people's hearts, which O'Connor absolutely refused to accept as her duty as a writer.

In O'Connor's late stories, posthumously published as *Everything That Rises Must Converge*, the title story sets the tone for the whole collection. The title seems to indicate something inevitable, a law of nature, where "convergence" at the story's closure has been prepared from the very first paragraph. The story is enormously rich in its brevity, and by no means does it depict just a strange relationship between an elderly mother and a grown-up son, ending in the mother's death and with the son, who formerly saw no future for himself and now can only postpone "his entry into the world of guilt and sorrow" (*CW* 500). The story is a superb example, one of the best in O'Connor's work, of narrative economy, which allows the text to comment on matters of race and class by dwelling on a family member who had been a governor or owned a plantation and two hundred slaves. Yet it concentrates on what this heritage has done to Julian's mother, and consequently to Julian, although it seems beyond him to understand any of this until it is too late. As in so many O'Connor stories, the sorrow and pain experienced or lying in store are related to *what might have been*—chances not offered, risks not taken, kindnesses not shown, compassion denied, friendship withheld. So Julian retreats into "the inner compartment of his mind where he spent most of his time" (*CW* 491).

We may suggest that O'Connor's short fiction is a kind of forced realism, in the sense that there is an explicit setting, a well-known world, people interacting with one another, yet from the very outset we know that this is a surface and that her stories take place beneath the surface, in the margin, outside of ordinary and organized life. The familiar becomes threatening so that suddenly the safety and security of everyday life cannot be taken for granted. O'Connor probes beneath the surface of our perceptions and conceptions, and suddenly the interchangeability of obvious facts and phenomena does not function. Intersubjectivity no longer works the way we expect it to do. When this happens, her characters live through uncanny moments where their value systems are questioned and where death, violent or tragic or both, comes as the end. When communication breaks down, we meet characters who are basically and essentially alone and lonely. The great accomplishment in O'Connor's best stories is that her characters appear to be singularly alone, even in the midst of their familiar social world. Her stories belong to a subgroup of the modern literary short story in which the very brevity of the texts is invariably linked to the kind of experience they convey, and which I elsewhere have called existential experience, and which others might develop further in religious terms. How does this relate to modern short story theory in general?

It has become a commonplace to maintain that short story definitions are essentialistic, but through the work of American critics from the 1970s onward, they have changed and have become relational. The question is not now what a short story is, but what it is *in relation to* other texts. A good example of this kind of approach is found in Mary Louise Pratt's seminal 1981 essay, "The Short Story: The Long and the Short of It."[2] Even if her errand is a defense of the short story, her main point is that genres are not essences but are based in different ways on theme, narrative handling, language, effect, and so forth. In the late 1950s Norman Friedman had insisted on the significance of the brevity of the short story to the exclusion of almost all other possible distinctive factors.[3] In the 1980s he repeated this view, asserting that we do not need a more precise definition than "a short fictional narrative in prose"—nor is one possible.[4] But this insistence on defining the genre on the basis of a single distinctive trait does not work, and hence Friedman calls for a set of multiple *differentiae,* a cluster of distinguishing traits, never insisting that they define the genre once and for all, but only that they show central tendencies, perhaps limited to one subgroup, one period, one national literature. We also need to be open to the fact that short stories and their close relatives in literature can be expected to overlap at the edges, and that we must adjust our descriptions when writers and texts modify the genre. I firmly support this understanding and approach but would add that it is vitally important that we do not move freely between formal and thematic categories, claiming for example that the short story has a particular subject matter that demands a certain structure. Charles May, one of the most productive and influential short story theorists, does this, insisting that the short story deals with epiphanic moments of revelation or myth or profound experience, and that this has structural consequences that explain the brevity of the story. A single defining characteristic is taken by Charles May to be constitutive of a whole genre, whereas I insist it describes a subgroup of the genre. It is within this group of short fiction, where brevity and existential experience go hand in hand, that I have placed William Faulkner's best short stories,[5] and I do not hesitate to place most of O'Connor's short fiction here as well, especially the stories in her posthumous collection, *Everything That Rises Must Converge.*

The limited world of O'Connor's short stories, her concentration on relatively few themes, and her preoccupation with similar if not identical characters may tempt scholars and critics to find such unity in and coherence between the stories that they deem them to be a short story *cycle.* Let us therefore turn to the question of whether *Everything That Rises Must Converge* can be described as a short story cycle, short story sequence, or short story composite, to use the most common terms for a collection of stories that is more unified than a mere collection and seems to be deliberately intended to function as a whole. I suggest that we should not only look for unity and study the contextual influence of individual stories on one another in the book but also insist that the sum of the whole must be larger than the parts added together.

Critics who have studied, described, and generalized about short story cycles seem to think that they have found a new field of study that promises great rewards. I am not convinced. Obviously one may achieve much by relating the short story cycle to, on the one hand, the individual short story and, on the other hand, to the novel. But I find it surprising that critics largely study the "new form" as a conflict between the individuality of short stories and the larger structure of a unified cycle that threatens to subsume the stories. They quarrel among themselves and with other critics over whether a certain book—for example Faulkner's *Go Down, Moses* or Eudora Welty's *The Golden Apples*—is a cycle or a novel.[6] We must be aware that texts may belong to more than one genre, may function in more than one capacity, and that the very idea of a strictly defined, stable genre is an impossibility. In other words, studying the short story, the short story cycle that short stories may form, and even novels created on the basis of previously published short stories demonstrates the usefulness as well as the inadequacy of genre concepts.

It was in 1971 that Forrest L. Ingram claimed that he had discovered a new literary genre: the short story cycle. Ingram, in his *Representative Short Story Cycles of the Twentieth Century,* discusses the balance that must be sought between the individuality of each story and the demands of the larger unit, and he points to patterns of recurrence and of development that operate concurrently. While his essentialist definitions become rather rigid and normative, the concept of unity with numerous unifying factors seems to have been basic also to Susan Garland Mann in her *The Short Story Cycle: A Genre Companion and Reference Guide* from 1989. Later theorists have tried to be more relational, more open to the great possibilities of variety and renewal the form offers. Robert Luscher states that a short story *sequence*—he prefers this term because the reader's experience of such collections is sequential— "should be viewed, not as failed novels, but as unique hybrids that combine two distinct reading pleasures: the patterned closure of individual stories and the discovery of larger unifying strategies that transcend the apparent gaps between stories." He also lists a number of simple textual strategies employed: a title, a preface, an epigraph, or framing stories, and "more organic unities such as common narrators, characters, images, locale, and themes" (Luscher 150). Rolf Lundén insists in his study, *The United Stories of America,* on the open nature of the short story composite, so that the inherent tension between discontinuity and fragmentation, on the one hand, and the totalizing demands, on the other, informs his reading. We all know of numerous short story collections that may not satisfy the expectations of unity of the critics of this subgroup of the short story genre, yet these books do benefit from a reading that emphasizes the autonomy of individual stories *and* the unifying strategies that provide coherence.

It is obviously possible and perhaps legitimate to dismiss *Everything That Rises Must Converge* as a short story cycle, since we do not know the full authorial intention behind the book. We may agree that a short story cycle must be "an authentic composite, intended to be thus structured," to quote one of Rolf Lundén's basic requirements for the genre (Lundén 49), and then we must say of this collection: it simply cannot be a short story cycle since the book was partly constructed by an editor. One may ask how rigid our definitions ought to be, when the proper question to ask is whether it would yield interpretive help to view the volume as a cycle of stories. J. Gerald Kennedy is unwilling to see *Everything that Rises Must Converge* as a short story cycle in the same sense that O'Connor's deliberately arranged *A Good Man Is Hard to Find* is, not only because she did not entirely compose or arrange the volume herself, but because she did not "leave instructions for its arrangement, nor did she mention a conceptual scheme."[7] We know that O'Connor brought the final stories with her to the hospital where she died and that her editor put together the collection. We know at least that the author had planned this as a collection of stories, and there is every reason to think that she was as careful in her planning as she had been all through her career. She had indicated both its title and title story as early as in March 1963. She mentions "Everything That Rises Must Converge" in a letter to Maryat Lee on March 25, saying that it "touches on certain topical issues in these parts and takes place on a bus" (*CW* 1147). The next day she wrote her literary agent, Elizabeth McKee, mentioning the new story and adding "and this is the title I want to put on my next collection" (*CW* 1258). She admits elsewhere that the title is taken from Pierre Teilhard de Chardin, although she does not understand "the scientific end of it or the philosophical" (*CW* 1152). Yet she must have thought that the expression indicated the inevitable convergence, perhaps even collision, of persons or objects, so that an ultimate fall is implied if one rises or dreams or aspires beyond the acceptable or permissible. Perhaps the title is deliberately vague; we had better read the stories and look more closely for possible unifying aspects and only then try to explain the title—rather than using the title as a key to unlock the whole book.

There may be other reasons why we should not insist on the unity of O'Connor's collection and should be cautious about establishing interrelatedness and dependency between the stories on the basis of minor details. O'Connor's stories are obviously very literary short stories, so we study imagery and symbols and characters and events in order to find similarities and parallels. Perhaps we should instead speculate why *Everything That Rises Must Converge* is less of a cycle of stories than some readers would wish and why it, in the end, must be regarded as a collection of individual stories. I write this, well aware that a larger pattern is discernible because of the limitations of O'Connor's locale and themes. Yet to "create" a unified whole on the basis of the stories in the collection would probably go against everything in the stories themselves, in the author's life at the time she wrote them, and it may even be in conflict with her ideas, beliefs, and the terrors of contemporary life as she saw them. In other words, if we insist that there is nothing but the text and remain inside the texts, we may find similarities and parallels enough to create some sort of unity and hence claim that the book approximates a short story cycle; but if we look outside the text—to other contexts and other demands than those of genre, style, and tradition—we experience something different.

The brevity of texts, the choice to condense, dramatize, and present texts in a mixture of suddenness and profound reflection, is not only a question of the availability of a literary form and an established mastery of it. O'Connor had every reason to stick closely and almost exclusively to what we may call an aesthetics of brevity. The most obvious reason, seldom acknowledged, was the threat of sudden death. She was well aware that her life would be brief and that to create art that would endure, she might have to make her works of art brief. She could not expect wholeness in her own life. She clearly saw that most things around her were fragmented and disjointed, often lacking the beauty and goodness that life on earth should offer, perhaps because religion no longer provided the stable comfort and solace it once had. She saw how people wasted their lives fighting for things they did not cherish in the end, and she reacted with fury and anger, more so than most writers since life to her was precious. She would have neither the time nor the opportunity to really absorb the world outside her native Georgia, so she had better stick to what she knew intimately. She would have to base her fictions in the world she knew and place her characters in conflicts and confrontations within the racially segregated South of the 1940s and 1950s. She often limited herself to family situations, in which the conflicts on the contemporary scene could also reflect the conflicts of the human heart.

The short stories in O'Connor's last collection owe their individuality to their fragmented nature, and they resist efforts to be categorized as a cycle of stories because the brief prose fiction narrative was O'Connor's preferred genre. She had an understanding of brevity in most areas of life and experience. Many events on the contemporary scene seemed to require a fictional representation in which condensation and concentration were the most efficient tools in getting the story told and bringing the message through. One may even venture the idea that her stories, revised again and again, often over a long period of time, became almost exemplary tales that offer us "fear in a handful of dust."

In a time of rapid transition from an old, seemingly unchangeable system to a new way of life, these changes could be recorded in brief and pointed tales: the minimal changes recorded in a short story could reflect the great changes in the world. O'Connor's stories are preoccupied with religion and with race, and clearly the dramatic changes brought about by the civil rights movement are important in her short fiction. The terrors and threats and uncertainties depicted in her fiction may also be grounded in the large-scale uncertainties of the world—the cold war, the shadow of the atomic bomb, the strain of relating to people and events that must have appeared to be small and of little consequence when the final question was "when shall I be blown up?"

On one hand, we have the question, then, of the impact of contemporary issues on O'Connor as a person; on the other hand, we have the question of how she transformed these issues into fiction and of whether such issues really were of major concern in her fiction. I think that they were but also that she hid them in stories about people and their shortcomings with great care and subtlety. The fact that everything happened so quickly, that changes were so many and so rapid, worked against long narrative structures even to the point where it would be wrong to link stories and to claim coherence when the individual stories in fact show the fragmentation, disruption, and the brevity of most things in human life. Accordingly *Everything That Rises Must Converge* achieves some of its power and richness from the tension between the connections, similarities, contrasts, and parallels that establish some unification in the collection *and* the uniqueness, singularity, and individuality of each story. The short stories relate to and, in profound ways, discuss contemporary issues, and as such they are transformed and become more than instances of an author's experience in her fragmented day and time.

The stories in *Everything That Rises Must Converge* are all told with ease and full control by a third-person narrator who remains outside the text and allows the narrative to focus on one or more characters at a time, so that often the point of view is located with a character whereas the voice is the narrator's or what may appear to be a combination of the character's and the narrator's. Characters are often introduced in the very first sentence of a story, and we are in the midst of the events of the story as it opens. Stories often include brief capsule stories that relate incidents and events from the central characters' pasts. Past events and previous confrontations may help explain the inevitable and deadly confrontations we find in so many stories. The main story may simply pause and halt for some time, to let the minor but decisive stories from the past be told. Or we may simply be allowed to follow the thoughts of a character, rendered in a straightforward narrative, similar to a narrated monologue. This technique, deceptively simple, enables the narrator to manipulate the distance to characters and events, from intimate and shocking closeness to a character, to the broader and more general revelations of shortcomings and evil, through a use of irony that reveals the characters' total misunderstanding of themselves and the world around them. In this particular collection of stories by O'Connor we meet numerous mothers and unmarried sons in deadly struggles of which they seem to be unaware when we watch their polite ways and listen to their ceaseless platitudes.

The stories in *Everything That Rises Must Converge* are stories about families and family life of a kind we seldom find in southern literature, even if they may be said to belong to the school of the grotesque. We meet a number of widowed mothers with shiftless, unmarried sons who are totally dependent on their mothers. In "The Lame Shall Enter First," we even have a child who longs for his dead mother and *a father*, but the conflict and the final resolution is even more chilling and horrifying than in the stories with mothers and sons. There is no understanding between parent and child, only remorse, rejection, and anger. No matter how different the conflicts, they lead to violence of an extreme kind. There is rarely a hint of the possibility of understanding, of resolving the conflict, or of establishing a meaningful existence, if not a worthwhile life. A title like "The Comforts of Home" is blatantly ironic, even if Thomas acts in order to salvage a peaceful existence in his mother's house when it is threatened by Sarah Ham. The conflict is even more complex in psychological terms: his mother tries to help Sarah, as a result Thomas fears that he will lose his mother's full attention, and at the same time all his thoughts relate to what his dead father would have done. For once, the story's conclusion is not on a par with the rest of the text. The sheriff's misreading of the scene with the smoking gun and the dead mother seems too glib a conclusion to O'Connor's probing analysis of a troubled male, who in his lack of masculinity, father complex, and total dependence on his mother is a sad and troubled figure. Perhaps we should have been allowed to remain inside Thomas's head also at this juncture: most of the other stories in the volume allow us to watch the main characters very closely.

Everything that rises and converges seems to be located within the family, but there are other themes that are worked out in the stories to explain the horrors of family life as well as the lack of communication and understanding. One important theme, perhaps the single most important in all of O'Connor's fiction, is race. If we add to this the preoccupation that so many characters show with property and class, with status, with appearances and correct behavior, we have a limited but strong cluster of themes that can be varied and used in new combinations in story after story. Moreover, religion, often represented through preachers and revival meetings, is crucial and destructive. The family is a dark place, the small towns and settlements and farms are equally somber and threatening. Only in Tanner's dream of the South that destroyed him but that he desperately wants to go back to, even if only to be buried there, do we glimpse a different South, a South that may become possible only on "Judgment Day." Thoughts of racial superiority, rigid demands for correct behavior, and a debilitating class consciousness linked to ownership of property lie behind many of the conflicts between mothers and sons, between young people who have been to college and those who stayed at home. This relates not only to the South as a region, but to the time of the stories, which was a period of transition, of changing values, and of a necessary adjustment to a changing world. Many of O'Connor's characters are proud of their families' pasts, when they owned slaves and were much better off than they are now that they have to pay their African American farmhands decent wages and may even risk meeting them on the bus. In the title story, the conflict between Julian and his mother may also be seen as a generational conflict, since Julian is ashamed of his mother's condescending ways toward black people. In "The Lame Shall Enter First," the good and righteous Mr. Sheppard, who is white, tries to save Rufus Johnson, a black youth, from his criminal ways but is completely ineffectual both because of his own self-righteousness and because Johnson is beyond his comprehension.

Violence erupts, death comes as the end in most of the stories in *Everything That Rises Must Converge,* and the author clearly intended this to be so. Some of the stories seem rather forced in the sense that the final confrontation is not an inevitable or natural result of the events leading up to a rendezvous with death. This is clearly the case in "Greenleaf," as it is with "A View of the Woods." Even in short stories with characters we come to know well, there are limits to what we as readers will think possible. If we accept the story because it is "just literary," literature has not achieved its goal. If we accept that Asbury in "The Enduring Chill" is not dying, we still have only three stories in the collection without death of one kind or another—ranging from suicide to murder and to natural death of old age. In "Revelation" we have violent fights and madness, but at the end we watch Mrs. Turpin in her vision of an ascension as she tries to reach an understanding of herself that will make her life bearable. In the strange story "Parker's Back," there is fighting and thrashing and violence, but also a married life that may even go on after the confrontation over the tattoo of a Byzantine Christ covering Parker's back. In "Judgment Day," the last story of the volume, a southerner's bones are dug up from a northern grave, so that they can be buried and be at peace in his beloved South. Read in the light of this final story, one might say that no characters come to rest or achieve peace unless they die and experience their judgment day. Since the stories clearly transcend their time and place, one might even come to the conclusion that the human heart, in conflict with itself or with the hearts of others, is a deep and dark place. But great literature does not need to brighten our days or lift up our hearts. It may show how pervasive the darkness all around us is, but it may also help us find our bearings, see a ray of hope and a narrow path out of the darkness, and to come to a better understanding of ourselves and our fellow human beings.

I hope this survey of themes, conflicts, confrontations, and their possible meanings in the individual stories in *Everything That Rises Must Converge* has indicated that the collection may be more unified than the average collection of short fictional pieces. We know the book is probably not in the final shape that authorial intention would have given it. We also know that the last text in the volume, "Judgment Day," was being revised during O'Connor's final days and would have been revised further had she been able to. Fortunately, Karl-Heinz Westarp has seen to it that a text with O'Connor's late changes is now available in the Library of America's edition of

O'Connor's complete works (*CW* 676–95, 1259–60). We may assume that the arrangement of stories in the volume, based more or less on chronology of publication, would also have been the author's own. One may of course speculate that with the author's limited output, her singularity of purpose, her limited number of themes, and little variation in the time and place of her stories, we should expect to find a high degree of unity in any collection of O'Connor stories, but we must also accept that the unity is not of the kind that scholars of the short story cycle ask for. Some find a strong thematic unity, for instance, a preoccupation with religious questions; others would find that the high number of elderly, widowed mothers, fighting to cope with a changing world and with good-for-nothing sons, demonstrates an early preoccupation with questions of gender. For me the time and place of her stories, the South in the postwar decades, explain at least some of the stories' emphasis on a deteriorating white ruling class, with poor whites and black characters thrown in. Violence, class consciousness, racial problems, as well as those of love and marriage and wider family relationships, come to dominate. It is striking how much of the characters' troubled lives is related to the racial problems of the South. I say this well aware that O'Connor transcends the actual setting of her stories to deal with matters far removed from what might have happened once upon a place in rural Georgia; I am convinced that her stories compress, condense, and dramatize more material and more significant insights than the stories of most American short story writers, the minimalists included.

Let me note that in a detailed study of the possible unity and coherence of *Everything That Rises Must Converge,* the significance of the almost optimistic "Revelation" and the inclusion of the strange "Parker's Back" must be studied as juxtapositions or antithetical texts in a collection dominated by death, although some, even here, would find a kind of grace. "The Lame Shall Enter First" is also a strange, maybe even a threatening story compared to most of its neighboring stories, with its mixture of social rehabilitation, religion, and a young boy's suicide. The stories that seem to belong together and support and contrast one another— "Everything That Rises Must Converge," "Greenleaf," "The Enduring Chill," and "The Comforts of Home"—should not make us overlook important connections between, for instance, "Judgment Day" and "The Enduring Chill," or between "Revelation" and the title story. Yet whatever we do, no matter how many unifying traits we find in this collection, it will never be a cycle like *Go Down, Moses* or *The Golden Apples,* where the sum of the stories approximates a novel. We are somehow in the same world throughout O'Connor's last collection, but we get acquainted with this world and its strange characters through a number of individual stories. *Everything That Rises Must Converge* is perhaps considered a short story sequence by some, but such labeling presupposes that the short story sequence is defined as simply a unique hybrid that combines the pleasure of reading one short story with the discovery in the collection as a whole of a larger pattern, such as a shared world, recurrent themes, or similar narrative strategies. Theories of the short story cycle only offer interpretive help if the insight, experience, discovery, and pleasure of the collection as a whole is larger than the sum of the experiences of its individual stories. Whether this is true of *Everything That Rises Must Converge* as a collection can only be answered by the individual reader.

Scholars of the short story sequence seem to have felt a compulsion to make short story cycles unified. We should rather approach a sequence of short stories with an open mind, a willingness to see whether the tension between the sequence as a whole and the individual stories is creative and productive. An awareness of structure, the interrelatedness of parts, similarities, juxtapositions, and antithetical positions is clearly helpful in an interpretation of *Winesburg, Ohio; In Our Time;* and *The Golden Apples,* but perhaps it is less helpful in reading Flannery O'Connor's short story collection *Everything That Rises Must Converge.*

Notes

1. Charles E. May, "The Nature of Knowledge in Short Fiction," in *The New Short Story Theories,* ed. Charles E. May, 131–43 (Athens: Ohio University Press, 1994); quotation on 139.

2. Mary Louise Pratt, "The Short Story: The Long and the Short of It," in *The New Short Story Theories,* ed. Charles E. May, 91–113 (Athens: Ohio University Press, 1994).

3. Norman Friedman, "What Makes a Short Story Short?" *Modern Fiction Studies* 4 (1958/59): 103–17.

4. Norman Friedman, "Recent Short Story Theories: Problems in Definition" in *Short Story Theory at a Crossroads,* ed. Susan Lohafer and Jo Ellyn Clarey, 13–31 (Baton Rouge: Louisiana State University Press, 1989); quotation on 29.

5. Hans Skei, *Reading Faulkner's Best Short Stories* (Columbia: University of South Carolina Press, 1999).

6. Examples can be found in Forrest L. Ingram, *Representative Short Story Cycles of the Twentieth Century* (The Hague: Mouton, 1971); Robert M. Luscher, "The Short Story Sequence: An Open Book," in *Short Story Theory at a Crossroads,* ed. Susan Lohafer and Jo Ellyn Clarey, 148–67 (Baton Rouge: Louisiana State University Press, 1989); Rolf Lundén, *The United Stories of America: Studies in the Short Story Composite* (Amsterdam and Atlanta: Rodopi, 1999); and Susan Garland Mann, *The Short Story Cycle: A Genre Companion and Reference Guide* (Westport, Conn.: Greenwood Press, 1989).

7. J. Gerald Kennedy, "Towards a Poetics of the Short Story Cycle," *Journal of the Short Story in English* 11 (Autumn 1988): 12.

Flannery O'Connor as Communicant

A Constant Devotion

Jean W. Cash

In his memorial tribute in *Esprit* in 1964, Cleanth Brooks said of Flannery O'Connor, "In her instance, I find it hard to separate the person from the artist. Certainly the character of both was an invincible integrity" (Brooks 17). Spiritual certainty established the basis of O'Connor's "invincible integrity." She possessed a deep and abiding faith that transcended the formal boundaries of Roman Catholicism. Her heritage, on both sides of her family, was Roman Catholic, and although O'Connor could look a bit critically at a few of the restrictions of the church, she did not falter in her fundamental Christian belief or in her practice of that faith. Little evidence exists to suggest that O'Connor ever suffered from any serious religious doubt. Only once in a letter to Alfred Corn, then a young student at Emory University who was having serious religious doubts himself, did she reveal that she herself experienced some problems with faith when she studied other religions in college. She told him that the "clash of different religions was a difficulty for me. What kept me a skeptic in college was precisely my Christian faith. It always said: wait, don't bite on this, get a wider picture, continue to read" (*HB* 477). The only other evidence that I found—and it is clearly tangential—that might indicate any sort of spiritual lapses occurs in O'Connor's letters to Fr. James McCown in the O'Connor Collection at Duke University. Before he placed the letters in the collection, he literally cut two or three sentences from individual letters that he felt might have been too personal for public exposure.[1]

O'Connor's deep spiritual commitment was both personal and intellectual; at the personal level, she practiced her faith with an almost obsessive dedication. Wherever she was—at Iowa, in Connecticut with the Fitzgeralds, or in Milledgeville—she attended Mass nearly every day. Although she insisted that she did not pray in a conventional, dogmatic sense, she kept *A Short Breviary* by her bed: "I say Prime in the morning and sometimes I say Compline at night" (*HB* 159). She also found other, less conventional ways to practice her belief.

Her parents and other relatives in Savannah were devout, practicing Roman Catholics, and Mary Flannery O'Connor herself early developed strong faith. Years later she wrote to William Sessions about the ease with which she took her first Communion. It was "as natural" to her, she said, "as brushing my teeth" (*HB* 164). The insularity of the Catholic community in Savannah also had a lasting impact on O'Connor's life. Of being a "born" Catholic, she wrote, "what one has as a born Catholic is something given and accepted before it is experienced" (*HB* 97). Because

Catholics in Savannah were a definite minority, they were devoted to the church and to one another. The O'Connor home, located as it was on Lafayette Square just a block from St. John's Cathedral, placed Mary Flannery in the center of this community. St. Vincent's Grammar School for Girls, which she attended through the fifth grade, was adjacent to the cathedral. Diagonal to St. Vincent's was the Marist Brothers School for Boys. Sister Consolata, a Mercy nun, who was Mary Flannery's third-grade teacher at St. Vincent's, comments on the overall religious atmosphere in which Mary Flannery grew up: "There was a very close relationship between the people and the church in those days, it [the Catholic community] was not large and the people knew each other." Mary Flannery's childhood playmates recall that "she and her family seemed to be devout Roman Catholics, as was the whole neighborhood," and that she was "raised very religious" (Hoynes interview). Sister Consolata says, "She had a very deep religious background even within her own home and with her associates. All of her relationships, like with the Dowlings—they are very religious—[and] the Feugers were very religious, the Persses were very religious. I think that her association with those people had a lot to do with Mary Flannery's religious training" (interview).

O'Connor began school in Savannah in 1931, entering first grade at St. Vincent's Grammar School, just across the square from her family's home. The Mercy nuns who ran the school were mostly young Irish girls brought to the United States, trained briefly in Baltimore, and then sent to teach in grammar schools like St. Vincent's. Sister Consolata was one of these neophytes. O'Connor's Savannah cousins, the three Persse sisters, spent all of their elementary school years at the Sacred Heart Academy to which Mary Flannery transferred in 1936. They have clear recollections of what Catholic elementary schools in Savannah were like in the 1930s, emphasizing the parochial atmosphere as being highly disciplined. In every classroom, the school day began with a formal prayer. Through the seventh grade, the same nun taught her class every subject. Behavior, they assert, was regimented in a positive sense. The sisters at St. Vincent's provided their students with religious instruction, preparing them for their first Communion. They used the Baltimore Catechism, then the official explanation of church doctrine in parochial schools. Another part of the religious training was, according to the Persse cousins, early participation in church ritual. They sang the complicated Latin Masses, participated in a children's choir, and learned to sing anthems. Though they learned to recite Masses, the Persse sisters do not recall reading any treatises by Catholic scholars.

When in 1938, at the age of thirteen, Mary Flannery moved to Milledgeville with her parents, she could no longer attend a parochial school because the Catholic community there was too small to support one; Regina Cline O'Connor had no choice but to send her daughter to the public Peabody High School. O'Connor, along with her Roman Catholic kin, continued to attend Mass in Milledgeville and to receive religious instruction from nuns who came to Milledgeville every Sunday from Mount DeSalles in Macon. Her neighbor Kitty Smith Kellam recalls how alien she felt as a Roman Catholic child in a predominantly Protestant town: "You didn't know what was wrong with you. . . . [I felt there] were a lot of misconceptions. Things that seemed perfectly normal to me seemed like voodoo to other people and I didn't understand why because I had never been to a Protestant church so I couldn't understand all the mysticism that they felt and the secrecy involved, when to me it made perfect sense" (interview). Elizabeth Horne, a friend of O'Connor, believes, however, that the small number of Catholics in Milledgeville helped to draw them closer together in their practice and in their faith. Horne, absolutely certain that O'Connor's faith never wavered throughout her life, remembers O'Connor's explanation for her lifetime of steadfast belief: "I heard her say once, in a conversation, she had investigated as thoroughly as she could the background of the Church, the credentials of the Church and had accepted them and as far as she was concerned from that point on in the Church, that was it, and I've always felt the same way" (interview). Throughout her high school and undergraduate years in Milledgeville, O'Connor's dedication to the church remained stable. Only once—years later—in the above-mentioned letter to Alfred Corn did she reveal that she experienced some problems with faith when she was in college.

When O'Connor attended the University of Iowa between 1945 and 1948, her religious practice was no doubt as simple, regular, and private as the rest of her life in Iowa City. Her friend Jean Wylder wrote that it was not until several years after O'Connor left Iowa that she learned of her Catholicism. The church O'Connor attended, St. Mary's, still sits on East Jefferson Street, within easy walking distance of both the Currier House Annex and Mrs. Guzeman's boarding house, in both of which O'Connor lived during her years at Iowa. Of her attendance at Mass, she wrote to Roslyn Barnes in December 1960 that she went to St. Mary's "practically every morning [for] three years and never knew a soul in that congregation or any of the priests, but it was not necessary. As soon as I went in the door I was home" (*HB* 422). Robie Macauley, who knew O'Connor well during her last year at Iowa, was not aware that she attended Mass every day but felt that her religious faith was the most serious thing in her life: O'Connor "was interested in theology and knew much more about it than I did. At Kenyon, I'd had an intensive course in *The Divine Comedy*, which encompassed a lot of reading in theology and history as well as reading Dante in Italian. That was about the extent of my knowledge of Catholicism. I remember some very interesting talks we had about Dante and how knowledgeable she was" (interview). Walter Sullivan, another of O'Connor's acquaintances at Iowa, recalls that in class and out she was generally reticent about expressing opinions about religion but provided commentary when required: "She and I were in a [Henry] James and [James] Joyce seminar and Austin Warren decided that she would have to be the Catholic authority in the class when we were looking at *The Portrait of the Artist as a Young Man*. She never volunteered anything, but he would say, 'Now Miss O'Connor, what are we talking about here?' And she would not seem at all reluctant to answer. She would give him the answer and we would go on from there until we came onto some other point and she'd give the answer" (interview). Of the overall importance of religion to O'Connor, Sullivan says, "She had this wonderful experience of never losing her faith. This was wonderful for her" (interview).

From Iowa, O'Connor traveled, as did many aspiring writers in the post–World War II era, to New York to further her career as a writer. She first spent about eight months at Yaddo, where she expressed concern with the lax personal habits of many of the artists there during the summer of 1948; one of these writers was Alfred Kazin, who was impressed with her reserved dedication to her faith and to her writing. Of her absolute religious faith, he said, "This is so rare in America that it makes her stand out in every possible way. To me she is one of the few writers of that postwar generation who will live for a very long time" (interview).

After O'Connor left Yaddo in March 1949, she lived briefly in New York City, where she continued her friendships with Elizabeth Hardwick and Robert Lowell, whom she had met at Yaddo. They introduced her to Mary McCarthy. Certainly one of the most interesting episodes in O'Connor's life in New York concerns her famous interaction with McCarthy, a former Catholic, and her friends. O'Connor spent one particularly memorable evening at McCarthy's apartment, described in a 1955 letter to Betty Hester: "Well, toward morning the conversation turned on the Eucharist, which I, being the Catholic, was obviously supposed to defend. Mrs. Broadwater said when she was a child and received the Host, she thought of it as the Holy Ghost. He being the 'most portable' person of the Trinity; now she thought of it as a symbol and implied that it was a pretty good one. I then said, in a very shaky voice, 'Well, if it's a symbol, to hell with it.' That was all the defense I was capable of but I realize now that this is all I will ever be able to say about it, outside of a story, except that it is the center of existence for me; all the rest of life is expendable" (*HB* 125). Of the episode, Hardwick said, "I don't remember this, but I read about it later. I don't think the memory is particularly damning to Mary McCarthy, the 'Real Presence' is indeed a matter of some perplexity. Flannery O'Connor clearly believed in it with the ardor she expresses" (interview). In an unpublished 1959 letter to Fr. James McCown, O'Connor again recounted the occasion: "I didn't open my mouth all evening. It was powerful intellecchul talk that went on." She then retold the rest of the story in words identical to those in her letter to Hester. In both accounts, O'Connor's strong defense of her faith clearly shows how little she had in common with the secular "literati" of New York City in the late 1940s. The strength of Catholic faith that marked her personal sensibility was clearly out of place in the spiritually empty metropolis; in fact, she expressed *her* devotion to Catholicism by joining the Catholic Unity League while she lived in New York.

In New York City, Robert Lowell also introduced O'Connor to Robert and Sally Fitzgerald, devout Roman Catholics, who soon invited her to live in their garage apartment in Connecticut. The Fitzgeralds then practiced Catholicism with a devotion at least equal to that of O'Connor; Robert Fitzgerald recalled that the family's day began with early Mass in Georgetown, a town four miles from their home. He and Sally alternated driving with O'Connor to Mass (Fitzgerald xiv). In a letter to Betty Hester in June 1956, she described the Fitzgeralds as "very intense Catholics and their religion covers everything they do. When I lived with them, they said the Benedictine grace before meals in Latin every day while the dinner got cold" (*HB* 161).

When illness forced her return to Milledgeville and her mother, O'Connor, by necessity, rejoined the community of practicing Roman Catholics there, picking up again the habits of practice that had characterized her girlhood in the town. Having recovered her health and realizing that she would live in Milledgeville for the rest of her life, O'Connor began to form, primarily through her correspondence, friendships with people from throughout the United States, many of them Roman Catholics. One of these connections was with Caroline Gordon, a convert to Roman Catholicism, who became a literary mentor to O'Connor. It was through Gordon that she met Brainard "Lon" and Frances "Fannie" Cheney from Nashville, also new Catholic communicants.

When *Wise Blood* came out in 1952, Brainard Cheney wrote a positive and sympathetic review of the book in *Shenandoah*. Having read the review, O'Connor asked Gordon about Cheney; Gordon immediately wrote to him on February 2, 1953, expressing her hope that the Cheneys would meet O'Connor:

> I think you'd both like her. Cal Lowell says she is a saint, but then he is given to extravagance. She may be, though, at that. She is a cradle Catholic, raised in Milledgeville where there are so few other Catholics . . . ; she sure is a powerful Catholic. No nonsense about her! She has some dire disease—some form of arthritis—and is kept going only by huge doses of something called ACTH. We are expected to adore all the Lord's doing, but it does give you pause when you reflect that this gifted girl will probably not be with us long whereas Truman Capote will live to a ripe old age, laden down with honours.

It seems logical then, that O'Connor, encouraged by Gordon, soon communicated with Cheney. Her February letter to him was uncharacteristically warm. She thanked him not just for the review but also for insights into the novel that helped increase her own awareness of its meaning. In his return letter to her, written in March 1953, Cheney wrote of the recent conversion of his wife and himself to Roman Catholicism. He also told O'Connor of his long friendship with Caroline Gordon Tate and suggested that he and O'Connor should meet: "There are not so many of us that we should set the common bent at naught" (Stephens 5). The Cheneys, either together or separately, often visited O'Connor at Andalusia; an unpublished letter that Lon wrote to Fannie while he was spending a weekend with

O'Connor and her mother gives insights into the quality of their practice of Catholicism: "We went in to town (since I was there to drive at night) to confession Saturday evening—and to bed by 10:30 P.M. And to Mass the following morning at 7:15 (which is really 6:15) in N[ashville] and I might say, drove in that four miles, in the pink dawn at somewhere close to zero—at least the frost was so heavy it looked like snow!"

Another Roman Catholic with whom O'Connor established a warm and enduring relationship was Fr. James McCown, whom she met in the mid-1950s. It seems particularly fitting that she should have formed one of her earliest close friendships with this jolly, affable priest, apparently so different from the priest then resident in Milledgeville. In a letter to Father McCown in the O'Connor collection at Duke, O'Connor wrote about the excessive Irishness of this priest who decorated the church with green carnations and a statue of Saint Patrick and objected to Roman Catholic girls at GSCW attending the baccalaureate sermon at the college. McCown was a native southerner, who had come to Macon, Georgia, in the early 1950s as assistant priest at St. Joseph's Catholic Church in Macon. At the church, McCown felt impelled to raise the "cultural level" of his congregation, particularly after one of his "literary" parishioners mentioned Flannery O'Connor: "I decided to get on the O'Connor trail. I read her two books and their reviews. Like the rest, I thought *Wise Blood* gripping but too concerned with bizarre, freakish people. *A Good Man Is Hard to Find* was more to my tastes" (McCown 1979, 86). When Father McCown decided to visit O'Connor, he had to "hitch" a ride to Milledgeville with "Horace Ridley, a fat, big-hearted unacademic whiskey salesman." For O'Connor the result of this visit was a strong and enduring relationship; this sympathetic priest served her as both friend and spiritual adviser. He became, in effect, her "personal priest."

After their first visit, Father McCown was so impressed with O'Connor's literary acumen that he recommended her to Harold Gardiner, S.J., then literary editor of *America*, who immediately asked O'Connor to write an article for the Catholic journal. The result was "The Church and the Fiction Writer," published in the magazine on March 30, 1957, with one sentence edited by Father Gardiner. McCown recalled her reaction as furious. "Flannery, bless her heart, thought boldly and straight, and was not intimidated by the rigorist-neurotic cast of much Catholic moral theology of the time" (McCown 1979, 87). Through the years Father McCown also served, he said, as a sort of "moral guide and dogmatic advisor" to O'Connor. When the literary group that she hosted at Andalusia between 1957 and 1960 wanted to read Gide, whose works were on the Catholic Index of Forbidden Books, she asked Father McCown to help her: "This minister is equipped with a list of what he would like us to read and upon the list is naturally Gide also listed on the Index. I despise Gide but if they read him I want to be able to put in my two cents worth.... You said once you would see if you had the faculties to get me permission to read such as this. Do you and will you? All these Protestants will be shocked if I say I can't get permission to read Gide" (*HB* 259). In his published memoir of O'Connor, McCown described how he solved the problem posed by the "terrible Catholic Index of Forbidden Books": "I wrote my old morals professor, Gerald Kelly, S.J. His satisfactory response was that a Catholic has an obligation to obey church law, yes. But she has an even higher obligation to protect the church from ridicule. He suggested that she use an *epeikia,* a reasonable interpretation of a law here and now patently inapplicable" (McCown 1979, 88). O'Connor reacted enthusiastically to the loophole McCown created: "I am very much obliged for your taking the time to find out about the permissions etc. I will use the *epeikia* and also invoke that word, which is very fancy" (*HB* 263).

Father McCown also recalled his position as her private priest, she "wrote me about problems in her spiritual life. I can only go so far as to say they were of the scope and seriousness found in a convent-bred high school girl" (McCown 1985, 18); in September 1959, she consulted him about inadvertently breaking the Catholic dietary law that forbade eating meat on Fridays. She was worried about having eaten vegetables at the Sanford House that she suspected had been cooked in ham stock; she wrote, "I am always afraid of sacrilege. It turned out they were cooked in ham stock. I enquired after I had eaten them. There is something about you can use drippings but you can't use stock. I hate this kind of question" (O'Connor, unpublished letter). To undercut her excessive concern, however, O'Connor also wrote in the letter that she knew she would not go to hell "over a plate of butter beans."

O'Connor's friendships with people who were struggling with spiritual problems also allowed her to use her knowledge about religious faith during her years in Milledgeville. Two of these friendships were with women who either were Catholic by birth (Cecil Dawkins) or were in the process of converting to the church (Betty Hester). Hester, a young woman from Atlanta, first wrote to O'Connor in the mid-1950s. A major feature of the early correspondence was their discussion of spiritual issues. Peter S. Hawkins has written of O'Connor's role as spiritual adviser to Hester: "The Defender of the Faith in O'Connor clearly had her work cut out; in fact, the correspondence produced an outpouring of theological reflection and spiritual wisdom not only outstanding in the context of O'Connor's collected letters, but on par with anything in Baron von Hügel or C. S. Lewis. It was also an outpouring that would change directions several times in response to [Hester]'s move from an initial wariness toward Catholicism (Summer, 1955), to her decision to be baptized (Winter, 1956) and confirmed (Spring, 1956), to the announcement of her leaving the Church (Autumn, 1961)" (Hawkins 99).

In a letter from early in the correspondence, O'Connor reacted to a questioning statement that Hester had apparently made about church dogma: "Dogma can in no way limit a limitless God.... For me a dogma is only a gateway to contemplation and is an instrument of freedom and not restriction" (*HB* 92). In the same letter, she also analyzed the role of the individual communicant in the church. She asserted that any member is, "no matter how worthless himself, a part of the Body of Christ and a participator in the Redemption. There is no blueprint the Church gives for understanding this. It is a matter of Faith and the Church can force no one to believe it" (*HB* 92). Later O'Connor also explained her ideas about any supposed emotional content of religion: "I must say that the thought on everyone lolling about in an emotionally satisfying faith is repugnant to me. I believe that we are ultimately directed Godward but that this journey is often impeded by emotion" (*HB* 100). In these early letters, she also clearly delineated her belief as being entirely different from that of a pantheist who worships God in nature, asserting that "for me the visible universe is a reflection of the invisible universe. Somewhere St. Augustine says that the things of the world poured forth from God in a double way: intellectually into the minds of the angels and physically into the world of things" (*HB* 128). Through their discussion of "A Temple of the Holy Ghost," they also began a dialogue on the meaning of sexual purity within the church. O'Connor explained her own feelings on the issue: "Purity strikes me as the most mysterious of the virtues and the more I think about it the less I know about it. "A Temple of the Holy Ghost" all revolves around what is purity" (*HB* 117). O'Connor saw the spiritual advice she gave Hester as an extension of her own religious practice; in advising her friend, she was helping lead another person toward spiritual truth. Though the friendship between them continued until O'Connor's death, it changed dramatically when Hester left the church in 1961. On hearing of her decision, O'Connor wrote to her: "I don't know anything that could grieve us here like this news. I know that what you do you do because you think it is right, and I don't think any the less of you outside the Church than in it, but what is painful is the true realization that this means a narrowing of life for you and a lessening of the desire for life" (*HB* 452). She also told Hester that her "unbelief" would eventually wane as she had now lost faith. "Leaving the Church is not the solution," she asserted, and urged her to return when her desire for faith reasserted itself.

Cecil Dawkins, a "cradle Catholic" like O'Connor, also became a close friend in the late 1950s. One serious subject of their correspondence, particularly in the first year or so, was Catholicism. During this time Dawkins was gradually retreating from the church. In several letters O'Connor used her own faith to try to encourage her friend to hold on to *her* faith. Realizing that Dawkins was a woman of intelligence, O'Connor suggested that she might strengthen her belief through reading modern Catholic novelists and theologians; she recommended those who had most affected her own religious life: the Catholic novelists Bloy, Bernanos, and Mauriac; and the philosophers Gilson, Maritain, Marcel, Picard, Guardini, and Karl Adam (*HB* 231). Later O'Connor sent Dawkins one of Mauriac's books, hoping it would help her friend solve her "difficulties with the Church. Maybe time will settle this for you in a better way. I hope so" (*HB* 264). She also urged Dawkins to read Pierre Teilhard de Chardin's *The Phenomenon of Man.*

Another correspondence in which O'Connor adopted the role of a spiritual adviser to a younger person was with Alfred Corn, whom she met after she gave a lecture at Emory University in 1962. Corn heard her speak and later wrote to her to solicit her advice concerning his doubts about Christianity: "I had seen . . . the Protestant fundamentalism of my upbringing crumble away from me under the flood of new ideas proposed in various undergraduate courses. . . . What I wanted to know was how she, with her sharp and cultivated mind, had retained her faith" (Corn 106–7). O'Connor replied, responding generously, both literally and figuratively, to his questions. She told him that his fear of losing his faith was actually evidence of the high value he placed on it and reminded him that Saint Peter had prayed: "'Lord, I believe. Help my unbelief.' It is the most natural and most human and most agonizing prayer in the gospels, and I think it is the foundation proper of faith" (*HB* 476). She encouraged Corn to realize that studying different religions does not require a Christian to justify them with his own belief: "Students get so bound up with difficulties such as reconciling the clashing of so many different faiths . . . that they cease to look for God in other ways." O'Connor even admitted to Corn her own early difficulties with the "clash" of religions. She told him that the clash no longer bothered her because she had "got, over the years, a sense of the immense sweep of creation, of the evolutionary process in everything, of how incomprehensible God must necessarily be to be the God of heaven and earth." She recommended that he read Teilhard's *The Phenomenon of Man.* She later lent him her copy of the book and admitted to him that what had kept her faith alive in college was her skepticism, "It always said: wait, don't bite on this, get a wider picture, continue to read." In the letter she also told him that he must work to maintain his faith: "It is a gift, but for very few of us is it a gift given without any demand for equal time devoted to its cultivation." Echoing a host of other Christians, she also urged him to realize that "in the life of a Christian, faith rises and falls like the tides of an invisible sea" (*HB* 476–77).

Further evidence of O'Connor's spiritual practice emerged during the trip she and her mother took to Lourdes in 1958. A Savannah cousin and patron, Katie Semmes, paid for the trip on the condition that O'Connor bathe in the healing waters at Lourdes. As her many comments in letters reveal, O'Connor, from the beginning, had mixed feelings about both foreign travel and joining the supplicants at Lourdes. One reason that she agreed to the trip to Europe in 1958 was that Sally and Robert Fitzgerald were then living in Levanto, Italy, and the pilgrimage would give her the opportunity to visit her longtime friends. Sally Fitzgerald traveled with the O'Connors to Paris, Lourdes, and Rome, and she also insisted that O'Connor take the waters at Lourdes. From Rome, O'Connor wrote Hester that "Lourdes was not as bad as I expected" and that she had agreed to the bath "because it seemed at the time that it must be what was wanted of me" (*HB* 280). After her return to the United States, she told Hester that the only reason that she bathed in the waters was Sally Fitzgerald's insistence: "She has a hyperthyroid moral imagination. If I hadn't taken it she said it would have been a failure to cooperate with grace and me, seeing myself plagued in the future by a bad conscience, took it" (*HB* 282). In retrospect, O'Connor gave her immersion at Lourdes credit for what proved to be a temporary improvement in the density of her hip bones. In November 1958 she wrote to Caroline Gordon that her doctor had told her that her hip bone was "recalcifying." "Maybe," she said, "this is Lourdes" (*HB* 305). A week later she also reported to Betty Hester that Katie Semmes was dying but had felt relieved at knowing "that the trip to Lourdes has effected some improvement in my bones" (*HB* 306). The Lourdes experience stayed with O'Connor; in February 1963 she wrote to a new friend, Janet McKane, about both having been there and the effect of "taking the waters" on her completion of *The Violent Bear It Away*: "I prayed there for the novel I was working on, not for my bones which I care about less, but I guess my prayers were answered about the novel, inasmuch as I finished it" (*HB* 509).

Still another way that O'Connor practiced her faith from the mid-1950s through the end of her life was through the book reviews she wrote for the diocesan publications, the *Bulletin* and *Southern Cross*. She began to write these reviews at least partly because of what she viewed as her responsibility as a Catholic writer. She wrote to Betty Hester in April 1957, "Doing these things is doing the only corporal work of mercy open to me. My mother takes care of all the visiting the sick and burying the dead that goes on around here. I can't fast on acct. of what I've got. I can't even kneel down to say my prayers. Every opportunity for performing any kind of charity is something to be snatched at" (*HB* 214). At the personal level, writing regular reviews gave her an excuse both to read and to comment on books that she probably would have found and read anyway; however, writing about them helped focus her understanding of the Catholic theologians whom she most admired, among them Romano Guardini, Baron Friedrich von Hügel, Karl Adam, Gustave Weigle, and Pierre Teilhard de Chardin. Reading and reviewing these works, in addition, added weight to her correspondence with various intellectual friends. Her reviews of novels by Catholic writers gave her the opportunity to set forth significant ideas about what she considered to be the mission of the Catholic novelist. She was averse to both too strict an adherence to the dogmatic and too much sentimental sugar-coating.

Somewhat allied with the reviews she wrote is the introduction she wrote in 1960 for the publication of *A Memoir of Mary Ann*, a book about a young girl who had died of cancer at Our Lady of Perpetual Help Home in Atlanta, a hospice run by the Dominican nuns. In an unpublished paragraph in a letter to Cecil Dawkins in November 1960, O'Connor told how she became involved in the project: "Right now I am writing an introduction to a book by some Dominican nuns in Atlanta about a child that they had in their free cancer home up there.... The child herself is worth writing about. One side of her face was quite beautiful, the other almost monstrous, particularly toward the end of her life. Anyway, she bore this outsize cross with considerable charm. Their book is by no means adequate to the subject, but of course, it isn't my dish of tea. I couldn't do it for them. But I am enjoying writing the introduction." The introduction she wrote for the book is one of her most engaging essays: she describes how she became involved in the project and explains her reluctance to write a book about a dying child. Later she retells the story of how Nathaniel Hawthorne, by reputation a reserved, even cold man, was touched by the plight of a repulsive child in an orphanage he visited in Italy. Hawthorne's daughter, Rose Hawthorne Lathrop, O'Connor wrote, founded the order of Dominican Nuns, the Servants of Relief for Incurable Cancer. Probably most significantly in the essay, O'Connor asserts that talking with the sisters about the project helped her to better understand her own use of the grotesque:

> This opened up for me also a new perspective on the grotesque. Most of us have learned to be dispassionate about evil, to look it in the face and find, as often as not, our own grinning reflections with which we do not argue, but good is another matter. Few have stared at that long enough to accept the fact that its face too is grotesque, that in us the good is something under construction. The modes of evil usually receive worthy expression. The modes of good have to be satisfied with a cliché or a smoothing-down that will soften their real look. When we look into the face of good, we are liable to see a face like Mary Ann's, full of promise. (*MM* 226)

Finally, nowhere is O'Connor's faith more evident than in her attitude toward her chronic illness, lupus erythematosus. None of her friends recall that she ever complained about her bad health. Her most poignant and revealing comment on the personal importance of her illness occurred in a letter she wrote to Betty Hester in June 1956: "I have never been anywhere but sick. In a sense sickness is a place more instructive than a long trip to Europe, and it's always a place where there's no company, where nobody can follow. Sickness before death is a very appropriate thing and I think those who don't have it miss one of God's mercies" (*HB* 163). In this deeply moving statement, she revealed her ability to endure the illness with admirable courage based on acceptance and faith. Although she wanted to live a long life in order to fulfill her vocation as a Catholic writer, she faced her final illness in 1964 with both fortitude and faith. By July 8, when she wrote to Janet McKane, she realized how serious her condition had become: "Yesterday the priest brought me Communion as it looks like a long time before I'm afoot. I also had him give me the now-called Sacrament of the Sick. Once known as Extreme Unction" (*HB* 591). About the same time, she also told Sister Mariella Gable, "I'll count on your prayers" (*HB* 591). A few weeks later, on August 3, 1964, at 12:40 A.M. in the Baldwin County Hospital, O'Connor died of kidney failure brought on by the lupus; her mother found her last note, dated July 28, 1964, to Maryat Lee, on her bedside table:

> Dear Raybat,
>
> Cowards can be just as vicious as those who declare themselves—more so. Don't take any romantic attitude toward the call. Be properly scared and go on doing what you have to do, but take the necessary precautions. And call the police. That might be a lead for them. Don't know when I'll send those stories. I've felt too bad to type them.
>
> Cheers, Tarfunk (HB 596)

It seems typical that, even as O'Connor was dying, she was more concerned about the welfare of her New York friend, who had just received an obscene telephone call, than about her own impending death. This heroic lack of self-concern shows just how well her faith allowed Flannery O'Connor to adapt to the disease that finally killed her.

Notes

1. Certain readers and critics of O'Connor and her work have long expressed doubts about both her spiritual conviction and the treatment of Christian themes in her work. John Hawkes may have been the first to question O'Connor's faith, telling her directly that she spoke with the devil's voice in his article, "Flannery O'Connor's Devil," *Sewanee Review* 70 (June 1962): 395–402. Others with similar outlooks include Martha Stephens, *The Question of Flannery O'Connor* (Baton Rouge: Louisiana State University Press, 1973); André Bleikasten, "The Heresy of Flannery O'Connor," in *Les Américanistes: New French Criticism on Modern American Fiction*, ed. Ira D. and Christiane Johnson, 53–70 (Port Washington, N.Y.: Kennikat Press, 1978); Suzanne Morrow Paulson, *Flannery O'Connor: A Study of the Short Fiction* (Boston: G. K. Hall, 1988); Ben Satterfield, "*Wise Blood*, Artistic Anemia, and the Hemorrhaging of O'Connor Criticism," *Studies in American Fiction* 17, no. 1 (1989): 33–50; Michael Kreyling, introduction to *New Essays on Wise Blood*, edited by Michael Kreyling, 1–24 (New York: Cambridge University Press, 1995); and, Joanne Halleran McMullen, *Writing against God: Language as Message in the Literature of Flannery O'Connor* (Macon, Ga.: Mercer University Press, 1996).

Works Cited

Brooks, Cleanth. "Flannery O'Connor—a Tribute." *Esprit* 8 (Winter 1964): 17.

Certificate of membership (1949) of Flannery O'Connor in the Catholic Unity League, New York. O'Connor Collection. Ina Dillard Russell Library, Georgia College and State University, Milledgeville.

Cheney, Brainard. Unpublished letter to Frances Cheney, December 3, 1956. Brainard and Frances Cheney Collection. Jean and Alexander Heard Library, Vanderbilt University, Nashville, Tenn.

Consolata, Sister. Interview by the author. August 8, 1990.

Corn, Alfred. "An Encounter with O'Connor and 'Parker's Back.'" *Flannery O'Connor Bulletin* 24 (1995–96): 104–18.

Fitzgerald, Robert. Introduction to *Everything That Rises Must Converge*, by Flannery O'Connor. New York: Farrar, Straus and Giroux, 1965.
Gordon, Caroline. Unpublished letter to Brainard Cheney, February 4, 1953. Cheney Collection. Jean and Alexander Heard Library, Vanderbilt University, Nashville, Tenn.
Hardwick, Elizabeth. Interview by the author. June 1992.
Hawkins, Peter S. "Faith and Doubt First Class: The Letters of Flannery O'Connor." *Southern Humanities Review* 26 (Spring 1982): 91–103.
Horne, Elizabeth. Interview by the author. October 5, 1992.
Hoynes, Loretta Feuger. Telephone interview by the author. August 6, 1990.
Kazin, Alfred. Telephone interview by the author. July 27, 1994.
Kellam, Kitty Smith. Interview by the author. October 7, 1992.
Macauley, Robie. Interview by the author. December 4, 1992.
McCown, James H. "Flannery O'Connor." Typescript of lecture presented at the University of Alabama, Mobile, April 26, 1985, pp. 1–19.
———. "Remembering Flannery O'Connor." *America*, September 8, 1979, 86–88.
O'Connor, Flannery. Unpublished autobiographical sketch (Iowa). O'Connor Collection. Ina Dillard Russell Library, Georgia College and State University, Milledgeville.
———. Unpublished correspondence with Cecil Dawkins. Cecil Dawkins File. McFarlin Library, University of Tulsa, Tulsa, Okla.
———. Unpublished letters to Fr. James McCown: March 3, 1958; April 3, 1959; September 20, 1959; June 23, 1961; and April 11, 1963. O'Connor Collection. William E. Perkins Library, Duke University, Durham, N.C.
Persse, Patricia, Winifred Persse, and Margaret P. Trexler. Interview by the author. August 6, 1990.
Stephens, Ralph C., ed. *The Correspondence of Flannery O'Connor and the Brainard Cheneys*. Jackson: University of Mississippi Press, 1986.
Sullivan, Walter. Interview by the author. August 8, 1992.
Wylder, Jean. "Flannery O'Connor: A Reminiscence and Some Letters." *North American Review* 225 (Spring 1970): 58–65.

Toward Discerning How Flannery O'Connor's Fiction Can Be Considered "Roman Catholic"

Patrick Samway, S.J.

Were you to have accompanied Flannery O'Connor to Sacred Heart Church in Milledgeville, Georgia, anytime after she had moved there in 1938 at age thirteen, you would have entered a simple, Congregationalist-looking, brick structure, topped by a steeple and surmounted with a cross.[1] Inside you would have been struck by the rather confined, unpretentious liturgical space, which allowed for close, almost intimate, contact between the congregation and the sanctuary. To the left, behind the altar rail, stood a baptismal font, and to the right a free-standing ambo—thus visually reminding the congregation of the importance of both baptism and the proclamation of the Word of God. In the center stood the main altar at which the priest celebrated Mass in Latin with his back to the congregation. As a reminder of the sacrificial nature of the Mass, he could look up to a nearly life-size, loincloth-draped Christus plaintively staring down on him. It is worth noting, too, that two statues, one of Jesus pointing to his Sacred Heart and the other of Our Lady standing on a globe, completed the sanctuary's spiritual decor.

Each time that Flannery entered Sacred Heart Church, passing by the unobtrusive confessional box, to attend Mass as a silent participant, what she saw and heard happening beyond the altar rail greatly enhanced her own spiritual life. Although her pastor/confessor once called her a "holy person," O'Connor made no pretense of cultivating mysticism in any form, though undoubtedly from her Catholic grade-school education and later catechetical instruction she would have known while looking at the two statues from her customary vantage point in the fifth pew on the right side, that they were inspired by two French mystics, Margaret Mary Alacoque, a Visitandine in the monastery at Paray-le-Monial, and Catherine Labouré, a novice in the community of the Daughters of Charity in Paris (Kilcourse 2).[2] As she prayed with these statuary reminders of the Mystical Body and the Communion of Saints before her, she did so, not in a vacuum, but as someone who had throughout her adult life read and admired such French writers, theologians, poets, and novelists as Louis Bouyer, Pierre Teilhard de Chardin, S.J., Yves Congar, O.P., Henri Daniel-Rops, Jean Daniélou, S.J., Henri DeLubac, S.J., Étienne Gilson, André Malraux, Jean Guitton, Jacques Maritain, François Mauriac, Emmanuel Mounier, Charles Péguy, and George Tavard, A.A., Denis de Rougemont, Simone Weil, as well as the Italian-German Romano Guardini (Hollandsworth, Zuber, Sessions, Kilcourse, *HB* [passim]). These two spiritual sources—that is, the ecclesial (baptism, confession, the

Mass, and belief in the mystical dimension of the church) and the extra-ecclesial (her private reading of French writers, especially those who interpreted Thomism for the modern world)—served as a larger apperceptive background by which O'Connor could evaluate the tug-and-pull of her own immediate experiences. Like Saint Augustine, who desired that his faith have an intellectual basis, O'Connor deliberately informed herself about ways of discerning and imagining God's mysteriously dramatic, eternal, and ineffable kingdom, proleptically lived in each moment of one's life but that reaches beyond the borders of one's earthly existence. "Faith," she acknowledged, "is what you have in the absence of knowledge," especially at the end of exhaustive enquiry (*HB* 477).

Raised in a church that curiously allows only six of its seven sacraments to women, O'Connor's spiritual and liturgical world was further informed by the theological discussions of the First Vatican Council (1869–70), which was preceded by years of theological reflection, particularly concerning the often decidedly unpopular notion of papal infallibility, commonly thought of as emanating from a sense of Roman triumphalism, and the less polemical belief of the immaculate conception of the Blessed Virgin Mary, both of which could and did, at times, have deleterious effects in promoting ecumenism, as O'Connor knew firsthand as a citizen of the Protestant South. Not surprisingly her fiction never mentions either dogma. Out of this council came a mentality that opposed what were called the errors of modern rationalism, materialism, and atheism—in short, the tenets of free-thinking, uninformed by divine revelation. Rather, as a practicing Catholic in the widening wake of Vatican I, O'Connor believed God creates his creatures out of nothing, manifests his perfection to them, and leads them to their intended, freely chosen destination. In asserting the relationship between faith and reason, she believed, as did other Catholics of her day, following the teaching of Thomas Aquinas, that the full impact of the mysteries of faith could not be grasped by natural reason alone, though revealed truth would never contradict the results of reasonable investigation. As a result every assertion is false, at least in a Thomistic framework, which contradicts the truth of an enlightened faith entrusted to the church for protection and interpretation. Miracles, of course, confirm divine revelation. Unlike the final decrees of the Second Vatican Council (1962–65), not in full force during O'Connor's lifetime, those of the First Vatican Council tended to be prescriptive rather than descriptive, based on what it considered to be assured, rock-solid, absolute certainty that could easily sniff out anything to the contrary.

In light of this theology, part and parcel of the preaching of her day, it is no wonder that Flannery O'Connor actively pursued Thomism—albeit as a "hillbilly Thomist" (*HB* 81)—in order to have a grounding in realistic metaphysical thinking, even if at a remove (*HB* 439).[3] In August 1955, O'Connor admitted to Betty Hester (a convert to Catholicism, who, while still a correspondent with O'Connor, left the church and subsequently committed suicide) that she was reading the *Summa*

Theologiae of Thomas Aquinas about twenty minutes a day, just before going to bed (*HB* 93). In another letter to Hester, O'Connor wove together her basic theological beliefs:

> I believe too that there is only one Reality and that that is the end of it, but the term, "Christian Realism," has become necessary for me, perhaps in a purely academic way, because I find myself in a world where everybody has his compartment, puts you in yours, shuts the door and departs. One of the awful things about writing when you are a Christian is that for you the ultimate reality is the Incarnation, the present reality is the Incarnation, and nobody believes in the Incarnation; that is, nobody in your audience. . . . As for Jesus' being a realist: if He was not God, He was no realist, only a liar, and the crucifixion an act of justice. (*HB* 92)

For O'Connor and her contemporaries, Jacques Maritain stands out as the most influential lay theologian in promoting a renascence in Catholic intellectual circles. A convert to Catholicism and philosopher who taught in Canada and the United States, he believed that the thought of Thomas Aquinas provided the basis for understanding a realistic existential metaphysics relating man's ontological structure and dignity to his relationship with God, which, in turn, served to explain the identification of the consecrated bread and wine at Mass and the person of Jesus the Christ. (Parenthetically it should be noted that Maritain admired O'Connor's works [*HB* 417]). O'Connor's celebrated retort to Mary McCarthy embodies this fundamental belief in the Catholic doctrine of the Eucharist: "Well, if it's a symbol, to hell with it" (*HB* 124–25, 479). Using the thought of Aristotle, Saint Thomas elaborated a theory of hylomorphism, employing the concepts of act and potency, matter and form, which demonstrates how the substance of a being could remain the same, though its accidents might have different appearances. For Saint Thomas, the act of Eucharistic transubstantiation provided a metaphysical guarantee—and not just for Catholics—that Jesus was really present in the consecrated bread and wine.

Maritain, however, went further by showing the relevance of metaphysics to art, poetry, and science, which restored, for some at least, the loss of the sense of being in the modern world, a phenomenon considered deplorable in certain Catholic circles. In both *Art and Scholasticism* and *Creative Intuition in Art and Poetry*, texts that O'Connor read and marked up, Maritain provides a bridge between a specific tradition of theological thought and a generalized world of culture—in essence, a dialogue integrating Thomism and a classical sense of humanism. O'Connor underlined the following passage in Maritain's *Creative Intuition in Art and Poetry*: "We may observe at this point that art endeavors to imitate in its own way the conditions peculiar to the pure spirits: it draws beauty from ugly things and monsters, it tries to overcome the division between beautiful and ugly by absorbing ugliness in a superior species of beauty, and by transferring us beyond the [aesthetic] beautiful and ugly"

(Andretta 7; see note 3 below). Informed thus by Maritain and others, such as Étienne Gilson, O'Connor, as she relates in her essay "The Nature and Aim of Fiction," remained steadfastly intent on explaining how her fiction and her theological creed flow from the same truthful spring: art glorifies God and reflects his being: "The basis of art is truth, both in matter and in mode. The person who aims after art in his work aims after truth, in an imaginative sense, no more and no less" (*MM* 65).[4] For Maritain, as for O'Connor, a searcher begins with concrete events and situations that at first appear small, perhaps insignificant, until the searcher experiences their expansive nature and theological fullness. In this way, O'Connor's protagonists gradually move closer and closer to an unspecified, but nevertheless felt, mystical, beatific vision, though no one route is preferable in finding either one's heart or God. Maritain and O'Connor believed strongly in the spiritual unconscious that is part and parcel of the mysterious nature of the literary enterprise.

O'Connor was a consummate Catholic fiction writer endowed with prospicience, who, though an admirer of Xavier Rynne's letters concerning the sessions of Vatican II, alas, never felt its actual liberating forces (*HB* 583). Outside the mainstream of Catholic writers of the late 1940s, 50s, and early 60s, she never followed in the wake of other American writers, particularly those who had experienced the radical shift in aesthetic and cultural sensibilities evident in art and literature during the post–World War I period, many of whom, such as T. S. Eliot, James Joyce, Virginia Woolf, W. B. Yeats, and Ezra Pound, broke with so-called Victorian bourgeois morality. In their attempt to throw off the aesthetic burden of the realistic novel, these writers were wont to introduce a variety of literary tactics and devices, including the radical disruption of the linear flow of narrative, the frustration of conventional expectations concerning unity of plot and character, and the deployment of ironic and ambiguous juxtapositions to call into question a panoply of theological, philosophical, and literary assumptions. The fragmented, nonchronological poetic forms of Eliot and Pound, for example, revolutionized poetry, and, in turn, much of the American fiction of that period, as graphically embodied in Faulkner's 1930 novel, *As I Lay Dying,* particularly its cubistic structure, religious argumentation, and use of multiple narrative voices.

Moreover, certain theological and literary movements that were developing during O'Connor's lifetime—the incipient "Death of God" theology and growing debate about deconstructionism in literature readily come to mind—grounded themselves in their own self-presence, without a discernible axis, and certainly not of Otherness, upon which everything rotates. Yet as someone who kept her eyes and heart on a definite theological center, O'Connor resisted the temptation to depict her fictive world a-linguistically and a-historically; she maintained a definite focus on the Christ-haunted American South she understood so well. And what is astonishing, at least for me, is that she resisted enveloping her fiction in a prepackaged Thomistic theology, popularly imagined during her lifetime as a triangle with God at the top, bishops under him, then priests, nuns, and brothers under the bishops, and lastly the good, simple Catholic laity resting on the bottom. Rather, anticipating some of the dynamic thinking of Vatican II, O'Connor's characters are more than likely flawed, uninformed, or sinful ones in need of a conversion as they undertake a journey—a pilgrimage, holy or otherwise. O'Connor writes about those whom many writers of her generation repressed: the mystic, the prophetic, the marginalized. In short, she deals with otherness, difference, transgression, excess—contemporary notions (some even might say "buzz words") so much part of critical parlance today. And this explains, in part, why O'Connor is so beloved by adult readers, who understand her thematic preoccupations, but difficult for young adults, who seek conformity, similarity, acceptance, and control of their emotional environment.

More than anyone else, I believe, William Lynch, S.J., one of my former professors whose books *The Image Industries* and *Christ and Apollo: The Dimensions of the Literary Imagination* O'Connor reviewed, helped her in validating her particular postmodernist direction (*PG* 74, 94). In his development of the "analogical imagination," as articulated in his 1954 essay "Theology and Imagination" in the journal *Thought*, which O'Connor likewise read and commented upon (*HB* 132), Lynch brings together sameness and difference, stressing that the things of this world have their own reality but also participate, as George Kilcourse notes in a discussion of Lynch's thought, in the larger community of being (Kilcourse 114). For Lynch, the "analogical" is "that habit of perception which sees that different levels of being are also somehow one and can therefore be *associated in the same image*, in the same and single act of perception" (Kilcourse 75). As God became incarnate in Jesus, and as Jesus often presented the otherworldly in images of the worldly, so too the human imagination probes the finite, the particular, the limited as a way of describing the mysteries of the infinite God. Thus Catholic theology at once embraces the world and renounces it, as it seeks to go from the specific to the horizon of the eternal moment. As O'Connor knew so well, the Incarnation is not a temporary blessing but a Christification of the world that renders the human sacrosanct—as depicted, for example, in the nude child Jesus in the Christmas crèche and the nude Christus on a crucifix above an altar. Finite and infinite realities coalesce, for Lynch, and thus there is no need to pull together what has never been separated. "The resurrection of Christ seems the high point in the law of nature," O'Connor wrote (*HB* 100), a loaded observation implying that the resurrection of Jesus, like an earthly miracle, is a natural phenomenon, something within the laws of nature, an observation that coincides with Robert Fitzgerald's in his introduction to *Everything That Rises Must Converge:* "The lives of O'Connor's solitaries are perhaps rightly to be considered as an anticipation of death—or, rather, of the life that is born from death" (14). For O'Connor, the mystery of God in every part of the universe undergirds the Christian imagination.

But more is at stake, I believe. The Manichean temptation for the imagination, as Lynch notes, is "to win its freedom by seeking quick infinities through the rapid and clever manipulation of the finite" rather than passing through "all the rigors, density, limitations, and decisions of the actual" (Lynch 1955, 545). In a telling fashion, O'Connor says that Lynch "describes the true nature of the literary imagination as founded on [in] a penetration of the finite and the limited.... In genuine tragedy and comedy, the definite is explored to its extremity and man is shown to be the limited creature he is, and it is at this point of greatest penetration of the limited that the artist finds insight. Much modern so-called tragedy avoids this penetration and makes a leap toward transcendence, resulting in an unearned and spacious [sic] resolution of the work" (*PG* 94). Though O'Connor did not ascribe to the entirety of Lynch's thesis, she did agree with his general theory, developed in three other essays in the journal *Thought*, since she realized its potential for explaining the Christic imagination, which she saw linked to the "anagogical" interpretation of scripture as expressed in the Latin phrase "*Littera gesta docet, quod credas allegoria, moralia qui agas, quo tendas anagogia*" (The literal teaches events, allegory what you believe, the moral teaches what to do, the anagogical where you are headed), though I feel certain O'Connor would have changed her views given the hermeneutical developments in scripture since her death (*HB* 520, *MM* 72–73, 111). Her penchant for accepting a fourfold reading of scripture is not without merit, however, since Catholicism, which accepts the Hebrew Bible as part of its scriptural heritage, has always had layered relationships of one sort or another not only with Judaism but with other religions; its earliest churches, as is well documented, were sometimes built on the sites of former pagan temples.

Though O'Connor insists in essay after essay on the freedom the Catholic Church gives a Catholic writer, especially in fathoming the depths of mystery, revelation, and the dogmas of the church, she curiously has little to say about the nature of fiction that can be labeled "Catholic": "If I had to say what a 'Catholic novel' is," she writes in "Catholic Novelists," "I could only say that it is one that represents reality adequately as we see it manifested in this world of things and human relationships.... [A] Catholic novel is not necessarily about a Christianized or Catholicized world, but simply that it is one in which the truth as Christians know it has been used as a light to see the world by. This may or may not be a Catholic world, and it may or may not have been seen by a Catholic" (*MM* 172). Surprisingly, her rather generic comments on the Catholic novel disappear asymptotically in her essays and letters, as if the subject held little genuine interest for her, perhaps because any development of the topic would take her into the world of literary criticism, one that had too many pitfalls. She did have, however, the audacious commonsense to "trash" Cardinal Francis Spellman's *The Foundling* (*HB* 60). Since O'Connor expressed her interest in the fiction of such Catholic writers as Graham Greene, Evelyn Waugh, Muriel Spark, Walker Percy, and J. F. Powers, as well as the poetry of

Gerard Manley Hopkins, S.J., it seems legitimate and appropriate to analyze the Catholic nature of O'Connor's fiction, just as one might do with the poetry of Hopkins, in spite of the fact that there are no literary organizations, as far as I know, explicitly devoted to a study of Catholic poetry or fiction, most likely because such works, as the Catholic novelist and historian Peter Quinn notes, appeal far beyond the ranks of the authors' coreligionists.[5] Conversely, some non-Catholics or once-Catholic writers who have decided not to remain within the Catholic fold write fiction that devout Catholics find expressive of their religious values. Much depends on one's point of view; suffering, for a Christian writer or reader, can bring the Christian closer to an understanding of the Kingdom of God; for Darwinians, however, it is a fact, empty of metaphysical significance. And for many in a post-Auschwitz world, the holy water font has for ages been dry and dusty.

In his study of Catholic fiction, Ross Labrie is not alone in noting that "the institutional church, particularly the Catholic Church, plays little role in the lives of [O'Connor's] protagonists" (Labrie 231). As she wrote to her friend James H. McCown, S.J., "A Catholic has to have strong nerves to write about Catholics" (*HB* 130). "Writers like myself who don't use Catholic settings or characters, good or bad," she likewise wrote to Betty Hester, "are trying to make it plain that personal loyalty to the person of Christ is imperative, is the structure of man's nature, his necessary direction, etc. The Church, as institution, doesn't come into it one way or another" (*HB* 290). Her strength as a Catholic fiction writer is that she believed with her whole heart in the sacraments—particularly baptism, the Eucharist, and reconciliation, which were so integral to her spiritual life as a parishioner of Sacred Heart Church—as well as in the mystical experience of the saints and the power of the Word of God, whether written or spoken.

Nevertheless, in spite of her stated reluctance, O'Connor depicts characters and incidents in three of her stories that reveal her explicit belief in Catholicism. In "The Temple of the Holy Ghost," for example, she dramatizes from the viewpoint of a twelve-year-old girl, who acknowledges, as does her mother, that the Holy Ghost lives within her second cousins Joanne and Susan, though they find this concept (a perpetual one if the name of one of the nun's rings true) laughable. In addition they mock the singing of Saint Thomas Aquinas's hymn to the real presence of God in the Eucharist, the *Tantum Ergo*. What, one might well ask, should this little girl do or believe? "She would have to be a saint because that was the occupation that included everything you could know and yet she knew she would never be a saint" (*CW* 204). The girl eventually links her own interior life with the plight of the freaks at the fair, who accept the way God made them. In turn, her face mashed by the nun's crucifix makes her a freakish person as she places herself before Christ present in the monstrance at Benediction. Later, while being driven home, she sees the brilliant setting sun, bloody in its appearance, a reminder of the suffering and transcended Son of God in the consecrated host—thus ratifying a Christocentric world.

God's presence in and among his people is more indirectly portrayed in "The Displaced Person" when Father Flynn brings the aging and ailing Mrs. McIntyre not the *Viaticum,* as he did to Mr. Guizac, but a bag of breadcrumbs for her peacocks. He does, however, sit at her bedside and explain the doctrines of the church, which she might or might not hear and might or might not accept. This "idiotic" old man had previously stood slack-jawed before a peacock whose tail was in full display with "small pregnant suns" floating in a "green-gold haze over his head." "Christ will come like that!" he says, making explicit that the Second Coming of the resurrected Christ will have a majesty we can only barely imagine, and then only imperfectly. Well does the priest know that Christ had once transfigured himself before three of his disciples, and they were blinded by his appearance (Matt. 17:2–5). In a matter-of-fact way, yet which has for the reader a newness to it, he proclaims that Christ came "to redeem us" (*CW* 317).

As a Catholic, O'Connor knew that the sacraments a priest confers *ex opere operato* have an efficacy independent of his theological knowledge or lack of it, something that Asbury Fox in "The Enduring Chill" does not quite realize after meeting Ignatius Vogle, S.J., at a lecture on Indian philosophy. When Father Finn, another Jesuit who is partially blind and deaf, upsets the dying Asbury because he does not know the works of the Jesuit-trained James Joyce, one can only wonder if Asbury is prepared to accept the basic catechetical instruction that Joyce himself was taught— "None of us knows the hour Our Blessed Lord may call us. . . . Nothing is overcome without prayer. . . . God made you" (*CW* 565–66). In addition Father Finn attempts to counter Asbury's rejection of the Holy Ghost by saying that the third person of the Trinity might well be the "last thing" Asbury receives before he dies, a prophetically charged statement, given the last sentence in the story.

These three stories with unequivocal Catholic dogmatic and liturgical references —especially Father Finn's litany of admonitions—provide an entrée into considering the religious nature of the rest of O'Connor's fiction insofar as it is recognizable to Christians of other denominations or no denomination at all. Because Catholics share the Old and New Testaments with other Christians, not to mention belief in the validity of baptism as an entrance into God's kingdom, O'Connor's fiction, from one perspective, develops outward from an absolute belief in the dogmatic tenets of Catholicism as it dramatizes aspects of certain biblical stories, the nature of parables, and hearing and preaching the Word of God, even if told in ways that are superliteral or fascinatingly bizarre.

O'Connor often wrote about communicating a religious vision to those for whom the phrase was almost meaningless; in order to do that, however, she needed to lead her reader through the thicket of her fiction, often by means of religious code words, phrases, incidents, and situations. My argument concerning a specific way in which O'Connor as author communicates with her reader enhances the thesis clearly developed by John Desmond in his book *Risen Sons,* in that I recognize O'Connor's use of the analogical principle in the act of writing to create a sense of mystery, but I am intent on indicating an additional mode of communication not explicitly developed by other critics. In doing so, I do not mean to provide a reductionist critique of her fiction but rather to show but another dimension of her art that builds on close readings of her texts. In mentioning, for example, "A Temple of the Holy Ghost," Desmond notes that in this story O'Connor "creates vision implicitly through the details of the passage—the Host, the freak, the nun's crucifix, Alonzo's pig ears, the sun, the trees. O'Connor preserves the mystery of the scene by leaving it to the reader to envision the 'connection' between the literary details and the hierophany, and she thereby respects both the created fictional world *and* the reader" (Desmond 23). I would go one step further, and add that O'Connor actually helps the reader to the hierophany by planting verbal signposts along the way, in the spirit of Walker Percy, who believed that a novelist takes a stranger into a strange, fictive land and teaches him or her to read carefully the signs that are there.

Like C. Auguste Dupin in Edgar Allan Poe's mystery stories, who associates the terms "mob" with "readership," O'Connor invests her own subtle critical voice into the text through contextualized references precisely to give hints of a spiritual direction to the uninitiated that will develop into revelatory grace-filled moments.[6] Grace, O'Connor repeats in myriad ways, is always amazing, even if it is not at first recognized as such. She seemed to sense that the most poignant manner of demonstrating to readers their own insensitivity in reading and perhaps their own lack of susceptibility in discerning theological hermeneutics would be to guide them through their own processes of reading by means of particular narrative devices. Thus O'Connor's fiction has a distinctive mysteriously formulaic character to it, not dissimilar to the types of formulas found, for instance, in chemistry, something sensed by Thomas Merton, O.C.S.O., as revealed in a comment he made about the ways O'Connor composed a story: "she would put together all these elements of unreason and let them fly slowly and inexorably at one another" (Merton 70). But how do formulas work in O'Connor's fiction? Taking a cue from a statement about Bishop in *The Violent Bear It Away* ("The little boy was part of a simple equation that required no further solution, except at the moments when with little or no warning he would feel himself overwhelmed by the horrifying love" [*CW* 401]), let me cite one equation, or formula, we all think we know: $NaCl$ is the formula for salt, that is, one can create salt by bonding sodium and chloride. Clear enough, but wait, both sodium and chloride are toxic. Thus, two poisons bonded together can create a substance that makes food taste better! *Et voilà*, a moment of revelation.

Examples abound of how O'Connor bonds theological elements, not just those in her three demonstrably Catholic stories, but in most of her other fiction that originate from her belief in the tenets of Catholicism. She bonds those elements that are toxic and can lead to perdition with other elements that can lead to eternal life, even if it means the death, nay suicide, of an individual. In "Good Country People," O'Connor uses, as she does in her other stories, marker phrases, codes, linguistic symbols that, when read linearly and cumulatively, reveal something new, something that has been there all along in the story, but which adds up to a dramatically theological insight whose logic and truthfulness demand the visionary powers of a mystic. When a one-legged woman with a Ph.D. in philosophy who has named herself Hulga risks falling in love with Manley Pointer, a gigolo and a Bible salesman who runs off with her wooden leg just as they are about to enjoy a certain intimacy, the question arises: will Hulga, once radically disappointed in love, ever open herself up to love again, especially the love that God shares in his written word, the Bible? O'Connor explained in her essay "Writing Short Stories" that once she brought Manley Pointer into the story, she had no idea what she was going to do with him, and specifically she did not know he was going to steal Hulga's wooden leg until ten or twelve lines before he did it. But once she discovered what he was going to do, she found this action to be inevitable. "This is a story," O'Connor wrote, "that produces a shock for the reader and I think one reason for this is that it produced a shock for the writer" (*MM* 100).

As the story progresses, O'Connor provides the reader with appropriate but unexpected marker phrases and linguistic symbols: (1) O'Connor writes about Hulga: "She had a weak heart"; (2) Manley Pointer likewise says, "I got this heart condition"; (3) Hulga says to her mother, "If you want me, here I am—LIKE I AM!"; (4) "Woman," Hulga screams at her mother, "do you ever look inside and see what you are *not* . . . God!, Malebranche was right . . . we are not our own light"; (5) Hulga says, "We know nothing by wishing to know nothing of Nothing"; (6) Manley Pointer says, "You can never tell when you'll need the word of God, Hulga"; (7) At the end of the story, Manley Pointer says, "Hulga, you aint so smart. I been believing in nothing ever since I was born!"; (8) And most important, Pointer says, quoting scripture, "He who losest his life shall find it" (*CW* 263–84). When we bond all these phrases together through the progressive action of the story, we end up with O'Connor salt, or "shock" as she puts it, thus falling into a meditation about risking love and being deceived in the process. The reader is forced to make connections. "He may not even know that he makes the connection[s]," O'Connor wrote in her essay "Writing Short Stories," "but the connection[s are] there nevertheless and [they] have an effect on him" (*MM* 99). Should one who has a "heart condition" and philosophically sees through to Nothing risk love again? Should one lose one's life in order to find it, as the mystics, such as Margaret Mary Alacoque and Catherine Labouré have done? In O'Connor's salvific economy in this story, love is linked to the saving word of God—unread, by the way, by all the characters in this story (in fact, Hulga's mother keeps her Bible in the attic, out of sight and out of reach). Yet in "Good Country People," God's word implicitly and explicitly permeates the entire story.[7] Ironically, as Sarah Gordon points out, this story shows that Hulga's powers of insight are overrated in that she has been completely deceived by Manly Pointer (Gordon 177).

After years of praying and participating in the sacramental life of Sacred Heart Church, especially the sacraments of reconciliation and the Eucharist, as well as knowing about the efficacious grace bestowed by baptism and the sacrament of the sick (last rites), O'Connor never ceased to enter more and more deeply into these mysteries of the church. Her knowledge of church history, especially key dimensions of the thought of Saint Thomas Aquinas as framed by some of the best twentieth-century commentators on Thomistic theology, afforded her an interior freedom to depict from a fictional perspective God's interaction with creatures who have been nurtured, for better or worse, by southern culture and manners, concepts that O'Connor left as wide ranging as possible. Her imagination, peculiarly religious and formulaic in nature, links phrases, scenes, and situations that add up to a type of truthful probability known to a Catholic Christian or any believer who grapples with a fading memory of God's unprogrammed and unprogrammatic interaction with curious groupings of his people who might seem to have passed through Milledgeville but are really citizens of a larger world. Above all, such Christians know the logic of The Misfit's statement that if Jesus did what he said, "then it's nothing for you to do but follow Him" (*CW* 152). Hazel Motes's logic has a similar ring to it: "If there's no bottom in your eyes, they hold more" (*CW* 126). Each of these texts has a context to be sure, but the logic of such phrases often hovers above the immediate story, though a critic should avoid soaring too high and losing a sense of the story's place, as Eudora Welty wisely counsels us. O'Connor wants her readers to look carefully at what she has written, like Ruby Hill looking down the stairwell or Norton gazing through his telescope, though like Mrs. May, who, when held by the bull's unbearable grip, "had the look of a person whose sight had been suddenly restored but who finds the light unbearable," so we too might not be prepared to see what is finally there (*CW* 523). But what we do manage to see and figure out should, if all goes well, lead us further into mystery.

Thus, one way to approach the religious nature of O'Connor's fiction is to appreciate how her Roman Catholic characters, their words and actions, provide an initial but necessary ontological grounding that reveals an absolute assurance and acceptance, by the author, of God's genuine presence within and among his people. The religiously chemical elements, if you will, remain in constant tension with one another as the reader/critic tries to determine the ways they are and can be bonded together. What is particularly interesting, to me at least, is that the juxtaposition of these elements about theological ideas, dogmas, and situations could not be found in a theological treatise, but only in a work of fiction. Moreover the elements in one O'Connor work, such as baptism, can be found in other of her works, thus allowing an expanded intertextual analysis that permits a larger, more comprehensive critique of the works in question, much like the open-endedness of Charles Sanders Peirce's triadic sign system. At the end of her novels O'Connor does not return her readers to ground zero, as some have argued, but to an equal sign. Each of her works of fiction, individually and collectively, adds up to something. But what? Certainly not a theme or some reductionist's pablum, since the bonding process of the elements within a story only compound and increase the complexity of the fictive structure. But what is on the other side of the equal sign? That really is the question. Maybe one place to begin seeking an answer would be to follow it back to its origin, back to a young woman praying almost daily in Sacred Heart Church in Milledgeville, back to this southerner, who, as she knelt before the Blessed Sacrament, roamed the many byways of her creative imagination, back to this artist who knew she needed to shout and draw large pictures, back to this writer who had more to tell those willing to see and learn and understand.

Notes

1. Two pictures (interior and exterior views) of Sacred Heart Church can be found in Harold Fickett and Douglas R. Gilbert, *Flannery O'Connor: Images of Grace* (Grand Rapids, Mich.: William B. Eerdmans Publishing Company, 1986), 38. Prior to attending Sacred Heart Church, Flannery had been a parishioner at the Cathedral of St. John the Baptist in Savannah, except for less than six months when she lived in Atlanta. I have focused on Sacred Heart Church, since this was O'Connor's parish church throughout her discerning teenage years, and also during her adult years when she lived in Milledgeville. Mr. and Mrs. Hugh Donnelly Treanor, Flannery's great-grandparents, donated the land on which Sacred Heart Church (completed in April 1874) was built.

2. Monsignor John Toomey, the parish priest at Sacred Heart from 1943 to 1956, made this statement to William Sessions at the O'Connor farm, Andalusia, while Sessions was visiting Flannery O'Connor and her mother. Professor Sessions also attended Mass with the O'Connors in Sacred Heart and heard Monsignor Toomey preach (William Sessions, interviewed by Patrick Samway, S.J., May 31, 2002). Flannery O'Connor's piety is likewise attested to by Elizabeth G. Ferguson, a Milledgeville resident, in an unpublished letter to the Editorial Department, Harcourt, Brace and Company, New York, N.Y., dated April 21, 1952 (Archives of Robert Giroux at Harcourt, Inc.). See also *HB* 92. The devotion to the Sacred Heart gained prominence among the Catholic faithful due in large part to the numerous visions of Margaret Mary Alacoque. It is believed that during one mystical vision in particular, which occurred on June 16, 1675, Jesus explained the love he had toward those in the world and asked, in return, for an expression of reciprocal love in and through the reception of Communion on the first Friday of each month. The statue of Our Lady, arms outstretched with the dazzling rays of light streaming from her fingers, depicts her as she appeared in a vision on November 27, 1830, to Catherine Labouré, and as subsequently portrayed on what is known as the Miraculous Medal.

3. For an analysis of O'Connor's views of Thomism, see "A Thomist's Letters to 'A,'" by Helen R. Andretta (an essay developed from a paper presented at the American Literature Association's Conference, May 30, 1998, San Diego, Calif.). I am grateful to Professor Andretta for sending me a copy of her essay.

4. Étienne Gilson, Maritain's contemporary, likewise a native Parisian, became director of studies for medieval philosophy at the École Pratique des Hautes Études in Paris. In 1926 he came

to the United States for the first time, lecturing at Harvard and the University of Virginia, before eventually becoming in 1929 the cofounder of the Institute of Mediaeval Studies in Toronto, Canada. In 1932 he became a professor at the Collège de France, and approximately twenty years later he returned to the institute in Toronto. Gilson particularly noted that medieval philosophy, under the influence of Christianity, opened up new ways of thinking to the extent that Christian revelation can serve as an indispensable aid to reason; in fact, Gilson, like some of his contemporaries, resisted synthesizing Thomism with philosophies not sympathetic with its spirit, such as the methodic doubt of Descartes, thus becoming a champion of a living unadulterated Thomism. O'Connor's admiration for Gilson can be seen in her letter to Betty Hester (*HB* 107). For an overview of Catholic theology as related to Flannery O'Connor I recommend the various essays in *The New Catholic Encyclopedia,* 15 vols. (New York: McGraw Hill, 1967), especially "Catholic Church," "Étienne Gilson," "Jacques Maritain," "Sacraments," and "Thomism."

5. See *HB* 570. Journals such as *Religion and Literature, Christianity and Literature, Religion and the Arts, Literature and Theology,* and *Renascence* bear witness to the fact that there is interest among certain critics in seeing relationships between theology and literary criticism, but this does not mean that there is a School of Catholic Literary Criticism. See also "Is There Such a Thing as a Catholic Novel?" by Peter Quinn (lecture at Fordham University's School of Law, New York, N.Y., April 18, 2002).

6. See "Detecting the Critic: The Presence of Poe's Critical Voice in the Dupin Tales" by Warren Kelly (talk delivered at the American Literature Association's Conference, May 30, 2002, Long Beach, Calif.). I am grateful to Professor Warren for sending me a copy of this talk and I willingly acknowledge my debt to him. It should be noted that O'Connor went through a period of reading Poe (*HB* 98).

7. To cite another example, O'Connor employs the same formulaic technique in "A Good Man Is Hard to Find." Some marker phrases that lead the reader: (1) "These days you don't know who to trust," [Sammy says]. "Aint that the truth"; (2) "'People are certainly not more like they used to be,' said the grandmother"; (3) "'A good man is hard to find,' Red Sammy said"; (4) "'I know you're a good man,' [the grandmother says to The Misfit.] 'You don't look a bit like you have common blood. I know you must come from nice people.' 'Nome,' [he replies], 'I aint a good man, but I aint the worst in the world either'"; (5) "'Jesus, Jesus,' the grandmother prays. 'Meaning Jesus will you help me, but the way she said it, it sounded as if she might be cursing'"; (6) "'Maybe he didn't raise the dead,' the old lady mumbled"; (7) The Misfit has the last line of the story: "It's no real pleasure in life" (*CW* 153). Where is the O'Connor salt here? It certainly has to do with meeting death unexpectedly and questioning the ultimate power of Jesus to raise others from the dead. At the end of life, after one has confronted evil personified, does Jesus's own death have value? O'Connor seems to be asking. "The heroine of this story, the Grandmother," O'Connor wrote in her essay "On Her Own Work," "is in the most significant position life offers a Christian. She is facing death. And to all appearances she, like the rest of us, is *not* too well prepared for it. She would like to see the event postponed. Indefinitely" (*MM* 110). Is there really a divinely good man to help us? And does the grandmother receive the grace of a happy death?

Works Cited

Desmond, John. *Risen Sons: Flannery O'Connor's Vision of History.* Athens: University of Georgia Press, 1987.

Faulkner, William. *As I Lay Dying.* New York: Jonathan Cape and Harrison Smith, 1930.

Gordon, Sarah. *Flannery O'Connor: The Obedient Imagination.* Athens: University of Georgia Press, 2000.

Hollandsworth, Linda. "'Sophisticated acts': The Friendship of Flannery O'Connor and William Sessions." *Southern Quarterly* 38 (Summer 2000): 93–100.

Kilcourse, George A., Jr. *Flannery O'Connor's Religious Imagination*. Mahwah, N.J.: Paulist Press, 2001.

Labrie, Ross. *The Catholic Imagination in American Literature*. Columbia: University of Missouri Press, 1997.

Lynch, William, S.J. *Christ and Apollo: The Dimensions of the Literary Imagination*. New York: Sheed and Ward, 1960.

———. *The Image Industries*. New York: Sheed and Ward, 1959.

———. "Theology and Imagination." *Thought* 29 (Spring 1954): 61–86; "Theology and Imagination II: The Evocative Symbol." *Thought* 29 (Winter 1954–55): 529–54; "Theology and Imagination III: The Problem of Comedy." *Thought* 30 (Spring 1955): 18–36; "The Imagination and the Finite." *Thought* 33 (Summer 1958): 205–28.

Maritain, Jacques. *Creative Intuition in Art and Poetry*. New York: Meridian, 1955.

Merton, Thomas, O.C.S.O. "Flannery O'Connor: A Prose Elegy." In *Critical Essays on Flannery O'Connor*, edited by Melvin J. Friedman and Beverly Lyon Clark, 68–70. Boston: G. K. Hall and Company, 1985.

Rynne, Xavier. *Letters from Vatican City*. 4 vols. New York: Farrar, Straus and Giroux, 1963–66.

Life at Andalusia

Ashley Brown

This essay is a sequel to "Flannery O'Connor: A Literary Memoir," which I wrote in 1984.[1] In that essay I related some of the details of my friendship with Flannery O'Connor, which began through correspondence in 1952. I first met her the following year at the home of Brainard and Frances Cheney in Tennessee; they had made her acquaintance and invited both of us to a house party. O'Connor visited the hospitable Cheneys several times, and the correspondence between them continued for the rest of her life. Ralph C. Stephens of the University of Maryland collected, edited, and published it.[2]

I first visited the O'Connors in April 1955 in the company of a friend at the University of Georgia in Athens, Fred Bornhauser. Fred, a high school friend of mine and later a Rhodes Scholar, seemed to have read most of the stories that would soon be included in *A Good Man Is Hard to Find*. This was not easily done because three of the ten stories were first published in *Harper's Bazaar*, not usual reading matter for an intellectual youth. It is to the credit of Alice Morris, in those days the literary editor of the magazine, that she was able to include stories of the caliber of "Good Country People" among the illustrations of haute couture. Flannery's response was characteristic: "A lady in Macon told me she read me under the dryer. I was gratified." Alice Morris could not resist putting this wry comment in a quite perceptive contributor's note that she wrote to accompany an unusual photograph of Flannery O'Connor. The fact is that O'Connor's stories sometimes turned up in unexpected places. She and her agent usually tried to place them in journals with a fairly large circulation. In a letter of April 11, 1954, to the Cheneys she reports that Monroe Spears is going to print "The Displaced Person," and she mentions that "the Atlantic kept it 4 months and decided it wasn't their dish" (Stephens 15). I find it astonishing that the *Atlantic Monthly*, once a highly esteemed American literary journal, should have rejected a masterpiece like "The Displaced Person," surely one of the most accessible of the stories. In any event, it was quickly accepted by the *Sewanee Review* and, once published there in October 1954, was soon revised and expanded into the version that we have in *A Good Man Is Hard to Find*.

It was an easy drive from Athens to Milledgeville on a fine Sunday afternoon in April. Andalusia lies outside the town on Highway 441 to Eatonton, which thus connects the homes of two famous Georgia authors, O'Connor and Joel Chandler Harris. A quick glance at *The Habit of Being* reveals that Flannery almost never mentioned Harris in her letters, but occasionally in conversation a visitor would bring up his name, and she would indicate that he was a writer whom she had enjoyed and taken for granted. More recently I have learned that another writer, Alice Walker, lived briefly along the Eatonton highway when she was a child; she belongs to a later generation, who would probably not have heard of Flannery while she was alive. Walker's fine essay "Beyond the Peacock: The Reconstruction of Flannery O'Connor" describes a visit that she and her mother made to Andalusia and her own nearby childhood home in 1974. Both houses were abandoned; one was only a ruin, whereas Andalusia had a caretaker who kept it locked. Alice Walker momentarily resents being excluded: "Her house becomes—in an instant—the symbol of my own disinheritance." But then, she says, "I remind myself of her courage and how much —in her art—she has helped me to see." Her essay, at times reminiscent of "The Displaced Person," ends with an "inspiring" view of the peacocks who were still roaming across the yard.[3]

When Fred and I drove up the rough dirt road to the house, we might have expected something grander to complement this large farm of perhaps twelve hundred acres, much larger than the farms we were familiar with in Kentucky. We saw cattle across the pasture, a barn, some small unpainted buildings, and the house itself, standing on a rise overlooking a pond. The driveway circled the house and led to the back door. Flannery may have mentioned this in her instructions for our trip; I gathered that most visitors, as well as the O'Connors themselves, entered the house from the rear. It is a rather plain white farmhouse, which probably has counterparts in various parts of the United States—perhaps in upstate New York or even along the Sevier River Valley in Utah where the early settlers from the East brought some of the architectural styles they were familiar with. The screened porch that runs across the front is perhaps more typical of southern houses, and not just in the countryside. I remember a hammock strung across the O'Connors' porch rather than the more customary porch swing, and there were rocking chairs for informal conversation or reading during the long seasons of warm weather.

Flannery was sometimes photographed on the brick steps leading up to the screened porch (for example in the photograph, much reproduced, on the jacket of *The Habit of Being*), but she almost never used the steps, even before she was on crutches. Indeed, the main reason she was living at Andalusia rather than in the Cline House in town was simply that she could enter or leave easily from the rear of the house. The first view that most visitors had of the interior was the kitchen. Here her mother, Regina O'Connor, presided over things. She welcomed visitors —a rather important matter, in my opinion. Life would have been difficult for Flannery if her mother had lacked what was only a conventional southern role as hostess. Regina was a perfectly able cook, who did not hesitate to take short cuts in the matter of cuisine. One knows about writers, like Wallace Stevens, who never invited friends to their homes simply because the "woman of the house" chose not to put up with the burden of entertaining strangers. Andalusia was a working dairy farm that Regina gradually learned to operate; she was, after all, used to the ways of town life, either in Savannah or Milledgeville. Despite her energy, there was a limit to what she could manage, and by 1957 she abandoned dairy farming for beef cattle, which did not require skilled labor. In the end she gave up cattle altogether and derived an income from the extensive pinewoods on the place.

I think some of Flannery's visitors expected intellectual conversations round the dinner table, or they even thought that Flannery lived under considerable constraint in her mother's company. For my part, I found Regina easy to get along with. I noticed on my first visit that she always called her daughter Mary Flannery, in the traditional southern manner, and Flannery usually referred to her mother by her first name, something I would never have done with my mother. I also noticed that as she grew a little older, during the decade or so that I knew her, Flannery increasingly used "we" to refer to her mother and herself. It may be that Regina only gradually accepted the fact that her daughter could move in a world different from the small-town society that had been the setting for her life. But I cannot speak for her.

On this first visit, Fred and I had a little tour of Milledgeville, especially its architectural gems. The town was "carved out of the wilderness," so people used to say, to be the post-Revolutionary capital of Georgia. In an effort to encourage the population to move inland from the old coastal cities, something like this happened in several other former colonies when they became states after the Revolution. Milledgeville, however, was the capital of Georgia for only two generations, and then Atlanta became the capital. Milledgeville was, unlike Atlanta, spared General Sherman's wrath in his march to the sea during the Civil War, and it retains a certain charm because of its history. Regina's family, the Clines, have had a part in its history. They were, I suppose, the preeminent Catholic family in the town, and their social status was assured by tradition rather than money.

One feature of Milledgeville during the 1950s should be mentioned. It was the site of the state asylum for the insane, which sat on the edge of the town, and the number of inmates there may well have exceeded the population of the town. I daresay the asylum contributed to the economy of the town, even though this was seldom mentioned. As one might expect, inmates occasionally escaped but were seldom pursued or brought back. When I first heard this, I thought that Flannery and Regina might be rather alarmed: they were, after all, two women living alone in the countryside, but evidently Milledgeville people accepted the situation and did not consider the fugitives dangerous. And then Flannery told me something that I was not to repeat to Regina. It seems that an inmate, a youth with literary interests, heard about her and initiated a correspondence. He broke out of the asylum, made his way to New York City, and continued to write to her. She was about to go to New York herself, probably to confer with her editor, Robert Giroux, and agreed to meet the youth in Bryant Park at the back of the public library at Fifth Avenue and Forty-second Street. I do not know what was said on that occasion, which was the only time that Flannery ever met the young man, but I thought it was an extreme example of the generosity of spirit that she could demonstrate. It must have been a hopeless situation. Incidentally, the general circumstances in Milledgeville, with fugitives from the asylum occasionally wandering across the fields, may have suggested some details for her story called "A Circle in the Fire," though, of course, the author complicates things by means of the child observer who thrusts herself into the action.

Back at Andalusia, before supper, we saw the famous peacocks showing their true colors against the pink twilight. I had never seen so many before, nor had I realized that they were capable of swooping up into the trees as unexpectedly as they did. They were only the most spectacular specimens of bird life on the scene, because Flannery also kept geese, ducks, a swan, various exotic chickens (some of them in cages), and feeding time was an important moment in the daily round of life at Andalusia. What about dogs and cats? Most authors I have known are devoted to one or the other, but not Flannery. I suspect that Pitty Sing, the cat responsible for the catastrophe in "A Good Man Is Hard to Find," represents her sentiments about the feline race. After I realized this, one day in a naughty moment I introduced her to Thomas Gray's little mock epic, "Ode on the Death of a Favourite Cat, Drowned in a Tub of Gold Fishes." "Served him right," she said.

Andalusia, the house and its environs, has been well described by a number of visitors, especially Sally Fitzgerald in an article, "The Andalusian Sibyl," that appeared in a popular magazine called *Southern Living* in May 1983. She never visited the place while Flannery was alive—Sally was living in Italy most of the time—but she had the advantage of often returning there once she had started research on *The Habit of Being* and the biography to be called *The Mansions of the South*. The article might have been preparatory for the biography. She was able to spend some time in Flannery's bedroom-study on the lower floor, to the left of the entrance, in a sense the most important room in the house. I was of course never admitted there, and I doubt whether other visitors were. There was much to interest me in the house, beginning with Flannery's books, a few of her paintings, including the self-portrait with a pheasant, and an upright piano, later removed. Clearly painting was her second art, even though her training was minimal. I am still convinced that a collection of her pictures, if published, would have something of the same interest that Elizabeth Bishop's paintings and Eudora Welty's photographs have.

As for the piano, I thought she might be an amateur musician, as I am, but that was not the case, and ordinarily she took no interest in music. On a later visit, when Regina was not around, I mentioned the Hollywood Bowl Easter Sunrise Service that I had attended in California. In order to illustrate the experience, I turned to the piano and beat out a number called "The Bible Tells Me So" by Dale Evans, wife of Roy Rogers, the cowboy star featured at the Hollywood Bowl. It began, I remember, with these lines: "Have faith, hope and charity— / That's the way to live successfully— / How do I know? / The Bible tells me so—." As sung by a line of cowboys in white costumes, this was one of the most astonishing quasi-rituals I have ever witnessed, as hilarious for Flannery as for me.

I saw Flannery several times in 1955; these were occasions when she visited the Cheneys at the house in Smyrna, Tennessee. I was finishing my doctorate at Vanderbilt and of course welcomed such diversions. At this time Flannery met Tom Carter, my former student at Washington and Lee University and then-editor of the *Shenandoah,* and found him to be a kindred spirit. He had published Brainard Cheney's review of *Wise Blood,* which started the friendship between Flannery and the Cheneys, as well as "A Stroke of Good Fortune," an early story that she wanted to keep in print. Brainard Cheney, or Lon, as he was known to hundreds of people in Tennessee, was actually from Georgia. He and his wife Frances, or Fannie, had been at Vanderbilt during the Fugitive days of the 1920s and kept up their literary associations with Robert Penn Warren, Allen and Caroline Gordon Tate, and many others. Andrew Lytle, another Tennessean, was a frequent visitor, and since he had known Flannery during her student days at Iowa, he was a connection between her and the Fugitive poets who were promoting her work at this time.

In 1955 *A Good Man Is Hard to Find* was published and widely reviewed. Flannery now had a modest fame and was soon invited to read her stories or sometimes to lecture at universities, and not just in the South. Caroline Gordon wrote the review for the *New York Times,* not a very long piece, perhaps one thousand words, but a decisive one. As a good reviewer, she makes a comparative judgment, in this case with Guy de Maupassant. Like him, she wrote, O'Connor "is very much of her time; and her stories, like his, have a certain glitter, as it were, of evil, which pervades them and astonishingly contributes to their lifelikeness."[4] Caroline Gordon points out that there are few landscapes in the stories; this is not to criticize them but to suggest one reason for the intensity of characterization that they share with Maupassant's stories. Caroline Gordon was being fair about this. Her own instinct as a writer was to set characters in landscape. Her first book of stories was called *The Forest of the South* (1945), and few American writers have dealt so lovingly and intelligently with their settings. Flannery would have been familiar with *The House of Fiction.* This anthology of stories and commentaries, first published in 1950, was a collaboration between the Tates, but it was mainly Caroline's book, and a generation of young readers and writers grew up knowing her name for this reason. Flannery herself was represented in the second edition by "A Good Man Is Hard to Find."[5] *The House of Fiction* proposes the existence of a modern tradition of fiction, running from Gustave Flaubert to certain contemporary writers, a tradition best described by a phrase from Henry James about a novel being "a direct impression of life." Flannery probably thought along these lines in any case, and she always invited and respected Caroline's criticism of her manuscripts. This was true all the way to the end, when Flannery was revising her last stories in the hospital.

Tom Carter and I visited the O'Connors in February 1956. The drive from Nashville was long, the weather was foul, and as we neared Milledgeville, we could hardly see the road because of the fog. This was the first time I stayed overnight at

Andalusia. Tom and I ascended the steep stairs to the upper floor, where a pair of bedrooms and a bathroom awaited visitors. They were finished and decorated in a minimal fashion but always looked comfortable to me after a long and exhausting drive. Somewhat later Regina added a small wing to the back of the house, which was usually set aside for guests. I remember being upstairs because this was where Irene Worth would later stand gazing over the fields. The distinguished actress, my favorite, played Mrs. McIntyre in an excellent television movie of "The Displaced Person" that was made some time after Flannery's death and filmed at Andalusia. I had seen Irene Worth on the stage a number of times in plays by T. S. Eliot, Noël Coward, Seneca (in *Oedipus* with John Gielgud), and Ibsen, among others. And now the great American actress was taking command of the O'Connors' house in a role created for her by Flannery.

This visit in early 1956 extended my knowledge of Flannery's family. Although Andalusia was important for her fiction, it was not always the center of her life. She spent some time, from about 1938 to 1945, at the Cline house in Milledgeville while she attended high school and college. As everyone knows, her formative years were spent in Savannah, where she was born. Mrs. O'Connor moved back to Milledgeville when her husband fell victim to lupus, the disease that would eventually take her daughter as well. During the 1950s the household at the Cline house on Greene Street was headed by Mary Cline, always called "Sister" by Regina, and their brother Louis, also unmarried. Uncle Louis was actually in the hardware business in Atlanta, but he unfailingly returned to Milledgeville on weekends and gave a certain balance to the family, I thought. At the luncheon table on Sunday, Miss Mary, as I called her, sat at the head of the table, Regina and Louis at the other end, and guests in the remaining places. At one time there was a quiet Presbyterian lady who seemed to live in this large house, probably to keep Sister company. It was the great family meal of the week and one of the high points of most visits. There could be no doubt about Sister's importance in the family.

I met several of Flannery's friends at Andalusia or at the house in town. Maryat Lee was a local girl in the sense that her family, her brother and his wife, lived on Greene Street near the Clines. I once visited their house, which was even grander than the Cline House. Her brother was president of the Georgia State College for Women, which Flannery had attended as an undergraduate. Maryat was a striking personality, rebellious in some ways; she always seemed to be moving back and forth between the South and New York City and what they represented. She reminded me of certain southern literary women of the 1920s, such as Evelyn Scott or Frances Newman. Once, when I was staying at Andalusia during the winter, she was invited out there for dinner. By the time she was preparing to leave, it was very dark along the highway, but she insisted on walking the several miles alone to Milledgeville and her brother's house. I had intended to drive her back; she absolutely refused. Regina was appalled; Flannery said nothing; Maryat had her way.

Another friend who figured in Flannery's life was Betty Hester, who chose to remain anonymous as "A" when Sally Fitzgerald edited *The Habit of Being*. I do not think any of us who were acquainted with her ever betrayed her anonymity, but now that she has ended her life, there is no reason to withhold her name. Flannery admired her because she managed to read widely and respond sensitively to many literary works, even though she lacked the superb education that friends like Robert Fitzgerald and Robie Macauley had. Even though Betty lived in Atlanta and could have driven with Louis Cline to Milledgeville on almost any weekend, Flannery and Betty seldom saw one another; hence their extensive correspondence. She had literary ambitions that came to nothing, but Flannery tried to encourage her without undue flattery even when there was some obvious disagreement. Caroline Gordon Tate had a friend from her youth named Sally Wood, also with literary ambitions. When Sally was very old, I helped her edit a volume of Caroline's letters written long ago and began to see the relationship more clearly. They were in effect sisters. Flannery, like Caroline, had no sister, and I do think that Betty had that role in her life. Sally Wood used to say that a woman writer needs such a confidante. She may have been correct.

A third young woman who went in and out of Flannery's life was Carol Johnson, a girl from the Midwest who was an ardent Roman Catholic for a time. During the late 1950s she was writing poems that were well regarded, and she had been taken up by several Catholic writers in New York. She had been corresponding with Flannery for several years; indeed it was Flannery who had started the correspondence after reading some of Carol's poems. I met her during the summer of 1959 at Caroline Tate's house in Princeton. She settled in Greensboro, North Carolina, for several years, during which I drove her to Milledgeville for a visit. But she was destined to be a woman of the world, and before long she was living in England to earn a doctorate at Bristol University. This was followed by academic periods in Paris and Rome and finally Victoria, British Columbia, where she has lived along the beach for many years. She was the first person I knew who journeyed to China when it was still an adventure to do so, and she traveled across Asia on the Trans-Siberian Express. Nowadays she is drawn to Antarctica, and one is not surprised to receive her postcards from the South Pole. It is truly an active life. She published a book of her early poems, but her mind tends to be analytical; consequently her best work is in two volumes of essays, mainly on poets of a "classical" persuasion. Flannery had a very wide range of friends. I occasionally wonder what she would think if she were alive to see us today. Of course if she *were* alive, we would probably have different ideas about *her*.

I also idly wonder about her early years in Savannah, a city that I have often visited since 1952. I know it partly through its literary associations, some of which Flannery knew about. As a young child she lived with her parents at 207 East Charlton Street on one side of Lafayette Square. The house is still there. You can stand on the front steps and look across the square at the Cathedral of St. John the Baptist, which obviously had some importance for this Catholic family, especially since it is so close. It is a handsome French Gothic building with its two spires; it was not completed until 1896, when the parish had been established already for a century. The original congregation was French. Although it was mostly destroyed by a fire in 1898, it was rebuilt the following year. A young boy named Conrad Aiken saw the fire from the balcony of his home on Oglethorpe Avenue and left a description of the event: "floating, burning wisps of cotton from a cotton wharf fire set innumerable fires that night. . . . The whole cathedral roof went in with one tremendous spout of flame—it was magnificent. Afterwards I collected bits of marble from the ruins which I put over the graves of our dead cats. It kept me supplied with cemetery material for years."[6] Conrad Aiken of course became a famous poet, a friend of T. S. Eliot and many others. In his late years, after living away from the South most of the time, he returned to Oglethorpe Avenue and the house next door to his boyhood home. I was commissioned to write a conversation piece with him for the *Shenandoah* and found him good company during several visits. At the same time I was aware that Flannery did not like him, even though she had never met him. I suspect that she acquired this attitude from Caroline Tate, who thought that Aiken was unfeeling, even cynical, about his several wives, whom he wrote about in his memoir called *Ushant*. She felt that he was a bad influence on Allen Tate, whom she had recently divorced.

Aiken mentioned St.-John Perse, the great French poet who spent the second half of his career in the United States; as an important diplomat, he had to flee France after Paris was occupied by the Germans during World War II. In 1942 he visited Savannah in the company of Francis Biddle, the attorney general of the United States, and Mrs. Biddle, also a poet. This is where he wrote a fine long poem, *Pluies*, or *Rains*, which draws on the imagery of the lowcountry around Savannah; in the background there is a tropical storm. According to Aiken, Perse "holed up" in the old Hotel Oglethorpe to write it. It was published in an English translation in the *Sewanee Review*, edited by Allen Tate, in 1944.

I discovered the presence of another French poet-diplomat in poking round the crumbling graves of the revolutionary heroes in the park across the street from Aiken's house. This is only a block or so from the cathedral. Near a wall I saw the grave of Denis Nicolas Cottineau, a French naval hero of the American Revolution. Above that is a plaque stating that Paul Claudel knelt here in homage in 1928. At that time Claudel, probably the most famous Catholic poet of the last century, was ambassador to the United States. I asked Flannery about this; did she remember the occasion? Certainly not, she was only three years old.

Finally there is Julian Green, born in Paris of American parents in 1900, a novelist who wrote mostly in French but who might be considered American, perhaps even southern, because of his ancestry. His family connections with Savannah were very close; his mother, especially, maintained a strong Confederate bias inherited by her son. His paternal grandfather, an Englishman in the cotton trade, built a fine house in Savannah, finished just as the Civil War broke out. Mr. Green, the grandfather, allowed Sherman to occupy his new house so that his Confederate friends would not be humiliated by having the invading general quartered with them. As for Julian, he attended the University of Virginia after the Great War and spent vacations in Savannah, which he describes in detail in his autobiography—the colonial cemetery, the cathedral, the squares. This is the part of Savannah where Flannery grew up; a few years after Julian's vacation (so I imagine), she would play in the cemetery and attend Mass in the cathedral. Flannery knew about Julian Green from Maurice Coindreau, a professor of French at Princeton and friend of Caroline Tate. He was famous for translating Faulkner into French, and he was to translate Flannery's novels. He visited Regina and Flannery at least twice and wrote a critical piece on her novels that may not have been translated into English.[7]

As a woman of letters, in both senses of the term, Flannery was in contact with a surprising number of people, some of whom offered a vigorous challenge to her. Despite the physical restrictions of her life at Andalusia, she had some rich intellectual resources to draw on. I doubt whether she would have done better if she had ended up on a university campus or in a metropolis, and she probably could not have stayed indefinitely with the Fitzgeralds in Connecticut or Italy. She always had a subject at hand, what she could see from the front porch at Andalusia or hear about in Milledgeville. I can see why she has been an inspiration to other writers, for example, Alice Munro from small-town Ontario and perhaps the best short story writer in North America today. Flannery exemplified the regional ideal of the local within the universal as well as any writer who comes to mind.

Notes

1. In *Realist of Distances: Flannery O'Connor Revisited*, ed. Karl-Heinz Westarp and Jan Nordby Gretlund, 18–29 (Aarhus: Aarhus University Press, 1987).

2. *The Correspondence of Flannery O'Connor and the Brainard Cheneys*, ed. Ralph C. Stephens (Jackson: University Press of Mississippi, 1986).

3. Alice Walker, "Beyond the Peacock: The Reconstruction of Flannery O'Connor," in *In Search of Our Mothers' Gardens*, 42–59 (San Diego: Harcourt Brace and Company, 1984). Quotations from pages 57, 59.

4. Caroline Gordon, "With a Glitter of Evil," *New York Times Book Review*, June 12, 1955, 5.

5. In *The House of Fiction: An Anthology of the Short Story with Commentary*, ed. Caroline Gordon and Allen Tate, 2nd ed., 370–86 (New York: Charles Scribner's Sons, 1960).

6. Ashley Brown, "An Interview with Conrad Aiken," *Shenandoah* 15 (Autumn 1963): 19–40 (quotation from 19–20).

7. Maurice-Edgar Coindreau, introduction to *La sagesse dans le sang*, by Flannery O'Connor, vii–xxiii (Paris: Gallimard, 1959).

Contributors

Jack Dillard Ashley received his Ph.D. from Vanderbilt University. Officially retired from the University of South Carolina, where he had been a William Shakespeare, John Milton, Emily Dickinson, and Flannery O'Connor scholar for forty years, he continues to teach there. He has written "The Narrator Voice in Flannery O'Connor's Stories" among other essays. He was a friend of Flannery O'Connor's and visited her at Andalusia.

Ashley Brown is professor emeritus at the University of South Carolina, where he still teaches. He has contributed many essays, reviews, and translations to journals in the United States and Great Britain. His translations of poetry from the Portuguese are particularly appreciated. A former editor of the journal *Shenandoah*, he has also edited several books, including *The Poetry Reviews of Allen Tate, 1924–1944*. He knew Flannery O'Connor during the last decade of her life and was a frequent guest at Andalusia, the subject of his essay in this volume and of his already published essay "Flannery O'Connor: A Literary Memoir."

Jean W. Cash is professor of English at James Madison University, Virginia. Since 1987 she has published essays on Flannery O'Connor, on subjects as diverse as O'Connor and Charles Dickens and O'Connor and Andrew Lytle. For the past ten years she has primarily devoted her research efforts to uncovering the facts of O'Connor's life, the topic of her essay in this collection as well as her most readable biography *Flannery O'Connor: A Life* (2002). She is currently editing a collection of essays on Mississippi writer Larry Brown and his work.

Marshall Bruce Gentry is professor of English at Georgia College and State University, where he teaches American literature with a special emphasis on the short story. He has published studies on gender dialogue in the works of E. L. Doctorow, Philip Roth, and Raymond Carver. He wrote the seminal work *Flannery O'Connor's Religion of the Grotesque* (1986). His review of three new books on Flannery O'Connor has recently appeared in the *International Fiction Review*, and he has contributed essays to *"On the Subject of the Feminist Business": Rereading Flannery O'Connor* (2004) and *Flannery O'Connor: New Perspectives* (1996). He is the editor of the *Flannery O'Connor Review*.

Kelly Gerald has written numerous articles, essays, and book reviews on southern writers. Her Ph.D. dissertation at Auburn University was on Flannery O'Connor as a visual artist, primarily examining O'Connor's achievement as a cartoonist, and this is also the topic for her essay in this volume. She currently resides in Arlington, Virginia.

Sarah Gordon has, since 1973, been teaching at Georgia College and State University in Milledgeville, O'Connor's alma mater and the repository of her manuscripts and personal library. Gordon was the editor of the *Flannery O'Connor*

Bulletin, and she is on the editorial board of the new journal *Flannery O'Connor Review.* She has chaired five Flannery O'Connor symposia. Her work includes a poetry collection, *Distances* (1999), as well as *Flannery O'Connor: In Celebration of Her Genius* (2000), which she edited, and the critical study *Flannery O'Connor: The Obedient Imagination* (2000). She is collaborating on a guide to Flannery O'Connor sites in Georgia and is one of the directors of the Flannery O'Connor–Andalusia Foundation.

Jan Nordby Gretlund is senior lecturer in American literature at the Center for American Studies, University of Southern Denmark. He is the literary editor of the European Association of American Studies' *Southern Studies Forum Newsletter* as well as the author of *Eudora Welty's Aesthetics of Place* (1997) and of *Frames of Southern Mind: Reflections on the Stoic, Bi-Racial & Existential South* (1998). He has edited (with Tony Badger and Walter B. Edgar) *Southern Landscapes* (1996) and (with Karl-Heinz Westarp) *Realist of Distances: Flannery O'Connor Revisited* (1987); *Walker Percy: Novelist and Philosopher* (1991); and *The Late Novels of Eudora Welty* (1998). He has also edited *The Southern State of Mind* (1999), a special "Southern" issue of *American Studies in Scandinavia* (33, no. 2 [2001]), and *Madison Jones' Garden of Innocence* (2005).

Michael Kreyling is professor of English at Vanderbilt University and has written three books on Eudora Welty, including *Understanding Eudora Welty* (1999). With Richard Ford he edited the two-volume Library of America edition of Welty's works. He is also the author of two books on southern literature in general, *Figures of the Hero in Southern Narrative* and a critical book that sparked much discussion, *Inventing Southern Literature* (1998). One of his contributions to O'Connor scholarship is the volume he edited on her first novel, *New Essays on "Wise Blood"* (1995).

Lila N. Meeks was educated at Auburn University. Although she has worked in the administration of the University of South Carolina Beaufort, where she served for almost twenty years as the dean for academic affairs, she never lost her interest in southern literature and has lectured on this topic extensively. Her favorite authors are William Faulkner, Walker Percy, the present-day Georgia writer Mary Hood (winner of the Flannery O'Connor Award for short fiction), and, of course, Flannery O'Connor herself. Meeks hopes to be able to return to teaching and writing about southern writers.

Marion Montgomery is professor emeritus of English at the University of Georgia. He was a friend of Flannery O'Connor's, they corresponded, and he visited with her. His many books include three novels, three volumes of poetry, and no less than three trilogies on American literature and intellectual history. His trilogy from the 1980s, *The Prophetic Poet and the Spirit of the Age,* begins with the volume *Why Flannery O'Connor Stayed Home.* The second trilogy, *Romancing Reality,* concludes with *Making: The Proper Habit of Our Being* (2000). The third trilogy, *Long, Long Thoughts on Love,* still awaits publication. He has written numerous other books, including *The Men I Have Chosen for Fathers* (1990) in which the chapter "Flannery O'Connor's Sacramental Vision" makes it clear that O'Connor is one of his elected "fathers." Montgomery's most recently published books are *Eudora Welty and Walker Percy: The Concept of Home in Their Lives and Literature* (2004) and *On Matters Southern: Essays about Literature and Culture, 1964–2000* (2005), and he currently has a book in press on Flannery O'Connor.

Patrick Samway, S.J., is professor of English at Saint Joseph's University, Philadelphia. Among his other degrees, he holds a Ph.D. in English from the University of North Carolina at Chapel Hill. Author of *William Faulkner's "Intruder in the Dust": A Critical Study of the Typescripts,* he has edited *Signposts in a Strange Land* (1991), Walker Percy's uncollected essays, as well as *A Thief of Peirce* (1995), Percy's exchange of letters with Kenneth Lane Ketner regarding the semiotics of Charles Sanders Peirce. He has also written the biography *Walker Percy: A Life* (1997). With Ben Forkner he has edited four anthologies of southern literature, and with Michel Gresset he has edited *Faulkner and Idealism* and *A Gathering of Evidence: Essays on William Faulkner's "Intruder in the Dust."* He is editing and annotating the letters of Robert Giroux, who was Flannery O'Connor's editor and publisher.

W. A. Sessions is retired Regents' Professor of English at Georgia State University. His Ph.D. is in English and comparative literature from Columbia University. He is a poet, a critic, and a playwright. His third play, *Words without End,* was produced as a Gateway Performance production (2002). He is the author or editor of seven books on Francis Bacon, Edmund Spenser, William Shakespeare, John Milton, and early modern English literature, and has written more than seventy-five essays, book chapters, and reviews. Perhaps his greatest success is *Henry Howard: The Poet Earl of Surrey* (1999), which was reprinted as a paperback. As is clear in his essay in this volume, Sessions was a friend of Flannery O'Connor's and corresponded with her for many years. He has been appointed by her estate to the board of directors of the Flannery O'Connor–Andalusia Foundation and is working on an official biography of O'Connor.

Hans H. Skei is professor of comparative literature at the University of Oslo in Norway. He is the author of *William Faulkner, the Short Story Career* (1981) and *William Faulkner, the Novelist as Short Story Writer* (1984). He also wrote the well-received *Reading Faulkner's Best Short Stories* (1999), translated Faulkner's Snopes trilogy into Norwegian, and edited the *Yearbook of Norwegian Literary Scholarship* from 1989 through 2002. He is the editor of *William Faulkner's Short Fiction: An International Symposium* (1997), and he is on the editorial board of the *Faulkner Journal.* A number of his essays on southern writers, among them Shelby Foote, Mary Chesnut, Eudora Welty, Madison Jones, and Flannery O'Connor, are now collected in *Faulkner and Other Southern Writers* (2004). He coedited and contributed to *The Art of Brevity: Excursions in Short Fiction Theory and Analysis* (2004).

Inger Thörnqvist holds a degree in church history from Lund University in Sweden, where her Ph.D. dissertation was published as *The Modern Alienation from Sacramental Religion as Displayed in Flannery O'Connor's Fiction* (2004). She has also published an essay comparing James Joyce and Flannery O'Connor.

Karl-Heinz Westarp holds a Dr.Phil. from Aarhus University, Denmark. He recently retired from the English department there, where he had been chair for more than ten years. He has published works on British and American drama, James Joyce, and the literature of the American South. Westarp has written *Flannery O'Connor: The Growing Craft* (1993) and *Precision and Depth in Flannery O'Connor's Short Stories* (2002). With Jan Nordby Gretlund he has edited *Walker Percy: Novelist and Philosopher* (1991); *The Late Novels of Eudora Welty* (1998); and *Realist of Distances: Flannery O'Connor Revisited* (1987).

Index

Adam, Karl, 57, 58, 156, 158
African Americans, 8, 10, 14–15, 59, 94–95, 146
Aiken, Conrad, 183, 184n6
Alacoque, Margaret Mary, 162, 171, 173n2
Ali, Muhammad, 10
Al-Qaeda, 2
Ambrose of Milan, 90, 99n7
America (periodical), 154, 161
Andalusia, xiv, 23, 46, 56, 57, 58, 64, 123–25, 130, 153, 154, 173n2, 176–84, 185, 186, 187
Angle, Kimberley Greene, 113, 120
Anselm of Canterbury, 63
Aquinas, Thomas, xii, xv, 56, 71, 72, 112, 127, 128, 131, 133, 134, 135, 136, 163–64, 172
Archer, Emily, 113, 120
Arendt, Hannah, 63
Aristotle, 61, 131, 132, 136, 164
Asals, Frederick, 51, 54, 113, 120
Ashley, Jack Dillard, xv, 185
Atlanta, 25, 64, 128, 130, 131, 155, 158, 159, 173n1, 178, 181, 182
Atlantic Monthly, 176
Augustine, 63, 85, 113, 131, 136, 156, 163

Bacon, Jon Lance, 1, 16
Baker, Robert J., 119, 120
Baldwin, James, 10, 16
Balthasar, Hans Urs von, 57, 63
Barnes, Roslyn, 151
Barth, Karl, 57, 63, 112
Baumgaertner, Jill P., 26, 40
Bawer, Bruce, 114, 119, 120
Béguin, Albert, 79, 84
Bellis, Jack De, 47, 54
Bergson, Henri, xiv, 70, 71–73, 74, 75, 76, 84
Berlin, xiv, 60, 61, 62, 63, 64, 66, 67n4

Bernanos, Georges, 70, 77, 80, 156
Bernard of Clairvaux, 92, 100
Betts, Doris, 114, 120
Bible, the, xv, 19, 53n1, 68, 70, 104, 105, 112, 113, 119, 167, 171, 179
Biddle, Francis, 183
Bishop, Elizabeth, 66
Bishop, John Peale, 74
Bleikasten, André, 160n1
Bloy, Léon Marie, xiv, 60, 70–71, 76–78, 79–84, 156
Bonaventura, 60
Boren, Max Edelman, 113, 120
Bornhauser, Fred, 176, 177, 178
Bouyer, Louis, 162
Bowie, David, 67
Brooks, Cleanth, 149, 160
Brown, Ashley, xvi, 184n6, 185
Buber, Martin, xiv, 58, 63, 84, 129, 136
Budy, Andrea Hollander, 117, 120
Bulletin (diocese of Savannah publication), 57, 67n6, 69, 76, 158
Bush, George W., 2

Capote, Truman, xiv, 42–55, 153; *Answered Prayers*, 45; "Handcarved Coffins," 42, 43, 47–49, 52, 53nn6–7, 54, 55; "The Headless Hawk," 43; *In Cold Blood*, xiv, 42–47, 49, 51, 52, 52–53nn1–2, 53nn4–5, 53n8, 54, 55
Carter, Tom, 180
Carver, Raymond, 185
Cash, Jean W., xv–xvi, 54, 185
Catholicism, 1, 2, 3, 5, 70, 71, 80, 85, 149–60
Cézanne, Paul, 74
Cheney, Brainard and Frances, xvi, 153, 160, 161, 180
Chesnut, Mary, 187
Chesterton, G. K., 126

Christensen, Peter G., 43, 54
church fathers, xv, 85, 88, 93, 96, 98
Clarke, Gerald, 47, 54
Claudel, Paul, xiv, 70, 80, 183
Clay, Cassius. *See* Ali, Muhammad
Coindreau, Maurice, 184, 184n7
cold war, xii, xiii, 1–17, 69, 144
Colonnade (Georgia College newspaper), 26–41
Communism, xiii, 2–10
Congar, Yves, 57, 162
Conrad, Joseph, 65, 74, 117
Copleston, Frederick, 103, 110
Corinthian (Georgia College journal), 26, 29, 35, 41
Corn, Alfred, 86, 120, 149, 151, 157, 160
Coulthard, A. R., 30, 40
Coward, Noël, 181
Creeger, George R., 46, 54
Criterion (periodical), 126
Cross, F. L., 87–88, 100
Curry, Walter Clyde, 59
Cyril of Jerusalem, xv, 19, 87–88, 92–93, 98, 99n9, 100

Daniélou, Jean, 162
Daniel-Rops, Henri, 162
Dante, Alighieri, 110, 124, 125, 132, 133, 151
Dawkins, Cecil, xvi, 23, 56, 67, 68, 112, 130, 155, 156–57, 158, 161
Day, Dorothy, 64
DeLubac, Henri, 162
Depression, the, 8
Desmond, John F., vii, 1, 16, 70, 169–70, 174
Dewey, Alvin, 45, 47
Dickens, Charles, 65, 185
Dickinson, Emily, 185
Dionysius the Areopagite, 85
Dostoevsky, Fyodor Mikhailovich, 63
Douglass, Paul, 84
Du Bos, Charles, 70

Duns Scotus, 72
Dyson, Peter J., 51, 54

Ehrman, Bart D., 91, 93, 94, 100
Eliot, T. S., 71, 76, 84, 114, 126, 137, 165, 181, 183
Ellis, Juniper, 26, 36, 41
Ellman, Richard, 102, 110
epiphany, 75, 102–3, 106, 114, 119, 133–35
Erigena, John Scotus, 103, 110
Esprit (periodical), 149, 160
Eusebius of Caesarea, 95, 100

Farmer, David, 26, 27, 28, 29, 30, 33, 34, 35, 38, 39, 41
Faulkner, William, 19, 63, 174, 184, 186, 187
Fickett, Harold, 116, 120, 173n1
Fitzgerald, Robert, xiv, 64, 152–53, 157, 182
Fitzgerald, Sally, xix, 152–53, 157, 179, 182
Flaubert, Gustave, 180
Foote, Shelby, 187
Fowlie, Wallace, 70, 84
Fox, Joe, 45
Freiburg, 57, 58, 60–61, 63, 67n4
Freud, Sigmund, 58
Friedman, Melvin J., 53n1, 54, 175
Friedman, Norman, 140, 148nn3–4

Gable, Sr. Mariella, 159–60
Galloway, David, 46, 54
Gardiner, Harold, 154
Garson, Helen, 43, 47, 54
Gentry, Marshall Bruce, xiv, 50, 51, 54, 185
Georgia College (and State University), xiv, 26, 27, 31, 84, 160, 185
Gerald, Kelly, xiii, 185
Gertrude of Helfta, 88, 96, 97, 99n5, 100
Getlein, Frank & Mary, 82, 83, 84
Getz, Lorine M., 112, 113, 118, 120
Giannone, Richard, 1, 16, 112, 120
Gide, André, 154–55

Gielgud, John, 181
Gill, Eric, 126
Gillies, Mary Ann, 71, 72, 73, 84
Gilson, Étienne, 4, 6, 12, 13, 17, 77, 156, 162, 165, 173–74n4
Giroux, Robert, 1, 3, 173n2, 178, 187
Gogh, Vincent van, 31
Gordon, Caroline (Tate), 1, 43, 54, 56, 66, 117, 126, 153, 158, 180, 182, 184n4
Gordon, Sarah, xiv, 120, 172, 185–86
Graham, Billy, 2, 11
Graulich, Melody, 114, 120
Gray, Richard, vii
Green, Julian, 183–84
Greene, Graham, 167
Gregory of Nyssa, 100
Gretlund, Jan Nordby, 184n1, 186, 188
Grillmeier, Aloys, 86, 87, 89, 93, 100
Grobel, Lawrence, 42, 53n3, 54
Guardini, Romano, xiv, 56–67, 67n4, 156, 158, 162
Guest, David, 44, 46–47, 54
Guitton, Jean, 57, 162

Hackett, Jerry, 103
Hall, Eileen, 112
Hardwick, Elizabeth, 152, 161
Harper's Bazaar, 176
Harris, Joel Chandler, 176
Hawkes, John, 49, 51, 75, 160n1
Hawkins, Peter S., 155, 161
Hawthorne, Nathaniel, 19, 62, 133, 159
Hawthorne-Lathrop, Rose, 159
Heidegger, Martin, xiv, 57, 58, 61, 63
Hendin, Josephine, 50, 54, 99n1
Herberg, Will, 72, 84
Herbert, Bob, 2, 17
Hester, Betty ("A" in *The Habit of Being*), xi, xvi, 9, 24, 39, 42, 49, 57, 64, 65, 67n1, 73, 77, 79, 87, 88, 89, 93, 112, 117, 119, 136, 152, 153, 155–56, 157–58, 159, 163, 164, 168, 174, 182
Hill, Pati, 42, 54

Hitchcock, Bert, vii
Hölderlin, J. Chr. Friedrich, 63
Holocaust, 34
Hopkins, Gerard Manley, 68, 72, 79, 111, 114, 168
Horne, Elizabeth, 151, 161
Hügel, Baron Friedrich von, 58, 65, 155, 158
Hussein, Saddam, 2
Huxley, Aldous, 6, 17
Huxley, Julian, 14, 17
Huysmans, Joris-Karl, 60
Hyman, Stanley Edgar, 85, 100

Ignatius of Antioch, 93, 94, 95, 98, 99n11
Ingram, Forrest L., 141, 148
Iowa, xi, 56, 149, 151, 152, 161, 180
Irenaeus (apologist) 89, 93, 96

James, Henry, 66, 151, 180
Jaspers, Karl, 63
Jerome, Eusebius Sophronius, 85, 95–96, 98, 100n14
Jesus Christ, 20, 23, 44, 79, 90, 95, 97, 98, 99, 105, 108, 111, 112, 117, 131, 136, 146, 156, 162, 164, 165, 166, 168–69, 172, 173n2, 174n7
John of the Cross, 85
John the Baptist (cathedral), 173n1, 183
Johnson, Carol, 182
Jones, David, 126
Jones, Madison, 188
Joyce, James A., 66, 71, 75, 76, 102–3, 110, 114, 120, 133, 151–52, 165, 169, 188
Julian of Norwich, 134, 136
Jung, Carl Gustav, xiv, 58
Justin (apologist), 86–87, 91, 93, 94, 96–97, 98, 99n8, 100n12

Kayser, Wolfgang, 36
Kazan, Elia, 3
Kazin, Alfred, 152, 161
Kennedy, J. Gerald, 142, 148n7

Kessler, Edward, 114, 115, 120
Kidd, Stuart, vii
Kierkegaard, Søren, 63, 117
Kilcourse, George, 119, 120, 162, 166, 175
King, Martin Luther, Jr., 10, 14
Kinney, Arthur F., 95, 96, 99n2, 100
Klevar, Harry, 96, 100
Kreyling, Michael, xiii, 160n1, 186
Krings, Heinrich, 112, 120
Kuryluk, Ewa, 36

Labouré, Catherine, 162, 171, 173n2
Labrie, Ross, 168, 175
Lawrence, D. H., 85
Lee, Harper, 14
Lee, Maryat, 142, 160, 181
Lerda, Valeria Gennaro, vii
Levie, Jean, 113
Lewis, C. S., 19, 155
Locke, John, 114
London, 4
Longinus, 118
Lourdes, 62, 157–58
Love, Betty Boyd, 26, 29, 41
Lowell, Robert, 152, 153
Lundén, Rolf, 141–42, 148
Luscher, Robert M., 141, 148
Lynch, William, 74, 166–67, 175
Lytle, Andrew, 49, 56, 59, 67, 180, 185

Macauley, Robie, 122, 151, 161, 182
Magny, Claude Edmond, 57
Malraux, André, 162
Manichean, 112, 167
Mann, Susan Garland, 141, 148
Marcel, Gabriel, 57, 70, 77, 99n1, 156
Marechal, Clothilde, 77
Maritain, Jacques, xiv, 4, 6, 70–73, 75, 76, 79, 80, 82–83, 84, 126, 162, 164, 174n4
Maritain, Raïssa, 70–72, 75–77, 79, 80, 84
Marx, Karl, 61
Maupassant, Guy de, 180
Mauriac, François, 70, 76–77, 80, 84, 156, 162

May, Charles, 138–39, 140
McCarthy, Joseph, 3
McCarthy, Mary, 152, 164
McCarthyism, xii
McCown, James, xvi, 77, 149, 152, 154–55, 161, 168
McKane, Janet, 158, 159
McKee, Elizabeth, 142
Meeks, Lila Nolen, xiii, 186
Melville, Herman, 62
Merton, Thomas, xiii, 1–17, 64, 170, 175
Milledgeville, Ga., xvi, 22, 26, 62, 68, 125, 149, 150–51, 153–55, 162, 172, 173, 173nn1–2, 176–84, 185
Milton, John, 110, 185, 187
Mindszenty, Joseph Cardinal, 3
Montgomery, Marion, xv, 114, 116, 120, 137, 186
Morris, Alice, 176
Morrison, Toni, 59–60, 67, 67n2, 67n7
Moss, Anita, ix
Mournier, Emmanuel, 162
Muller, Gilbert, 70
Munich, 57, 60
Munro, Alice, 184
Murphy, John J., 120–21
Musurillo, Herbert, 88, 89, 91, 94, 100

Nance, William L., 46, 55
New Criticism, 1
New York, 123, 124, 128, 130, 152, 160, 174n5, 177, 178, 180, 181, 182
New York Times, 2, 17, 180, 184n4
Newman, Frances, 181
Newman, John Cardinal, 60–61
Nietzsche, Friedrich, xi, 58
Nye, Harold, 45

O'Connor, Flannery
  as artist, xi, 9, 18, 26–41, 65, 73–74, 78–79, 83, 111–21, 126–28, 135, 138, 149, 167, 173
  —*A Memoir of Mary Ann*, 158

as believer, xiii, xvi, 2, 7, 8 64, 66, 98, 149–61, 162–75
as book reviewer, 58, 69, 112, 158
as correspondent, xiv, xvi, 13, 56, 123, 163
—*The Habit of Being,* 10, 176, 177, 179, 182
as critic, 8, 57, 95, 172, 174n6
—*Mystery and Manners,* 7–8, 36, 59, 127
as novelist, 18, 69, 116, 125–26, 133, 135, 158
—*The Violent Bear It Away,* xii, xiv, 32, 36, 59, 62, 64, 65, 85–86, 89, 90, 92, 94, 96–98, 131–32, 158, 170
—*Wise Blood,* xi, 14, 30, 35, 36, 46, 53n1, 68, 80, 86, 90, 97, 122, 130–31, 132, 153, 154, 160n1, 180, 186
as short story writer:
—*A Good Man Is Hard to Find,* 36, 142, 154, 176, 180; "The Artificial Nigger," 67, 13; "A Circle in the Fire," 107, 108, 179; "The Displaced Person," 10, 62, 92, 107–8, 169, 176–77, 181; "Good Country People," 40, 53n1, 107, 171, 176; "A Good Man Is Hard to Find," xiv, 20, 32, 42, 43, 45, 51–52, 61, 75, 129, 174n7, 179, 180; "A Late Encounter with the Enemy," 32, 52, 96; "The Life You Save May Be Your Own," 89, 97, 106, 130; "The River," 20, 42, 43, 47, 48, 51, 72, 90, 98, 107; "A Stroke of Good Fortune," 180; "A Temple of the Holy Ghost," 37, 52, 79, 88, 92, 97, 105, 156, 168, 170
—*Everything That Rises Must Converge,* xv, 138–48, 166; "The Comforts of Home," 35, 51, 95, 145, 147; "The Enduring Chill," 32, 87, 89, 97, 105, 124, 146, 147, 169; "Everything That Rises Must Converge," 13, 14, 31, 37, 105, 106, 147;
"Greenleaf," 21, 31, 32, 43, 92, 98, 105–6, 108, 146, 147; "Judgment Day," 10, 94–95, 145, 146, 147; "The Lame Shall Enter First," 49, 51–52, 75, 90, 95, 97, 106, 145, 146, 147; "Parker's Back," 31, 78, 105, 108, 119, 146, 147; "Revelation," 21, 31, 36–37, 38, 75, 91, 98, 102, 103, 108–9, 146, 147; "A View of the Woods," 38, 89–90, 91, 98, 106, 107, 108, 146
—*Collected Works:* "The Geranium," 118; "The Partridge Festival," 11–13, 14, 92; "Why Do the Heathen Rage?" 94, 95, 96, 98
technique of, 26, 38–39, 40, 62, 73, 81, 144, 174n7
—characters, xi, xiv, 10, 12, 20, 22–25, 33–38, 42, 45, 68, 85, 89, 96–97, 107–9, 117–19, 138–40, 141, 142–48, 166, 168, 171–72, 180
—epiphany, 102, 105–6, 133, 135
—humor, ix, 18, 22–25, 33, 37, 69–70
—images, 26–40, 105, 11, 116–20
—irony, 14, 15, 38, 39, 60–62, 65, 66, 129, 144
—language, x, xiii, 22, 40, 83, 111, 113–14, 117, 140
—metaphor, xv, 48, 79, 86, 90, 93–94, 106, 111–20
—place, 128–29, 131, 134, 147, 172
—symbol, xv, 14, 16, 29, 31, 66, 85–101, 103, 142, 152, 164, 171, 177
themes of:
—art, ix, xi, xiii, xv, 6, 9–10, 18, 23, 31, 32, 36, 61, 65, 68, 72–74, 77, 78, 82–83, 112, 115–17, 122–23, 126–27, 132–33, 135–36, 143, 164–65
—evil, x, xi, 75, 90, 97, 99, 119, 131, 135–36, 144, 159, 174n7
—the Fall, xii, xiii, 76, 82, 85
—grace, ix, x, xi, xii, xiii, xv, xvi, 7, 14, 18–22, 25, 49, 50, 60, 66–67, 72,

themes of (*continued*)
> 74, 75–77, 81, 84, 91, 111, 113, 118, 119, 129, 131–32, 134–36, 139, 147, 158, 170, 172
> —grotesque, ix–x, xii, xiii, xiv, 22, 35–37, 67, 69, 70, 75, 113, 139, 145, 159
> —incarnation, xv, 1, 68, 74–75, 112–16, 136, 164, 166
> —manners, 7, 14, 16, 20, 116, 123, 127–32, 172
> —mystery, ix, xiv, xv, 7–8, 16, 22, 25, 59, 60, 62, 65, 74, 76, 82, 88, 102, 103, 108–9, 115–16, 118–20, 127, 132, 134–36, 166–67, 170, 172
> —redemption, xi, 14, 19, 20, 76, 89–92, 97, 98, 99, 113, 138, 156
> —religion, 9, 14, 19, 21, 24, 44, 45, 69, 139, 143, 145, 147, 149, 151–52, 153, 156, 157, 167–68
> —revelation, 136, 140, 163, 167, 174n4
> —salvation, 18, 19, 21–22, 25, 84, 89, 90, 92, 96, 98, 112–13
> —sin, xiii, 14, 19, 21, 64, 68, 90–91, 98, 133, 138
> —social issues, ix, 3, 7, 14, 16, 30, 32, 36, 37–38, 147
> —South, the, 19, 21, 47, 52, 56, 69, 93, 98, 124, 125, 143, 145–47, 163, 165
> —vision, xiv, xvi, 1–2, 22, 23, 26, 31, 34, 88, 94, 97, 109, 116, 125, 131–32, 134, 146, 165, 169–70

O'Connor, Flannery Collection, the (Duke University), 149
O'Connor, Flannery Collection, the (Milledgeville), 26, 28, 84, 160, 161
O'Connor, Regina Cline, 24, 69, 124, 150, 177–81, 184

Pacelli, Eugenio, 63
Paris, 25, 71, 83, 157, 162, 173n4, 182, 183
Pascal, Blaise, 63
Paul (apostle), x, 53n7, 91, 94
Peabody High School, xiii, 27, 150
Peabody Palladium, 26, 28
Peale, Norman Vincent, 2
Péguy, Charles Pierre, xiv, 70–71, 80, 162
Peirce, Charles Sanders, 187
Percy, Walker, xvi, 18, 25n1, 83, 122–23, 126, 136, 167, 170, 186, 187, 188
Perkins, Judith, 93–94, 95, 100
Perse, St.-John, 183
Picard, Max, 57–58, 158
Pieper, Josef, 63, 135, 137
Piltz, Anders, 90, 100
Plato, 131
Plimpton, George, 45, 53n8, 55
Poe, Edgar Allan, 174n6,
Polycarp (bishop), 89, 97
Pope, Alexander, 102, 109, 110
Porter, Katherine Anne, 117
Pound, Ezra, 165
Powers, J. F., 167
Pratt, Mary Louise, 140, 148n2
Price, Reynolds, 62, 112, 120
Pseudo-Dionysius, xiv, 88, 94, 97, 98, 99n6, 101
Psichari, Ernest, 140

Quinn, Peter, 168, 174n5
Quinn, Robert Hawley, 47–49

Rahner, Karl, 58, 63, 112–13, 121
Ransom, John Crowe, 59
Rath, Sura Prasad, 30, 41, 99n1
Ratzinger, Karl, 63
Reisman, David, 3
Renzo, Anthony Di, 70
Ricoeur, Paul, 59
Riffaterre, Michael, 114, 121
Rilke, Rainer Maria, 63
Rome, 25, 67, 157, 182
Rorem, Ned, 45
Rorem, Paul, 88–89, 101

INDEX

Rouault, Georges, xiv, 70, 73, 79, 82, 83, 84
Rougemont, Denis de, 162
Rubenson, Samuel, 85, 92, 101
Ryan, Elizabeth Shreve, 26, 28, 41
Rynne, Xavier, 165, 175

Samway, Patrick, S.J., xvi, 173n2, 187
Savannah, Ga., xv–xvi, 24, 54, 62, 149–50, 157, 173n1, 177, 181, 182–84
Scheffczyk, Leo, 113, 121
Schleiermacher, Friedrich, 116
Scholasticism, 134
Scholes, Robert, 102
Scott, Evelyn, 181
Semmes, Katie, 157, 158
Seneca, 181
Sessions, William A., xiv, 57, 149, 162, 173n2, 187
Sewanee Review, 56, 160n1, 176, 183
Sexton, Anne, 64
Shakespeare, William, 59, 185, 187
Sheen, Fulton J. (bishop of Rochester, N.Y.), 2
Shenandoah (periodical), 153, 180, 183, 185
Skei, Hans, xv, 148n5, 187
Socrates, 63, 127, 131
Sophocles, 61, 132, 133
Southern Cross (periodical), 158
Southern Living (periodical), 179
Spark, Muriel, 167
Spectrum (Georgia College yearbook), 27, 29, 35, 37, 41
Spellman, Francis Cardinal, 2, 3
Spivey, Ted R., 43, 55, 85–86, 99n1, 101
Srigley, Susan, xi, xvii
Steinbeck, John, 18
Stensen, Niels (Steno), 118
Stephens, Martha, 160n1,
Stephens, Ralph C., 153, 161, 176, 184n2
Stevens, Wallace, 109, 110, 177
Streight, Irwin Howard, 113, 114–15, 121
Styron, William, 62

Sullivan, Walter, 151–52, 161
Swinburne, Algernon Charles, 18

Tate, Allen, 43, 54, 56, 59, 117, 125–26, 137, 183, 185
Tavard, George, 162
Teilhard de Chardin, Pierre, 13, 17, 18, 25, 113, 118, 142, 158, 162
terror, ix, x–xii, xiii, xv–xvi, 2, 90, 103, 109, 133
Tertullian, 94
theophany, xv, 102–10
Thörnqvist, Inger, xv, 188
Thought (journal), 166, 167, 175
Trowbridge, Clinton W., 119, 121
Tübingen, Ger., 58, 60
Tuttle, Jon, 43–44, 55
Tynan, Kathleen, 45
Tynan, Kenneth, 45

Van Doren, Mark, 4
Vatican Council I, 163
Vatican Council II, xvi, 63, 163, 165–66
Villon, François, 46, 53n5, 55, 99n1
Virgil, 90
Vögelin, Eric, xiv, 58

Walker, Alice, 59–60, 176–77, 184n3
Warren, Austin, 151
Warren, Robert Penn, 180
Waugh, Evelyn, 167
WAVES (Women Accepted for Volunteer Emergency Service in the U.S. Navy), 27
Weigle, Gustave, 158
Weil, Simone, 87, 162
Welty, Eudora, xvi, 62, 172, 186, 187, 188
Westarp, Karl-Heinz, xv, 146–47, 184n1, 188
Whitfield, Stephen J., xiii, 2–3, 10, 11–12, 17
Whitt, Margaret Earley, 118, 121
Wilson, Charles Reagan, 93–95, 101

Wood, Ralph C., 85, 101
Wood, Sally, 182
Woolf, Virginia, 71, 165
Wordsworth, William, 58
World War II, xii, 3, 64, 83, 126, 183
Wylder, Jean, 151, 161

Yaddo (artists' colony), 152
Yaeger, Patricia, xi, xvii, 1
Yeats, William Butler, x–xi, 127–28, 165

Zaidman, Laura Mandell, 50–51, 55
Zuber, Leo, 85, 162

www.ingramcontent.com/pod-product-compliance
Lightning Source LLC
Chambersburg PA
CBHW020231170426
43201CB00007B/388